1

Polis

*An Introduction to the
Ancient Greek City-State*

MOGENS HERMAN HANSEN

OXFORD
UNIVERSITY PRESS

OXFORD

UNIVERSITY PRESS

Great Clarendon Street, Oxford OX2 6DP

Oxford University Press is a department of the University of Oxford.
It furthers the University's objective of excellence in research, scholarship,
and education by publishing worldwide in

Oxford New York

Auckland Cape Town Dar es Salaam Hong Kong Karachi
Kuala Lumpur Madrid Melbourne Mexico City Nairobi
New Delhi Shanghai Taipei Toronto

With offices in

Argentina Austria Brazil Chile Czech Republic France Greece
Guatemala Hungary Italy Japan Poland Portugal Singapore
South Korea Switzerland Thailand Turkey Ukraine Vietnam

Oxford is a registered trade mark of Oxford University Press
in the UK and in certain other countries

Published in the United States
by Oxford University Press Inc., New York

British Library Cataloguing in Publication Data
Data available

Library of Congress Cataloging in Publication Data
Data available

Typeset by John Waś, Oxford
Printed in Great Britain
on acid-free paper by
Biddles Ltd., King's Lynn, Norfolk

ISBN 0–19–920849–2   978–0–19–920849–4
ISBN 0–19–920850–6 (Pbk.)   978–0–19–920850–0 (Pbk.)

1 3 5 7 9 10 8 6 4 2

FOR JOHN CROOK

This book is an enlarged and revised version of my Danish book: *Polis: den oldgræske bystatskultur* (Copenhagen, 2004). When it was published, I sent copies to colleagues and friends, including, of course, John Crook. He liked it and volunteered to produce an English version. Offered the opportunity, I accepted the proposal with gratitude; I remembered the happy time we had spent together in the winter and spring of 1990 working on the translation of *The Athenian Democracy in the Age of Demosthenes*. We had a repeat of that in August 2002 translating my essay on *The Triumph of Time: Reflections of a Historian about Time in History*. This spring we did it for the third time, and here is the result. Let me take this opportunity to thank John Crook for his friendship and all I have learned from him during more than thirty years and, of course, for the enjoyable days we spent together in Cambridge working on the translation and putting it onto my faithful follower: Ollie the Second.

Contents

Introduction   1

I. CITY-STATES IN WORLD HISTORY

1. Cities, States, City-States and City-State Cultures   7
2. A Sketch of the Thirty-Seven Identified City-State
   Cultures   17
3. 'Country-States' versus City-State Cultures   24

II. THE CITY-STATE CULTURE
IN ANCIENT GREECE

Introduction   31
4. The Unity of the City-State Culture of Ancient Greece   33
5. The Rise of the Ancient Greek City-State Culture   39
6. The End of the City-State Culture in Ancient Greece   48
7. How *Poleis* Arose and Disappeared   51
8. What is a *Polis*? An Investigation of the Concept of '*Polis*'   56
9. The *Polis* as City and State   62
10. *Polis* as City   66
11. The Settlement Pattern of the Ancient Greek City-States 67
12. The Size and Population of the Cities   73
13. The Demography of the Greek City-State Culture   77
14. The Economy of the Cities: Max Weber's 'Ideal Type'   85
15. *Polis* as City in the Archaic Period   98
16. The Greek Conception of *Polis* as a City with a Hinter-
    land   101
17. *Polis* as State   106

18. Army 116
19. Religion 118
20. State and Society 122
21. Civil War (*Stasis*) 125
22. Relationships between *Poleis* 127
23. The Hellenistic *Polis* 132

III. CONCLUSION

24. The *Polis* Compared with Other City-State Cultures 137

Notes 147
References 191
Index of Sources 215
Index of Names 226
General Index 235

Introduction

Polis is the ancient Greek word for 'city',[1] 'state'[2] and the combination of city and state, the 'city-state'.[3] It has often, quite rightly, been said that the *polis*, as a form of state and society, was the basis of the whole of Greek civilisation; and the implication of that is that one can only understand Greek civilisation if one understands the form of the society the Greeks lived under, i.e. the *polis*. However, this illuminating truth is, regrettably, seldom followed up by a description of what a *polis* actually is (or rather was, for the form of city-state culture that dominated Greece in antiquity no longer exists anywhere in the world). We have lacked comprehensive, fundamental studies of the *polis* both as a concept and as an actual phenomenon: earlier investigations have been subjective, and the examples chosen were mostly taken from sources that dealt with Athens. But Athens was only one of about 1,500 *poleis*, and was in many respects anomalous. So what about the roughly 1,499 other *poleis*? Very little has been written about them,[4] and that is one of the reasons why there goes on being deep disagreement about almost all the fundamental questions that can be asked about the *polis*: when it arose, when it came to an end, how many *poleis* there were and precisely where they were situated, whether it was a fusion of state and society or, on the contrary, a society but not a state, i.e. without the institutions that characterised a state. There is disagreement also as to how entirely a *polis* was a society of adult male citizens or whether it included women, children, outsiders, slaves and so on. All these unsolved—and often unaddressed—problems were the background that led to the setting up by the Danish National Research Foundation in 1993 of a centre for the study of the ancient Greek city-state: the Polis Centre. It was at Copenhagen University, in the Faculty of Humanities, and its primary remit was to describe the form of state and settlement typical of ancient Greece, the *polis*, the city-state. On the basis of a great number of published researches about the *polis*, both as form of state and as form of settlement, it has been for the first time possible to create an Inventory of all known Greek *poleis* in the Archaic and Classical periods (*c.*650 to 323 BC); and starting from that Inventory we have carried out an analysis of the ancient Greek *polis*-world. That has produced a new evaluation and a revision of many standard doctrines about the development and character of the Greek *polis*. The Inventory was published by Oxford University Press in 2004.[5]

The second task of the Centre was to understand the *polis* in a wider world-historical context. The ancient Greek *polis* was a city-state, and when historians nowadays talk about city-states, they are thinking first and foremost of ancient Greece and after that of the cities of north Italy in the Middle Ages. But there have been city-states in other places and at other times. A general analysis of urbanisation and state formation shows that in world history from antiquity to *c.*1900 two different types of state have existed: macro-states, with numerous cities included in the territory of each of them, as against regions divided into micro-states each of which consisted of one city and its hinterland. Such a micro-state is what is called a 'city-state', and regions divided into city-states form what the Polis Centre has called a 'city-state culture'. We have succeeded in identifying thirty-seven 'city-state cultures', from the Sumerians in Mesopotamia in the third millennium BC to several city-state cultures in West Africa which were only wiped out by the colonial powers a bit over a hundred years ago.[6] In this matter also, nobody has yet tried to get an overall picture of how many and what kind of city-state cultures there have been in the history of the world.

To sum up the results of the researches of the Polis Centre I single out four features. In city-state cultures, including that of ancient Greece, there has been (1) a degree of urbanisation unexampled in major states before the Industrial Revolution, which began in the second half of the eighteenth century; (2) an economy based on trade and centred on the city's market; (3) a political decision-making process whereby laws and decrees were not always dictated by a monarch, but were often passed by majority votes after a debate in an assembly, which mostly was a selection from among the better-class citizens but sometimes included them all; (4) interaction between city-states, which resulted in the rise of leagues of states and federal states. As a type of state, the federal state grew up within the city-state cultures, and only appeared as a macro-state with the foundation of the USA in 1787–9.

There is no longer any city-state culture remaining; the last of them vanished in *c.*1900. So it is an irony of history that the social, economic and political organisation that characterised the city-state cultures did not disappear when they disappeared, but came to dominate states and societies in the world we have today. In many important respects modern macro-states are more like the ancient city-state cultures than they are like the ancient macro-states.

This brief overview is designed for a broad band of interested readers and also for the narrower public of classical scholars, archaeologists, anthropologists, sociologists and historians, who in the course of their professional work have to come to terms with what is understood by a city, a state and a city-state. The present book is in three parts. The first is a relatively wide overview of the concepts of city-state and city-state culture and of the thirty-seven such cultures that we think we have uncovered in world history. The second is a specific description of the ancient Greek *polis*, and the third is a Conclusion, in which the Greek *polis* is compared with the thirty-six other city-state cultures and with the concept of city-state culture as such.

I

CITY-STATES IN
WORLD HISTORY

1

Cities, States, City-States and City-State Cultures

In the very long perspective there are three milestones in the history of mankind before the Industrial Revolution: (1) the change from hunting and fishing to agriculture and herding as the most important mode of getting a living, (2) the change from dispersed to nucleated settlement, first in villages and later in true cities, (3) the change in social structure from looser, family-based groups to institutionalised communities with first the tribe and later the state as the dominant political unit.[1]

(1) In our part of the world the 'agrarian revolution' began c.8000 BC, i.e. in the Neolithic period and in the Near East between Asia Minor and Mesopotamia.

(2) The 'agrarian revolution' was quickly followed by settlement in permanent villages: the first towns arose already in the Stone Age. One of the oldest is Çatal Höyük in Turkey, c.250 km south of Ankara, a Stone Age town of 16 ha covered with houses standing wall to wall without streets in between. It flourished in the period 6800–6300 BC, and had perhaps 5,000 inhabitants.[2]

(3) The close-knit form of settlement in villages and towns resulted in a need for regulation of people's social behaviour. Early tribal societies were typically ruled by assemblies of all the members of the tribe, by councils of the elders of the group, and in some cases by chieftains. Only later came the founding of real states, i.e. the creation of institutionalised and centralised political leadership with a legitimate monopoly of force to establish and maintain a legal order within a given territory and over a given population.[3]

The 'agrarian revolution' and settlement in villages and cities can be observed in the traces found by the archaeologists: pollen and animal bones, remains of buildings and household objects. It is harder to find archaeological traces of human social structures

and forms of political organisation. So usually we shall have secure knowledge of the actual growth of states only when they attain
to a knowledge of writing. In our part of the world the two oldest civilisations where we can find unassailable evidence for the
rise of states are in Mesopotamia and Egypt, where documents in
cuneiform (from *c*.3200 BC) and hieroglyphs (from about 3000 BC)
give us a detailed picture of the form of those societies. It cannot
be excluded that Çatal Höyük in the Stone Age may have had a
political organisation like some kind of state: we do not know and
perhaps we never shall.[4]

Very broadly stated, then, the pattern of development in world
history has been that agriculture led to fixed settlements and to a
population density that, in turn, created the possibility for urbanisation and the rise of states. But what is the relationship between
agriculture and urbanisation and the creation of states? Do the
three of them hang unbreakably together, or can one find societies
without growth of cities and states, or states without cities, or cities
without states?

There are plenty of examples of civilisations with absolutely no
agriculture, urbanisation or state formation (e.g. the North American Indian tribes and numerous nomadic societies). One can also
find examples of states without cities (e.g. the seven Anglo-Saxon
states in England between AD 500 and 700[5]), and of societies with
cities but no state (e.g. the Yakö people in Nigeria down to the
beginning of the twentieth century[6]). Nevertheless, we can at the
same time say truly that in by far the greatest number of civilisations we read about in world history, people were permanently
settled and were organised in states: they have mostly been agriculturalists living dispersed or in villages, but some of them in true
cities.

Urbanisation is closely connected with the growth of states, and
so the two processes often occur in a time-frame that indicates the
close relationship of the phenomena. While it often takes thousands
of years for an agricultural society to embark on state formation
and urbanisation, there is seldom a very long time between the
formation of states and the formation of cities, perhaps at most a few
hundred years; and usually the two phenomena are simultaneous,
each undoubtedly influencing the other. In Denmark agriculture
and herding can be traced back to *c*.4000 BC. It took about 5,000
years before Denmark became a state in the Viking Age, as is shown

inter alia by the Jelling stone on which Harald Bluetooth declared that 'he won for himself all Denmark and Norway and made the Danes into Christians'. And at the same time we can observe the growth of cities: first Hedeby and Ribe, and afterwards Ålborg, Århus and Odense, furthered by the new royal power.[7]

So city formation and state formation go hand in hand; but the relations between them vary. Often state formation covers very large areas, with several cities in the territory of each state: examples are Egypt in antiquity, Denmark in the Viking Age, and the Inca Empire in the late Middle Ages. However, there is a set of examples where there is a kind of one-to-one relationship between city formation and state formation, in which each city is the centre of a small state consisting of town plus hinterland and, looked at the other way round, each state is relatively small and has, typically, one single city as the centre of the society. And that is what we call a city-state. The oldest known examples are the Sumerian city-states in Mesopotamia from *c.*3100 BC, with Uruk as the largest among some fifty others. But there have been many other city-states in world history: Athens was one in antiquity, Venice was one until 1797, Bremen from 1741 to 1937. Danzig was still a city-state between the World Wars, 1919–39, and to this day Andorra in the Pyrenees is one.

However, it is not satisfactory to put all these city-states under one hat. Uruk, Athens and Venice were city-states lying amongst other city-states. Bremen, Danzig and Andorra were isolated city-states. Bremen lay between Oldenburg and Hannover, Danzig was hemmed in between Germany and Poland, and Andorra lies between Spain and France. So we must distinguish between a city-state and a cluster of city-states, which is, in the terminology of our project, called a 'city-state culture'. To distinguish the concept of 'city-state culture' from that of 'city-state' is one of the central aims in the research of the Polis Centre, and we define a city-state culture thus: a city-state culture arises when a region is inhabited by a people who have the same language (or a common *lingua franca*), the same religion, the same culture and the same traditions, but is divided politically into a large number of small states, each of which consists of a city and its immediate hinterland.[8]

A city-state culture arises typically in one of three ways. (a) After a period without state formation there occurs a period of economic and population growth, in which the whole territory is both ur-

banised and organised politically as a set of city-states. That is
what happened, for example, in the ancient Greek city-states in
the eighth century BC. (b) A larger state with many cities splits up,
and each city in it becomes a self-governing unit. That is how the
Chinese city-states came into existence in the Spring-and-Autumn
period, 771–481 BC. (c) An immigrant people settles itself into city-
states, or city-states arise shortly after colonisation. That happened
in the Aztec city-states in Mexico *c.* AD 1200.

Individual city-states in a city-state culture vary in geographical
and in population size, but as a rule none of them is strong enough to
subdue all the others and turn the whole region into a macro-state.

In a city-state culture there is war nearly all the time between at
least some of the city-states, but at the same time there is enormous
economic and cultural interaction between them.

In peacetime the city-states have diplomatic relationships with
each other. Rarely does a city-state culture consist only of independent city-states: most of them are collections of many small and
a few larger city-states, and the little ones often join themselves
into leagues and federations led by a bigger city-state, or else they
become dependencies under a big city-state or under the king of a
neighbouring kingdom.

City-state cultures often go under because there arises in the
neighbouring region a powerful macro-state which subdues to itself
the whole region of city-states. That is how the Sumerian city-states
came to an end *c.*2350 BC, being all swallowed up from the north by
King Sargon of Akkad.

City-state cultures are usually found in neighbouring regions,
and in a number of cases one can speak of clusters of city-state
cultures, e.g. in the Near East where the Sumerian, Babylonian,
Assyrian, Anatolian, Syrian, Phoenician, Neo-Hittite, Palestinian
and Philistine city-states, in the course of 2,500 years, produced
nine different city-state cultures that bordered on one another.

As a typical example of a city-state culture, a short description
is given here of a West African one. South of Lake Chad in the
northernmost part of Cameroon are the Kotoko people, in a region
of *c.*8,000 km². Their language belongs to the Chad family, they
are Muslim, and they live mostly by fishing. From the Middle
Ages to the beginning of the twentieth century the region was
divided into fourteen small kingdoms, each consisting of a city and
its surrounding territory. Originally they were entirely independent

of one another, but *c.*1600 they became dependencies under the Bornu Empire. And in the nineteenth century twelve of them were joined in two federal states: the seven most northerly ones became part of a federation ruled by the prince of the city Makari, while the five southernmost ones formed another federation under the ruler of the city Logone Birni. The political, economic and religious centre of each city-state was a town with a protecting wall around it, which, besides habitation quarters, had also a mosque, a sultan's palace and an assembly place with a *gudu*, a little tower from which the sultan could address the people. Each sultanate had a territory of 100–1,000 km². One of the bigger towns, Goulfeil, covers *c.*20 ha, and in 1873 the city-state had 8,000 inhabitants, of whom about half lived in the town itself.[9]

The city-state culture is a historical phenomenon. There are still, today, a few city-states, e.g. San Marino and Andorra, and it is common to classify, for example, Hamburg and Singapore as city-states. But they are all isolated cases, and there is no longer any city-state culture left anywhere in the world.

So much for the concept of a city-state culture. We will next change focus from the whole to the part, and study the individual items of which a city-state culture consists, i.e. the city-state itself.[10]

A city-state is a micro-state both territorially and in population. The smallest ancient Greek city-states had a territory of *c.*10 km² and a population of sometimes less than 1,000 inhabitants. The population in one of the smallest city-states in central Asia was, *c.*100 BC, counted as 190 persons! It is much more difficult to state an upper limit. The territory of a city-state is first and foremost the hinterland of the town, and a city-state that expands beyond its hinterland becomes less and less a city-state. If one tentatively puts a city's hinterland as at most a day's march from city to boundary, a radius of 30 km will give a territory of *c.*3,000 km² and a population of at most 300,000. Athens had a territory of 2,500 km² and, in the fourth century BC, a population of at least 200,000, of whom at least 30,000 were adult male full citizens.

A city-state consists typically of just one city and its hinterland. If there are other nucleated settlements within the territory, they mostly have the character of villages.

It is typical of city-states that the name of the state is the same as the name of the city—thus Athens, Venice, Andorra. In macro-states with many cities the state's name is the same as the name of the country, e.g. Denmark, Estonia, France.

A city-state is often described as a 'face-to-face society', a society, that is, in which everybody has personal contact with everybody else (at least the adult male citizens).

In contrast to nation-states, which ideally have a correspondence between political and ethnic identity, the population of a city-state will always have an ethnic identity different from the political identity. Ethnic identity the city's inhabitants share with the inhabitants of all the other city-states within the city-state culture, whereas political identity and patriotic sentiment are directed towards the individual city-state and have a force that separates one city-state from another.

As to the form of settlement, a city-state is characterised by a much higher level of urbanisation than any other pre-industrial society. In smaller city-states between 50 per cent and 90 per cent of the population often live within the city walls, whereas a city population of *c.*10 per cent of the total population was typical of many macro-states, in antiquity and the Middle Ages and in the Early Modern period down to *c.*1750.

Very small city-states may well have had something like a subsistence economy, in which each household produced, by and large, all that it needed; but medium and large city-states had division of labour, which led to a substantial production for a local market where the citizens bought or bartered for the greater part of their daily needs, apart from imported luxury wares. In 1521 the Spaniards were amazed at the enormous trade that went on every day in the markets of the Aztec city-states.

A city-state is ruled from its centre, and the government is not only heavily centralised but also extremely institutionalised. Many city-states have a republican form of government—for example, the Italian and Swiss ones in the Middle Ages and more recently—and some are even democracies, like Athens in antiquity.

A city-state is a self-governing state, but not necessarily an independent one. Many city-states possess what one might call 'internal' sovereignty, i.e. a government that wields a rule of law within a given territory over a given population, while 'external' sovereignty, i.e. independence, is missing. Miletos in Asia Minor was such a self-governing ancient Greek city-state, yet from *c.*545 BC it belonged to the Persian Empire, and subsequently to other big powers, and it was only an independent city-state quite briefly in the fifth century. Now, in what parts of the world have there been city-state cultures?[11] In the Near East, along the so-called Fertile Crescent, there were in antiquity a cluster of city-state cultures—the Sumerian, Babylonian, Assyrian, Anatolian, Syrian, Phoenician, Neo-Hittite, Palestinian and Philistine city-states. In south-west Asia Minor were the Lykians, who created a city-state culture in the sixth to fourth centuries BC. The whole sphere of ancient Greek civilisation from c.750 BC to about AD 500 was a city-state culture, with about 1,500 city-states. In Italy there was also in antiquity the Etruscan city-state culture north of Rome and the Latin one which comprised Rome and the cities of Latium south of Rome.

In the Middle Ages we can find city-state cultures in north Italy, south Germany and Switzerland; and the Dutch Republic was founded in 1579 as a kind of federal state comprising fifty-seven cities. Nor must it be forgotten that the Norwegian Vikings established a city-state culture in Ireland in the tenth century.

Going beyond Europe, we find no true city-state cultures in North or South America, but, on the other hand, in Mesoamerica there was a set of city-state cultures. The most important were the Maya in the Yucatan peninsula, the Mixtec and Zapotec city-states on the coast of the Pacific, and the Aztecs of central Mexico.

In West Africa there were city-state cultures in Nigeria, principally the Hausa kingdoms east of the Niger, the Yoruba kingdoms west of that river, and the slave-trading city-states in the Niger delta; also the Fante city-states along the Gold Coast and the Kotoko city-states south of Lake Chad. In the Swahili-speaking part of East Africa, in Kenya and Tanzania, there were the so-called stone cities; and in a great oasis in the middle of the Sahara there lay five small city-states inhabited from 1012 by a Berber tribe called the Mozabites.

In South-East Asia in the Middle Ages there was one city-state culture in Thailand and another in Indonesia in the period c.1400–1625. In Palembang in Sumatra there are traces of an earlier one c.700–1100. Central China was divided into more than 200 city-states in the Spring-and-Autumn Period, 771–481 BC. And in oases around the edge of the Taklamakan desert in Central Asia lay twenty-six little city-states that were integrated into the Chinese Empire only c.1780. What is more, the valley of Kathmandu in

Nepal in relatively recent times was split between from three to four little city-states.

Taken together, we have thirty-seven identifiable city-state cultures in world history. Our team of scholars at the Polis Centre has attempted for the first time ever to describe all of them, but we must presume that some have escaped our notice or will only be recognised as city-state cultures in the light of this investigation. This overview reveals that city-state cultures have occurred only in certain parts of the world. There never were any in Scandinavia or in England. In France and Spain one can find city-states, but only isolated and for short periods. In Germany before 1806 there were anything from sixty to a hundred, but many of them were isolated from one another and hemmed in by dukedoms and bishoprics: only in south Germany was there, in the late Middle Ages and the Renaissance, a true city-state culture like that in Switzerland.

So, in the major part of the world and for the major part of world history people did not live in city-states but in what, since the Peace of Westphalia in 1648, have been called 'territorial states'. And pursuing that concept, it has become standard to see city-states and territorial states as the two poles in a pair of opposites. But since all city-states had a well-defined territory, even if a small one, that terminology has taken people's minds in a wrong direction. I propose instead that we make the distinction between (small) city-states and (big) 'country-states'.[12]

What is the point of distinguishing the concepts of city-state culture and city-state? And of distinguishing between city-states and 'country-states'? Are there any major trends in world history that stand out more clearly if we contrast 'country-states' and city-state cultures? I believe that there are, and I advance three considerations.

First, throughout world history down to the eighteenth century, all 'country-states' have been monarchies. Many city-states were also monarchies, but the small scale of city-states meant that alongside monarchies there arose also oligarchies or democracies, i.e. states where the political decision-making process lay with councils and assemblies and where decisions were made on the basis of voting and debating. It is this political pattern that prevails in the world today, and it has its roots in the city-state cultures. In the oligarchies it was an elected council, in the democracies a people's assembly, that took the decisions. Common to both these types of constitution is that they are based on majority decisions after debate in assemblies, on selection of leaders, and on some degree of rotation amongst those entitled to take part in the political process. Before the nineteenth century, only in micro-states could such a system be practised, and the micro-states were city-states. The great upheaval in the political process occurred in the second half of the eighteenth century with the American War of Independence and the French Revolution.[13]

With the French Revolution democracy began to arrive in macro-states. The chief ideologue was Jean-Jacques Rousseau: his concept of democracy was entirely direct assembly democracy, which was known only from the city-states. His ideals were the constitution of Rome *c.*500 BC and the oligarchic constitution of his native city of Geneva, which he regarded as the ideal democracy. In that view he was mistaken; but in the present context that does not matter. Geneva in the eighteenth century was a city-state like ancient Rome, and thus the whole political ideology that grew up under Rousseau's inspiration under the French Revolution, and that we live under today has its roots in the city-state cultures.[14]

After the American War of Independence, in 1787–9, for the first time in modern times, the Americans created a federal state constitution in which the thirteen constituent states and the federation shared sovereignty amongst themselves, and there was therefore no sovereign at all in the classical sense, because, as we know, sovereignty is indivisible. Such a constitution was regarded by many at the time as an impossibility, but its champions were able to reply that there were historical examples of such a constitution functioning extremely well. Amongst the examples were the Achaian League and the Aitolian League, both founded in Greece in 280/79 BC, the Swiss confederacy of 1291, and the Dutch federal republic founded by the Treaty of Utrecht in 1579.[15] According to Montesquieu (1748) a federal state was typically a federation of small city-states,[16] and the Founding Fathers of the American Revolution were aware that they were transferring a historical political system from the micro-state to the macro-state level. Nowadays more than half the population of the world lives in federal states or in states with federal aspects. So once again our political civilisation is based on ideas and structures that have their roots in the city-states, and only afterwards were adapted to 'country-states'.[17]

Secondly, with the creation of federal states there opened up a

gap in the concept of a state. In the USA they distinguished between the states and the federation: New York and Pennsylvania
were states, but so was the whole federation. 'State' is typically defined as an institution possessing a legitimate monopoly of power to
uphold a given legal order within a specific territory over a specific
population. On that definition, a state that is part of a federation
is, of course, a state; but the whole federation is also a state, and
we can no longer say that a state is a state is a state, and that all
states are in principle equal. We have created, at base, a hierarchical
concept of state, and have thus reverted to the—often—hierarchical
structure of the city-state cultures, in which self-government was
a necessary requirement for being a city-state, but independence
was not necessarily required, and in which the federal state was the
preferred model for creating larger political units.[18]

Thirdly, one basis of the modern economy is urbanisation. In the
industrialised countries, about 80–90 per cent of the population live
in cities,[19] but 250 years ago the opposite was true: 80–90 per cent
of the population lived on the land or in villages, and only some 10–
20 per cent in the cities.[20] A subsistence economy is usually found
in communities with low urbanisation, whereas market economies
go with communities with high urbanisation. Now if there is one
thing that characterises city-state cultures in socio-economic terms,
it is urbanisation and markets. A nice example is the city-state of
Assur in northern Mesopotamia and its trading-station at Kanesh
in Asia Minor, which was in 1900 BC the centre for the whole
trade of the region, in gold, silver, tin and textiles.[21] The Polis
Centre's investigation of the thirty-seven city-state cultures shows
that the British economist John Hicks was right in his assertion
(often contradicted) that the modern market economy arose in the
city-states.[22]

2

A Sketch of the Thirty-Seven
Identified City-State Cultures

The Near East and Europe

(1) The oldest known city-state culture is that of the Sumerians in Mesopotamia, with Uruk, Ur and Lagash as three of the best-known city-states. They were city-states from c.3100 to c.2350 BC, when Sargon of Akkad conquered Sumer. The city-states arose again briefly after the collapse of the Akkadian dynasty c.2150, but the third dynasty of Ur (c.2100–2000) changed the city-states again into provinces within a larger kingdom. When the third dynasty of Ur collapsed, there was yet another city-state period from c.2000 to 1850 BC[1]

(2) In Syria in the third millennium BC there was a set of city-states, the best known being Ebla. They were destroyed and disappeared c.2300, but turned up again as city-states in the Middle Bronze Age (c.2000–1700) and a third time in the early Iron Age (c.1000).[2]

(3) In the periods 2900–2300 BC and again in 2000–1200 BC Palestine was divided into about fourteen city-states, of which Hazor was the most important.[3]

(4) In the Old Assyrian Period (c.1950–1700 BC) Assur was a city-state, as we know especially from thousands of inscribed clay tablets found in Assur's trading station, Kanesh, in Asia Minor. It is not known whether Assur was an isolated city-state or whether it was the southernmost of a group of city-states on both sides of the upper course of the Tigris.[4]

(5) During the early Middle Bronze Age (c.2000–1650 BC) Central Anatolia was divided into a large number of city-states, probably several hundred. They seem often to have formed a network of leagues or federations, each consisting of one hegemonic and

a number of smaller dependent city-states. The best known are Kanesh, Durhumit and Purushattum.[5]

(6) In the course of the second millennium BC a set of city-states arose along the coast of Phoenicia, including Arwad, Byblos, Sidon and Tyre; and in the first millennium BC they founded a number of colonies in Cyprus and the western Mediterranean, of which the greatest was Carthage, and Carthage in turn founded a set of colonies in Sardinia, Sicilia, North Africa and Spain.[6]

(7) When the Hittite Empire broke up c.1200 BC its southern part gradually split into a set of city-states which disappeared only when they were incorporated into the Assyrian empire in the second half of the eighth century BC. The biggest of them was Karkamis on the Euphrates; the southernmost was Hama.[7]

(8) After the collapse of the Kassite monarchy c.1100 BC the countryside of southern Mesopotamia became settled with Aramaic, Chaldean and Arab tribes, while many of the old cities became city-states once again. They formed, as it were, a network of 'islands' separated by the tribal communities, and in the ninth to seventh centuries BC they came under Assyrian overlordship.[8]

(9) c.1175 BC Ramesses III settled Philistines in five city-states in Palestine, from Ekron in the north to Gaza in the south. They disappeared in 605 BC, when they were conquered by the Neo-Babylonian Empire and their inhabitants were deported to Babylon.[9]

(10) The ancient Greek city-state culture covered the eastern Mediterranean world from c.750 BC to AD 550. It comprised some 1,500 city-states. Its centre was in Greece and Asia Minor, but in the Archaic period (c.750 to 500 BC) hundreds of city-states were founded along the coasts of the Mediterranean and the Black Sea; and in the early Hellenistic Age (c.330–200) several hundred new city-states were founded in the Near East.[10]

(11) In Asia Minor there may well have been a host of local city-state cultures before the whole region was Hellenised after Alexander the Great's conquest of the Persian Empire. One such can probably be found in Lykia in the Dynastic Period (c.550–330 BC), when part of the population was settled in self-governing city-states. In the Hellenistic period they were turned into *poleis*, and the 'Lykian Federation' was an integral part of the Greek city-state culture.[11]

(12) The Etruscans were settled in twelve city-states, including

Caere, Tarquinia and Vulci, until the whole region north of Rome was conquered by the Romans in the third century BC[12]

(13) Rome itself was the largest of about twenty city-states in Latium; amongst the others were Tibur and Praeneste. The Latin city-states were conquered by Rome and turned into self-governing *municipia*, the last after the Social War in 91–89 BC. Rome was still a city-state at the beginning of the fourth century BC, but changed over the following centuries into being the capital city of an empire consisting essentially of dependent city-states: *poleis* in the East and *civitates* in the West.[13]

(14) On the caravan route along the west coast of the Arabian peninsula there were a set of small cities in the oases. The most important were Medina and Mecca. They may have formed a city-state culture in the fifth and sixth centuries AD.[14]

(15) Vikings from Norway colonised the east coast of Ireland in the tenth century AD and established a set of cities, principally Dublin. The cities were city-states; at first they were independent, but they soon became dependencies under Irish kings, and were finally conquered by the English in 1171.[15]

(16) When the Carolingian kingdom of Louis II broke up in AD 875, the cities of northern Italy became city-states, most of them governed by the local bishop. From the end of the eleventh century they changed into republics governed by elected consuls and councils: in the High Middle Ages there were about 300 such city-states in north Italy. In the course of the fifteenth century most of them fell under the control of the three biggest ones, Florence, Milan and Venice, which in that way became by conquest no longer city-states but small 'country-states'.[16]

(17) In the German Reich in the late Middle Ages there were c.100 *Reichsstädte* and *Freie Städte*,[17] most of them in south Germany. There were also in the same region episcopal states and dukedoms, but in the period c.1350–1550 the cities created a set of city-leagues, and through the interaction of the cities in trade and production they formed during these two centuries a city-state culture that disappeared for good only with the end of the German Reich in 1806.[18]

(18) When the last duke of Zähringen died in 1218, Switzerland was freed from the feudal form of government which otherwise dominated the whole of Central Europe. Eight Swiss Free Cities

arose: they were city-states and formed a city-state culture from the fourteenth century until 1848.[19]

(19) The Dutch Republic founded by the Union of Utrecht in 1579 was a confederation of seven provinces, each province consisting of a number of self-governing cities. The Union can quite reasonably be regarded as a city-state culture consisting of fifty-seven dependent city-states.[20] See *supra*: The Near East and Europe.

Asia

(20) The Zhou monarchy in China came to an end in 771 BC, and the state was broken up into several hundred little states, most of them city-states. In the Spring-and-Autumn period the city-state was the most important form of state in central China, but a great many of them were swallowed up by their much bigger neighbours, and in the Warring States Period (481–221 BC) the city-states had all disappeared again.[21]

(21) In central Asia where the Silk Route went north and south round the Tarim Basin and on the edge of the Taklamakan desert there lay forty-seven little states, of which twenty-five were city-states. They arose in *c*.200 BC, and disappeared first definitely in AD 1800. At periods they were independent, but most of the time they were dependent states under China or Tibet or the Mongols.[22]

(22) From the seventh to the eleventh century AD there was in southern Sumatra a city-state called Sriwijaya which exercised a hegemony. It controlled a set of dependent city-states that lay along the rivers. Sriwijaya was a Malay city-state, possibly to be identified with Palembang.[23]

(23) In the same region there were a number of big harbour-cities, which created an Islamic city-state culture *c*.1450–1625, e.g. Melaka, Aceh and Brunei. They were called *negeri*, a Sanskrit word meaning 'city', but which in modern Malay has come to mean 'state'.[24]

(24) Besides the Malay city-states, there were in that region a number of other city-states, which had as their common language Thai or Javanese or Makassarese. The Thai city-states, at any rate, constituted a city-state culture from *c*. AD 800 to 1700.[25]

(25) The valley of Kathhmandu in Nepal was ruled, *c*.1200, by the Malla dynasty. Down until 1482 the whole valley was ruled by one king, but when Yaksa Malla died in 1482, his kingdom

was divided between his three sons. For the next 300 years the valley was fragmented into three small city-states, until in 1768-9 the Gurkhas conquered the region and turned the biggest of the city-states, Kathmandu, into the capital of the state of Nepal.[26]

Africa

(26) The Mozabites are a Berber tribe, who settled in the eleventh century AD in a large oasis in the northern Sahara. They founded an Islamic city-state culture with five, later seven, city-states. It lasted until 1882, when the whole region came under French rule.[27]

(27) Along the east coast of Africa, in southern Somalia, Kenya, Tanzania and northern Mozambique are a whole set of ancient 'stone cities', continuously occupied by a Swahili-speaking population. They arose c. AD 1000 and were self-governing city-states until the beginning of the nineteenth century. There was close connection between the cities along the coast, and they can all be regarded as part of the same city-state culture.[28]

(28) On the grassy plain south of the Sahara and east of the River Niger live the Hausa. From c.1415 their territory was divided between seven larger city-states and a lot of small ones, and all together they counted as an Islamic city-state culture. But in 1804 the Hausa were defeated by the Fulani and the city-states lost their independence and became provincial capitals in a new Caliphate.[29]

(29) Before the European colonisation of West Africa, the densest urbanisation south and west of the Niger was that of the Yoruba between c.1600 and 1900. Many of their cities constituted a city-state culture. In the seventeenth century Oyo, the largest of the city-states, conquered its smaller neighbours and was for a longer period the centre of a small empire of city-states.[30]

(30) On the Gold Coast, in what is now Ghana, the Fante people lived in city-states. They can be traced back to the fourteenth to sixteenth century and flourished in the seventeenth and eighteenth centuries, in which period they were organised in a federation led by Mankessim. At the beginning of the nineteenth century the federation was overturned by the Asante.[31]

(31) The twelve to fourteen city-states of the Kotoko have been mentioned above. In the seventeenth century they fell under the Bornu Empire, but kept their self-government, which still existed at the beginning of the twentieth century.[32]

(32) From *c*.1600 to 1800 the western delta of the Niger was divided between four city-states, and the little city-state culture was a centre of the Atlantic slave trade. It was still in existence in the nineteenth century but vanished with the European colonisation of the area in the 1890s.[33]

(33) The Konso are a small people who inhabit a zone of *c*.300 km² in the highlands of south-western Ethiopia. They number *c*.55,000 persons who live in some thirty-five close-set fortified towns. They are agriculturalists who have their homes in the towns and their fields in its hinterland. Until the end of the nineteenth century the towns were self-governing political communities, each ruled by an elected council of elders. In 1897 the Konso were subdued by the Abyssinians.[34]

Central America

(34) The decipherment of the Maya hieroglyphs, combined with new excavations using modern archaeological techniques, shows that in the Classic period (*c*. AD 250–900) there were about thirty Maya city-states on the Yucatan peninsula. The cities disappeared in the course of the tenth century, and with them the city-states; but when the kingdom ruled from Mayapan broke up *c*.1450, Yucatan was once more divided into city-states down to the Spanish conquest.[35]

(35) North-west of the Mayan territory lay Mixteca, a region organised as a city-state culture in the post-Classic period, *c*. AD 900–1521. It consisted of over 100 city-states, which were not reduced to mere cities until the end of the sixteenth century. From *c*.1450 the Mixtec city-states were no longer independent, but they remained self-governing throughout, though dominated first by the Aztecs and afterwards by the Spaniards.[36]

(36) And east of Mixteca lies the valley of Oaxaca, the Sierra Zapoteca and the isthmus of Tehuantepec, all in the region called Bènizàa. The state in the Oaxaca valley, which in the Classic period was ruled from Monte Alban, broke up in *c*. AD 800, and the region was divided into city-states. In the fifteenth century new city-states were created as colonies in the Sierra Zapoteca and the Tehuantepec. The city-state culture collapsed in the course of the sixteenth century after Spain's seizure of power.[37]

(37) The Aztecs invaded Mexico from the north in the course of

the twelfth century and straight away settled in cities which were politically run as city-states. The three largest, Tenochtitlan, Texcoco and Tlacopan, created in 1428 a triple alliance that extended its sway over large parts of Central America. When the Spaniards arrived in America in 1519–21, the triple alliance controlled c.500 dependent states, of which the majority continued as tribute-paying city-states.[38]

3

'Country-States' versus City-State Cultures

In the perspective of world history we can see that the mutual interreaction between the creation of cities and the creation of states brought to the fore two different types of state: macro-states, which each had a great number of cities spread out over the territory, and regions whose population had, indeed, the same culture, language, religion and traditions but were nevertheless divided into a large number of little states, each consisting of a city and its hinterland, often of under 100 and, at most, 1,000 or so km².

It is usual to call the macro-states 'territorial states' and to treat territorial states and city-states as antonyms.[1] But that is misleading, because every city-state had a territory, even if of modest size. It would be much more correct to distinguish between city-states and 'country-states'.[2] That terminology would also fit very well the fact that, roughly speaking, the names of all macro-states are the same as the country they are in, whereas almost all city-states are named after the city.[3]

But why did urbanisation and the creation of states give rise sometimes to the creation of a 'country-state' and sometimes to a city-state culture?[4] That question has never been studied systematically; but when the talk is of city-states, it is always geo-political reasons that are adduced. That is fair enough, but a look at the thirty-seven city-state cultures shows that geo-physical explanation is not, by itself, enough: it must give way to other factors. And, as always in history, it must be realised that mono-causality is a wild-goose chase, and only the play of different factors in different combinations can provide a general explanation of a phenomenon.

A. *The geo-political factor* It is usually asserted that city-states often arise in regions where little valleys and plateaux are like

pockets amongst mountains which divide them. Such an explanation well fits, for example, the Syrian and Greek city-states (nos.
2 and 10, ch. 2) and the Malay city-states where a number of coastal
cities were divided from one another by impenetrable jungle (nos.
22 and 23). But the Sumerian city-state culture arose in southern Mesopotamia, which is as flat as a pancake (no. 1), and the
Mozabites turned a big oasis into five city-states, although the geo-
physical situation could just as well have resulted in the whole oasis
being a 'country-state' with five cities (no. 26). And, vice versa,
large 'country-states' have arisen in mountainous regions where
one might have expected the creation of city-states if one insisted
on geo-political determinism. Norway in the Middle Ages is an
obvious example.

B. *The economic factor*   The creation of city-states may in numerous cases have resulted from a combination of economic and
geo-political factors. The thirty-seven city-state cultures show that
there is often a connection between city-state cultures and com-
merce.

The relationship arises in several, variant ways; (a) caravan routes
led through cities, or cities grew up on caravan routes. Some of those
cities lay in the 'country-states' through which the caravan route
passed, but when it went out into no man's land, city-states might
arise. Along the caravan route from Mesopotamia to Aden, there
were a number of cities on the south coast of the Arabian peninsula,
amongst them Medina and Mecca, and those cities were probably
city-states in the fourth to sixth century AD (no. 14). (b) Commercial
cities have often arisen in the interface between two civilisations and
such cities could develop into city-states. Examples are the Niger
Delta city-states, which arose in the sixteenth century in connection
with the Atlantic slave trade (no. 32).

C. *Colonisation*   When a population group was sent out to found
a colony (or did so under its own auspices), they had to settle
in foreign and often hostile territory. The result was often that, to
begin with, the colonists settled in a fortified town which controlled
only a limited hinterland. In some cases the colonists were governed
from the homeland, e.g. the European colonies in Africa and Asia;
in other cases they became self-governing societies, i.e. city-states.
Typical examples are the Phoenician and Greek colonial city-states
in antiquity (nos. 6 and 10). Sometimes a whole city-state culture

could arise through colonisation: the five Philistine city-states in
Palestine began as colonists sent out from Egypt by Ramesses III
*c.*1175 BC (no. 9), and the Aztec city-states were founded by invaders
from the north *c.* AD 1200 (no. 37).

D. *Sequence*   Everywhere in the world, and at all times, there has
been a close connection between the growth of cities and the growth
of states, but the two processes have not always begun simultaneously. Sometimes the state arose before the city, sometimes the other
way round. When state formation comes before city formation, the
result tends to be a 'country-state', whereas city-state cultures seem
to arise when the rise of cities comes before the rise of states or simultaneously. In Mesopotamia cities grew up very early, perhaps
quite a while before the rise of a real state (no. 1). In Egypt it is
not until dynastic times that we find cities that bear a resemblance
to the Mesopotamian ones. So it was in the Middle Ages. In England after the Anglo-Saxon immigration and in Scandinavia in the
Viking Age, the state arose at a period when the village was the
only known form of nucleated settlement, and real cities arose only
under the auspices of a monarchy. Contrariwise, in the Netherlands
and Italy cities arose early and kept well out of the way of powerful
'country-states'. Here the possibilities for a city-state culture were
notably better (nos. 19 and 16).

E. *Acculturation*   We know of clusters of city-state cultures in the
Near East and southern Europe, East Asia, West Africa and Central
America. There can be no doubt that the city-states in each of those
four zones arose spontaneously and without cross-influence from
any of the other zones. But within each of the four zones there is a
close relationship between the city-state cultures, and acculturation
from the older city-state cultures was, in those cases, a factor that
helped to create the younger ones. The many city-state cultures
along the Fertile Crescent always influenced one another, and it has
often been alleged that the Greeks got not only their alphabet from
the Phoenicians but also their city-state concept; and in the same
way a reasonable assumption can be made that the creation of the
Etruscan and Latin city-states took its inspiration from the Greek
city-states in south Italy and Sicily.

F. *Devolution*   In numerous cases a city-state culture did not arise
de novo in a region where before there had been no city or state cre-

ation, but by devolution—that is to say, by an urbanised 'country-state' collapsing and being broken up into a large number of city-states. The Neo-Hittite city-state culture in North Syria arose when the Hittite Empire collapsed *c.*1200 BC (no. 7). After the break-up of the Zhou dynasty in 771 BC there followed the Spring-and-Autumn period (771–481 BC) in which central China was for a period split into more than 200 city-states (no. 20). The Zapotec city-state culture arose in the ninth century AD in the vacuum left by the collapse of the big state that had been ruled from the great city of Monte Alban until *c.*800 (no. 36). On Louis II's death in 875 there was a power vacuum in north Italy which made possible the rise of the north Italian city-states (no. 16). And in Switzerland the city-states arose after the Zähringer dynasty died out in 1218 (no. 18).

G. Successive city-state cultures in the same region   In some cases a region was divided into city-states only once in world history: for example, the Greek city-state culture in the eastern Mediterranean from *c.*750 BC to AD 550 (no. 10) and the Chinese one in the Spring-and-Autumn period from 771 to 481 BC (no. 20). But in other regions a city-state culture vanished only to turn up again after an extended period. The Sumerian city-states disappeared when Sargon of Akkad conquered south Mesopotamia *c.*2350 BC (no. 1), but turned up again for three short periods: first when Assyria collapsed *c.*2250, and again after the third dynasty at Ur in 2000, and yet again after the end of the Kassite monarchy *c.*1100 BC.[5] The Etruscan city-states in Tuscany disappeared in the third to second centuries BC (no. 12), but after the collapse of the Roman Empire they came back again in the Middle Ages, with Pisa, Siena and Florence as the leading states (no. 16). In other cases not just the city-states but the cities themselves disappeared, and the city-state culture was followed by a 'Dark Age' which might last for hundreds of years until in the end it was succeeded by a new city-state culture. The city-states of Syria and Palestine (nos. 2 and 3) and the Mayan city-state culture in the Classic period *c.*200–900 and again after *c.*1450 (no. 34) are examples of such successive city-state cultures interrupted by 'Dark Ages'. By contrast, in Sumer the city-state periods were separated by periods in which Sumer became a unified state in which the former city-states were provincial capitals.

H. *Defence*   In a ground-breaking article the Israeli sociologist Azar Gat has emphasised defence and the protection of city walls as the single most important cause of the rise of city-states.[6] If we are looking at the causes of cities in general, there can be no doubt that he is right. But cities existed in 'country-states' as well as in city-state cultures, and defence and protection were surely an important motive for the rise of cities in both cases. Are there, then, any circumstances that make the role of defence even more important for city-state cultures than for 'country-states'? There may be good arguments for this: 'country-states' make war against each other but have peace internally; city-state cultures might sometimes wage wars against the 'country-states' on their boundaries, but at the same time every single city-state culture was plagued by constant wars with other city-states. Other things being equal, we can conjecture that war was a greater problem in the city-state cultures than in the 'country-states', and correspondingly, that the city-states had a greater need for fortified cities to which the population could flee for protection.[7]

II

THE CITY-STATE CULTURE
IN ANCIENT GREECE

Introduction

Both geographically and demographically the ancient Greek city-state culture was much the biggest of the thirty-seven cultures I have listed in the previous part.[1] The Greeks called a city-state *polis*, plural *poleis*,[2] and there were in all *c*.1,500 *poleis*. More than 600 are attested in Greece proper;[3] more than 400 were colonies or Hellenised communities along the coasts of the Mediterranean and the Black Sea,[4] to which must be added more than 300 Hellenistic foundations in the Near East as far as the River Indus.[5] But there were never 1,500 *poleis* at the same time. Throughout new *poleis* were being founded and old ones were disappearing. In *c*.400 BC we can trace about 850 *poleis* in the sources we have,[6] and we can guess that many others may have been named in all the sources that have been lost. At any given time in the Classical period there were at least 1,000 *poleis*, and that makes the ancient Greek city-state culture the biggest in world history: the next biggest was that of the Aztecs in Central America in the fifteenth century AD.[7]

There were Greek cities all over the Mediterranean world, from Emporion in the Pyrenees to Ai Khanoum in Afghanistan and from Olbia at the mouth of the river Bug in Ukraine to Kyrene in Libya. Almost all those *poleis* had arisen or been founded in the period from 750 to 200 BC, and as late as the sixth century AD some of them were still city-states, though most were just cities. Thus the ancient Greek city-state culture lasted for some 1,200 years, exceeded only by the thousands of years of history of the Sumerian and Babylonian city-states.[8] Population-wise there is no city-state culture that can measure up to that of ancient Greece. Precise figures we do not have but a cautious estimate is that in the fourth century BC the population of all the Greek *poleis* totalled at least 7.5 million people and in the time of the Roman Empire there were about 30 million Greek-speaking people living in *poleis*.[9]

The city-state culture of ancient Greece stretched so far in time, in space, in population and in number of cities that it can properly be asked: is it right to describe the history of 1,500 city-states over a period of 1,000 years as one and the same city-state culture? Without discussion or documentation, more or less all historians take it for granted that all the *poleis* belonged to the same civilisation and have so much in common that they can be treated as a unity.[10] Contrariwise, there is no agreement as to how long a period of time is covered by this unified picture.

4

The Unity of the City-State Culture of Ancient Greece

The unity of all the Greek city-states can best be illustrated by an example. We possess a small treatise on the geography of the Mediterranean and the Black Sea, written in the fourth century BC and wrongly attributed to the geographer Skylax of Karyanda, who really lived 200 years earlier, which is why it goes under the name of Pseudo-Skylax.[1] It is organised as a *periplous*, i.e. a journey by sail along the coasts of the Mediterranean and the Black Sea, and the writer enumerates, region by region, the most important settlements along the coast. In all, 733 toponyms are quoted, and most of them are classified, directly or indirectly, as *poleis*.[2] Pseudo-Skylax begins his voyage at the Pillars of Hercules (Gibraltar) and goes along the coasts of Spain, France, Italy and Illyria, as far as the river Acheron in southern Epeiros 'where Hellas begins to be continuous'. Then the voyage goes all the way south round Greece to the river Peneios in north Thessaly 'where continuous Hellas ends'.[3] Then it goes via Macedon, Thrace, Skythia, Asia Minor, Syria, Egypt, Libya and North Africa, and so back to the Pillars of Hercules. In his classification of cities Pesudo-Skylax distinguishes between Hellenic and barbarian, i.e. non-Hellenic, *poleis*. In the first and the last sections a Greek colony is called a *polis Hellenis*, while *polis* without qualification means a barbarian city: but in the central section, the section about Greece proper, a *polis* means a Hellenic city, and the addition *Hellenis* is superfluous. The list of Hellenic *poleis* is far from exhaustive—and does not pretend to be— but the whole treatise rests on the assumption that the Hellenic city-states comprise all Greek settlements in the whole Mediterranean. Hellas is not just 'continuous Hellas', i.e. roughly modern Greece and the west coast of Asia Minor, where all *poleis* were Hellenic, but is also the whole colonial world, where Hellas is divided up into little bits, all of them *poleis* divided from one another by territories inhabited by 'barbarians'. The division into Hellenic *poleis* and barbarian *poleis*,[4] and the conception that all Hellenic *poleis* belong together, is found in all our sources,[5] and can be traced back to the fragments we have of the oldest Greek historical geographer, Hekataios of Miletos, who wrote his description of the inhabited world at the end of the sixth century BC.[6]

In contrast to many other city-state cultures, the Greek *poleis* did not lie together in one large region so that communication between them could be by land. In this respect the Greek *poleis* were like the Phoenician and the Malayan ones: most Archaic and Classical Greek *poleis* were on the sea, and only in the Hellenistic period did the Greeks found a long row of colonies well into the Persian Empire and far from the coasts of the Mediterranean and the Black Sea. Most early Greek city-states were by the sea or near the sea, 'like frogs round a pond' in Plato's vivid phrase.[7] And his remark is borne out by Pseudo-Skylax, who lists his *poleis* in the order in which they lie along the coast: only occasionally is his list interrupted by the standard comment, 'there are also some *poleis* inland'.[8]

As the world looks today, it is sea that divides and land that binds together, but in antiquity it was the other way round: communication was easiest by sea, and land communication was complicated and costly.[9] The Greeks were a seafaring people, and after *polis* it is *limen*, the harbour, that is the commonest term for settlement in Pseudo-Skylax.[10] With Classical Sparta as the one notorious exception, the ancient Greek city-state was anything but a society of xenophobic stay-at-homes. The Greeks were, on the contrary, unbelievably mobile and unbelievably easy-going about letting strangers settle in their cities.

(a) From the eighth to the third century BC new *poleis* were created all the time, both in Greece and outside it: they were founded as colonies (*apoikiai*), usually by settlers sent from the big *poleis* in Greece, which were consequently regarded as a colony's 'mother-city' (*metropolis*). Many of the colonies subsequently got reinforcements of new colonists, partly from their own *metropolis* but also from other *poleis*.[11] Most of the colonies were politically independent of the mother-city, but there were strong religious and cultural links, kept alive by constant communication between colony and mother-city.[12] A large colony might often itself found new colonies in the region, thus acquiring a double status, as both a *metropolis* and an *apoikia*.[13]

(b) Many individual Greeks moved from one *polis* to another. Often they were traders or craftsmen, but the numerous civil wars also resulted in large groups of citizens being sentenced to exile or living as refuges in neighbouring city-states.[14] So besides citizens and the slaves of citizens there was in every *polis* a large population of free non-citizens who had settled in the city either permanently or for a period of years and were very seldom admitted to citizenship.[15]

(c) The army of a city-state was primarily a citizen militia, but it could be supplemented by professional mercenaries, and in the Classical and Hellenistic periods many Greeks served for years on end as mercenaries in foreign armies.[16]

(d) Inter-regional trade, especially sea trade, was a striking characteristic of the Greek city-state culture: trade was made necessary by the high degree of urbanisation, another typical feature, which also characterises other city-state cultures amongst our thirty-seven.[17]

(e) It was not only trade that caused Greeks to leave their native place for a more or less long period: Delphi and the other famous Greek oracles were consulted every year by thousands of people, who had often travelled for weeks to obtain the god's answers to their questions,[18] and thousands of Greeks met at two- or four-year intervals at the great pan-Hellenic festivals. At the Olympic Games there may have been as many as 40,000 or 50,000 spectators.[19]

This constant and intense communication between Greeks all over the Mediterranean world was the precondition for the ability of the Greeks who lived outside Greece to retain their ethnic identity, including their conviction that, as Greeks, they were superior to the barbarians who surrounded them.[20] In some colonies the colonists were virtually all males, who married and had children by local women.[21] But the Greeks described all non-Greeks as *barbaroi* or *barbarophonoi* (people speaking something unintelligible). They did not bother to learn the languages of other peoples,[22] and it was the women and the slaves who had to learn the language and conform to the culture of their husbands and owners. The colonies of ancient Greece are a rare example of it being the father's language that became the children's mother-tongue, and there are very few known cases where Greek colonists adapted themselves to the local language and culture and finally stopped speaking Greek or feeling themselves to be Greeks.[23]

In spite of the enormous distance from Spain to the Caucasus, the Greeks held fast to the conviction that they were a single people, and according to Herodotos (8.144.3) there were four things that bound them together: common origin, common language, common sacred places and cults, and common customs and traditions.

(a) Common origin was a myth: like most other peoples, the Greeks believed that at some time the human race had been wiped out by a flood sent by the gods, that the sole survivors were Deukalion and his family, and that all Hellenes were descended from Deukalion's son Hellen.[24] Although entirely mythical, this sense of a common origin must not be underrated: on the other hand, it should be stressed that the Greeks did not see themselves as a superior *race*. When the Greeks went on about how they were superior to all barbarians physically and mentally, they justified this by climate and surroundings: with its temperate climate Greece was the best place in the world, where its people combined *dianoia* (intelligence) with *thymos* (spirit). The hot climate of the East promoted intelligence, but was inimical to spirit, while the cold of the West gave people freedom of spirit, but was inimical to their intelligence.[25]

(b) If one takes into account the enormous spread of Greek civilisation, there were astonishingly few dialects, and there was relatively little difference between them.[26] If we can trust our sources, all Greeks could understand each other.[27] In his account of the *Anabasis*, the expedition against Persia, Xenophon tells of Prince Kyros, who in 401 BC assembled a mercenary army of Greeks 10,000 strong and marched eastwards to push his brother off the throne. The soldiers came from many different city-states and spoke different dialects, but when the army was called together each soldier addressed his fellow soldiers without interpreters, whereas interpreters are mentioned as soon as the Greeks come into contact with the Persians or other 'barbarians'.[28] Similarly, at Athens in the People's Court any non-local could speak his own dialect and expect to be understood by the jurors.[29] 'In the Archaic and Classical sources there is practically no evidence that local dialects were ever a hindrance to mutual comprehension':[30] the only source that qualifies this assertion is Thucydides in his description of the Eurytanes, a tribe in inner Aitolia 'who were extremely difficult to understand and who lived on raw meat' (3.94.5).

After Alexander the Great conquered the Persian Empire, the Greeks founded several hundred colonies in the Near East; nevertheless, the Greeks in the Hellenistic Age still maintained a strong linguistic convergence: they all used the same written form, a combination of the Attic and Ionian dialects. This new 'dialect' was called *koine* (common language), and it seems to have lived up to its name. As to the spoken language, we are almost entirely in the dark, but here, too, it seems that the dialects had to give way to a kind of standard Greek.[31]

(c) The 'common cult-places' that Herodotos speaks of were partly the great oracles that all the Greeks sought advice from, in Dodone, Delphi, Lebadeia, Abai, Oropos and Didyma,[32] partly the places that held pan-Hellenic competitions in sport, music, drama and recitation: Olympia, Delphi, the Isthmos and Nemea.[33] Herodotos' reference to common cults shows that the cults and the set of gods that turned up at the festivals must have had so much in common that they can all be regarded as manifestations of one and the same religion—a view to which the Greeks themselves gave expression in the sources we have.[34]

(d) Common customs and traditions can cover everything from recitation and reading of Homer to the use of coinage or the building of peripteral temples. In this connection we will limit ourselves to one example. Sporting contests were a feature of Greek culture that distinguished them from all their neighbours.[35] The Games were pan-Hellenic, which meant that all Greeks could participate—but also that *only* Greeks could participate. A participant had to state what *polis* he came from, and a victor was named in his proclamation as a citizen of the city-state he belonged to.[36] Amongst the Olympic victors whose names are preserved, 177 out of 736 came from Greek city-states outside Greece proper.[37]

So the Greeks had a common culture and a fixed belief that they were a single people. And that justifies the proposition that all 1,500 *poleis* belonged to one and the same city-state culture, a proposition formulated with force and brevity by the poet Poseidippos: 'there is only one Hellas, but there are many *poleis*' (fr. 30, *PCG*).

However, it must not be concluded that the city-state was a specifically Greek institution, a form of society that distinguished Greeks from barbarians. That is a view that can be read in modern works,[38] but, with Aristotle as the sole exception, it is not what the Greeks themselves believed. Aristotle argued that the only true humans were adult Greek males who were citizens of a *polis*, and that the *polis* was a specifically Greek form of society such as barbarians did not have the capacity to create.[39] But in Herodotos, Thucydides, Xenophon, Pseudo-Skylax and all the other sources we hear of hundreds of 'barbarian' *poleis*. The word *polis* is often used in the sense of 'city' rather than 'state'; but it is also often used of 'barbarian' city-states, e.g. Rome or the Etruscan or Phoenician city-states.[40] To use the word *polis* of a barbarian city was naturally often as misleading as when the Greeks identified foreign gods with their own, and called, e.g., the Skythian god Geitosyros 'Apollo';[41] but the language and concept the Greek writers used do not show that the Greeks themselves felt that their own division into *poleis* was one of the characteristic differences between Greeks and barbarians.

5

The Rise of the Ancient
Greek City-State Culture

Modern historians are still in conflict over the chronology of the Greek city-states. Can the *polis* be traced back to the Mycenean Age? Or did it arise in the Geometric period? And if one settles for the latter view, one still has to take a position about whether it began as early as *c*.900 BC or as late as 700. No consensus has yet been reached as to where and when the earliest *poleis* are to be found; and there is even less agreement still as to when the later ones died out.

In what follows I shall argue for the now widespread opinion that the Greek *polis* was not destroyed by the Macedonians at the end of the Classical period but continued as the leading form of state and society all through the Hellenistic Age and through most of the Roman Imperial period.[1] The *polis* died out only in late antiquity after a period of decline of several hundred years: its disappearance was gradual and imperceptible, as had been its arrival on the scene more than 1,000 years earlier.

We have three distinct types of evidence that can cast light on the rise of the *polis*: (1) etymological study of related words in other Indo-European languages; (2) literary and inscriptional sources from the eighth to the sixth century BC; (3) physical remains of early settlements.

(1) *Etymological evidence* An etymological investigation of the word *polis* is extremely important because by extrapolation it can take us back to the time before the oldest written sources. An earlier variant of *polis*, *ptolis*, is perhaps to be found on a Mycenean tablet in the form *po-to-ri-jo*; but unfortunately, the word is only a part of a proper name,[2] so we have no idea what *po-to-ri-jo* meant in Mycenean. Comparison with other Indo-European languages gives bet-

ter results. The Greek word *polis* is cognate with Old Indian *púr*, Lithuanian *pilìs* and Latvian *pils*.³ In all three languages its original meaning is 'fortified place', but in Old Indian it developed into 'city', while the original meaning stayed in the two Baltic languages.⁴

So we can conclude that *polis* originally meant a fortified place, and that idea is supported by our earliest written sources, where *polis* is sometimes used synonymously with *akropolis* in the sense 'fortified place'. But while *akropolis* signifies both an eminence used as a settlement and a fortified eminence with no settlement,⁵ *polis* seems always to have meant a settlement, high-lying and usually fortified,⁶ not just a high-lying place of refuge.

Remains of such fortified settlements from the period *c*.1000–800 BC are found at Dreros and Anavlochos in Crete,⁷ and in numerous other places where we have remains from the Proto-Geometric and Geometric periods.⁸ We shall never have it confirmed, but it is a qualified guess that such settlements were called *polis* by their inhabitants.⁹ The Indo-European terminology points to the conclusion that the original meaning of the word *polis* was not 'city' or 'state' but 'fortified place', specifically a small fortified settlement on a height.

This brief survey of the word *polis* shows that the question 'How old is the *polis*?' is meaningless in so short a form. In the sense 'fortified place', *polis* may indeed have a history stretching back to Mycenean times; but that is not what historians mean when they ask how old the *polis* is: they want to know how old the Greek city-state is, i.e. how far back we can trace the *polis* that we know from the Archaic and Classical sources. But even in this form the question is hard to answer, because the development of the form of a society is a process that often stretches over hundreds of years. When is it appropriate to call a settlement a city? And when is it appropriate to call its political organisation a state?¹⁰ The only way forward is to cut the Gordian knot and set up a provisional definition (or, rather, a provisional 'ideal type') of the Classical Greek *polis* and ask how far back in history that form of state and society can be traced. Thus: a *polis* was a small institutionalised self-governing society, a political community of adult male citizens (*politai* or *astoi*), who along with their families lived in a—usually—fortified city (also called *polis* or sometimes *asty*) or in its hinterland (*chora* or *ge*) along with two

other sets of inhabitants, free non-citizens (*xenoi* or often *metoikoi*)
and slaves (*douloi*).

It is still a disputed question whether the *polis* in that sense can
be traced back to the Mycenean Age. I am one of those who believe
that there was a break in development at the end of the Bronze Age
and that we should not expect any continuity in types of society.[11] It
cannot be excluded, however, that each of the Minoan palace-cities
on Crete was the centre of a city-state in the New Palace Period
(*c.*1750–1550 BC),[12] so that Crete at the beginning of the late Bronze
Age ought to be counted amongst the city-state cultures; but with
the sources we have, we cannot take the Mycenean palaces in Knossos, Pylos, Mykenai, Thebes and Athens to have been centres of
city-states that disappeared in the Dark Ages but reappeared in the
ninth and eighth centuries.[13] The *polis* seems to have arisen in the
Geometric period, *c.*900–700, not by devolution as a result of the
collapse of the Mycenean states but by evolution as a result of a
great rise in population, prosperity and civilisation. City formation
and state formation took off at more or less the same time, and
with constant interaction between them. So to answer the question 'When did the *polis* arise?' we must begin *c.*500 BC and work
backwards as far as the sources will take us.

(2) *Written sources*   The oldest pieces of inescapable evidence that
individual named communities were called *poleis* in the sense of
city-state are Thasos (named by Archilochos[14]), Sparta (named by
Tyrtaios[15]) and Dreros on Crete (named in the oldest Greek law
preserved on stone[16]). In these sources *polis* is used both to mean
'state', with reference to the political community of citizens, and to
mean 'city', with reference to the urban centre.[17] All three sources
are more or less contemporaneous, going back to the middle of the
seventh century BC, and we can therefore take as our starting-point
that *c.*650 BC must be the *terminus ante quem* for *polis* as a city-state.

What about Homer? Fifty years ago Moses Finley—and many
in his wake—believed that there was no trace of the Classical *polis*
in the Homeric poems. The word *polis* or *ptolis* is certainly to be
found in the poems, but only in the sense of a fortified settlement,
not one that could be called a city or a state in the later sense of
those words.[18] Nowadays everybody accepts that *polis* in the sense
of city-state *is* to be found in the poems,[19] and there can be no
doubt at all that a public that listened, in the sixth century BC, to

a recitation of the *Odyssey* would instinctively have seen the *polis* of the Phaiakians as a Greek colony founded by Nausithoos (*Od.* 6.7–10, 262–72); and the description in the *Iliad* of the two *poleis* on the shield of Achilleus (*Il.* 18.490–540) would at once have been understood as a description of contemporary fortified cities.

The problem is that we cannot give a precise date to the Homeric poems. Comparison with epic poems in other civilisations shows that orally transmitted verse is being refashioned all the time, until one particular version gets frozen by being written down.[20] The written version is like a coin-hoard: the latest coin dates the hoard to a few years before the hoard was deposited, while the oldest coins may have been struck hundreds of years earlier. Similarly, the society and material culture described in an epic that has been transmitted orally may belong to different layers and create a mixture of new and old.

Here is just one example, one usually not noticed by historians.[21] The Homeric *polis* is full of palaces,[22] and sometimes has a temple as well.[23] The Homeric palaces are, up to a point, reminiscent of the ones that have been excavated at Pylos, Mykenai, Tiryns and Knossos.[24] Those palaces disappeared at the end of the Bronze Age, *c.*1200–1100 BC, and the earliest known Greek palace in a *polis* is that of Dionysios I at Syracuse *c.*400 BC.[25] Temples, by contrast, are unknown in the Mycenean civilisation, but are the best-known form of monumental architecture in Greece from the second half of the eighth century onwards.[26]

There are not many temples in the Homeric *polis*, but they are mentioned in the description of Troy and of the city of the Phaiakians on the island of Scheria. It is pretty unlikely that an early *polis* had both a palace and a temple inside its walls. The Greeks who listened to recitations of Homer *c.*600 BC would hear about all the wonderful palaces, but there would be virtually no mention of temples: yet, when they went home after the recitation, what they saw were temples and never palaces. It would be mistaken to look for any historical city that corresponded altogether to the *polis* described in Homer. Homer must be read as poetry.[27] In many ways the poems reflect the society of the eighth and seventh centuries BC: temples are just one example. But the Homeric *polis* also included reminiscences of walled palaces of the Bronze Age and of weapons and chariots used in the Mycenean Age.[28] And we can also conjecture that the epic poets had a vague idea of the great cities of the

Near Eastern empires—for example, Babylon and Nimrud—and those three different elements were mixed up also with fairy-tale cities that were products of poetic fantasy. To sort out the strands in such a complicated net is well-nigh impossible and will not be attempted here.

We cannot, therefore, expect the picture of the society described in the *Iliad* and the *Odyssey* to be historically correct. In Book 2 of the *Iliad* are listed all the contingents of the Greek fleet that sailed to Troy, in a long sequence traditionally known as the Catalogue of the Ships (*Il.* 2.484–759). These lines contain the largest collection of named *poleis/ptoleis* in the Homeric poems. But the listed *poleis* are not city-states; they are cities that are part of larger states ruled by kings. Crete is thus described as an island with a hundred *poleis*, all ruled by Idomeneus (*Il.* 2.645–52). Close study of the cities listed in the Catalogue of the Ships shows also that they mostly belonged to the Mycenean Age, not the Geometric or the Archaic.[29] There are, naturally, some exceptions—as in my comparison of the poems with a coin-hoard—and such exceptions show that the poems do not give a true picture of the world of the Mycenean states either.[30]

Worst of all, perhaps, is that we cannot fix any *terminus ante quem*, because we do not know when the poems were written down. Some historians are taken with Barry Powell's idea that the Greek alphabet was created by a man from Euboia *c.*800–750 BC with the specific purpose of writing down the Homeric poems.[31] But a much later dating is championed by Minna Skafte Jensen, who argues that the Homeric poems were written down in Athens only in the sixth century BC in connection with the Peisistratid reform of the festival of the Panathenaia.[32]

The conclusion of this investigation is that I cannot be a party to the prevailing ideas of a 'Homeric Society' understood as a society of the early Iron Age described in the Homeric epics with an astonishing consistency and no disturbing anachronisms of any significance.[33] My cautious conclusion is that in the written sources the essential elements of the Classical *polis* can be traced back to *c.*650 BC as a *terminus ante quem*.[34]

(3) *Archaeological remains*   In Homeric studies it is new interpretations of well-known texts that cause the picture to change. The case is different when we come to archaeological research in Greece, where newly found remains of cities and settlements can take us a

step or two forward—or, rather, back. Many early settlements have been found on islands in the Aegean: Zagora on Andros, Koukounaris on Paros, and Vathy Limenari on Donoussa, to name just some of the more important. Most are little fortified settlements on the slopes of a mountain. They appeared and flourished *c.*1000–700 BC, but had all been abandoned by *c.*700 BC.[35] Were they centres of the earliest *poleis* we know? If *polis* is understood as a fortified place or a little fortified settlement, the answer is 'Yes'. But if *polis* is understood as an early form of a Classical *polis*, the answer is rather, 'Well . . .'. There is no trace of administrative structures,[36] and the material remains cannot tell us anything about the political organisation of those early settlements: we have no idea how Zagora was governed. It may have been a small self-governing community, but without the political institutions that are a prerequisite for us speaking of city-states; or Zagora may have been the political centre for the whole of Andros, or a settlement in a much bigger state covering many of the Kyklades: we don't know and probably never will.

So the little fortified Iron Age settlements in the Aegean cannot get us any further: but study of the Greek colonies *can* do so, especially the ones in Sicily and south Italy, which were the earliest founded by the Greeks. Until recently historians were agreed that the rise of *poleis* in Greece was a precondition for the founding of all the colonies outside Greece.[37] Today the opposite viewpoint is gaining support: that the *polis* arose as a *result* of colonisation, and that it was the rise of *poleis* in the colonies that was the efficient cause of their rise in Greece proper.[38]

In every single case Greek colonisation led to the founding of a city, to a confrontation between the local inhabitants and the Greek colonists, who came to form the privileged citizen body, and to the introduction of laws and political institutions for the new society. All three functions are central elements in a *polis* in the sense of a city-state. Colonisation may have resulted in all three being accentuated and developed earliest in the colonies and then being copied back at home shortly after.

It is in any case certain that in the Greek colonies in Sicily and south Italy there are remains of imposing city centres, which in some cases can be traced right back to the foundation of the colony in the eighth century BC or the immediately succeeding period.[39] Syracuse and Megara Hyblaia are two striking examples.[40] And all those colonies are known as self-governing communities as far back as our written sources go, i.e. to the end of the sixth century BC. By combining the archaeological evidence for city formation in the eighth century with written evidence of their status as *poleis* in the sixth, we can conclude that those colonies were *poleis* in the Classical sense of the word either simultaneously with their foundation or shortly afterwards. Syracuse and Megara Hyblaia must thus have been *poleis* in the sense of city-states from their foundation in 734 and 728 BC respectively, or at any rate from 700 BC.

The sending out of colonists was not necessarily an action taken by the state. Colonists might well go out on their own initiative from a community that was not itself yet urbanised (compare the foundation of the Irish city-states by Norwegian Vikings) and had not even yet created a real state for itself (compare the Anglo-Saxon colonisation of England in the Iron Age).[41] The despatch of colonists from Corinth in 734 BC may not necessarily have been a political decision by the citizens of Corinth.[42] It is also worth noting that the people of Achaia in the northern Peloponnese were very active in colonisation in the eighth century, while Achaia itself does not seem to have been organised in *poleis* before the end of the sixth.[43]

The question of *when* the Greek city-state culture began goes with the question of *where* it began. There is much to suggest that the *polis* arose c.850–750 BC more or less at the same time as the Greeks borrowed the Phoenician alphabet and developed a written language. Some of the oldest *poleis* we know were in Cyprus, side by side with city-states founded by the Phoenicians. The Greek cities Paphos and Salamis had city walls already in the eighth century BC and were neighbours of Kition, which was a colony founded by Phoenicians from Tyre. It is a likely supposition that the *polis*, both as city and as state, arose in Cyprus with the Phoenician city-states as models.[44]

Alternatively, one might think that the *polis* arose, or at any rate developed, in connection with the founding of the earliest Greek colonies in Sicily and South Italy and spread out from there to the regions the colonists came from: Euboia, Achaia and the Isthmos.[45] And the theory that the *polis* arose in connection with colonisation can also be linked to the eastern part of the Greek city-state culture. In Asia Minor Ionia was colonised by Greeks in the Dark Age 1050–800 BC; and although new archaeological discoveries are all the time

extending our knowledge of that period, those centuries are still so
dark that we simply do not know how and when the colonisation
of Ionia took place. But we do know that Smyrna was a fortified
city already in the ninth century BC, and that Miletos was *c.*700.[46]
If the Ionian cities in the early Archaic Age were self-governing
communities, we can conjecture that the *polis* arose in connection
with the Ionian colonisation of Asia Minor in the early Iron Age.[47]

A third possibility would be to stick to the traditional idea that
the beginning of the Greek city-state is to be sought in the eastern
part of Greece proper, i.e. the region *from* which colonisation orig-
inated:[48] Chalkis and Eretria in Euboia, Corinth and Megara on
the Isthmos, Sparta in Lakedaimon, Argos in the Argolid, Athens
in Attika, and some of the Aegean islands, including Paros, Naxos
and Crete. Crete especially has been pointed to very recently as the
island where Greek city-state culture began. The oldest laws that
have come down to us come from city-states in Crete, and some
of the oldest known fortified settlements were on high places in
the eastern part of Crete. Continuity between the Bronze Age and
the Iron Age is also much closer on Crete than anywhere else in
Greece.[49] If one chooses Crete as the cradle of Greek city-state culture, one needs also to reconsider to what extent the city-states in
the first millennium BC are the refoundation of a city-state culture
of the second Millennium BC. Crete, and Greece as a whole, may
thus have been one of the places where there have been city-state
cultures in two different periods.[50]

With the sources we have at present, it is not possible to make
a secure choice between the different suggestions. And we must
not forget that they are not impossible to combine: perhaps further
research will show that a fusion of several suggestions is the best
explanation. But one thing is certain: the city-state did not arise all
over the Greek world at one go.[51] Even if we are in doubt about
the origins of the city-state, we can find traces of its development—
for example, by shifting our focus from *c.*800–700 BC to *c.*600–
550, for which we have more sources. In the first half of the sixth
century BC there were *poleis* everywhere along the shores of the
Aegean and on the islands off its coast. The colonies in the western
Mediterranean, along the north coast of the Aegean, and in the
Black Sea region were also *poleis*. But the western and northern part
of Greece proper and the lands in south-western Asia Minor lay
outside the Greek city-state culture. In the Peloponnese it seems

likely that there were no *poleis* in Achaia, Elis or Messenia, and except for a few Corinthian colonies there were no *poleis* in western Greece in Lokris, Aitolia, Akarnania and Epeiros. It is doubtful whether there were *poleis* in Thessaly or the neighbouring regions. And in south-west Asia Minor there were a few Greek colonies in Karia and Lykia, but otherwise those regions were Hellenised only in the late Classical and Hellenistic periods.[52]

6

The End of the City-State Culture in Ancient Greece

The lack of agreement as to when the epoch of the Greek city-states came to an end is even greater than that as to its beginning. Some historians still hold that the city-state flourished in the Archaic and Classical periods but was destroyed by the Macedonians in the second half of the fourth century BC. Independence (*autonomia*) is regarded as the most important characteristic of a city-state, and city-states lost their independence at the beginning of the Hellenistic period.[1] Indeed, it is often supposed that the city-state disappeared at a single blow, the blow being the Battle of Chaironeia on 7 Metageitnion = 2 August 338,[2] probably at *c*.3 o'clock in the afternoon when the defeat of the Thebans and Athenians by the Macedonians under Philip II was a reality—and that was what rang the referee's bell for the city-state.

That point of view goes closely with the belief that, by losing their *autonomia*, the city-states lost their identity as *poleis*. But many city-states were already subordinate to other city-states 150 years before the defeat of Chaironeia, and *autonomia* was not, ever, an irreducible characteristic for a *polis* to be a *polis*.[3] Even in the Archaic Age there were *poleis* that were dependencies: for example, the *poleis* of the Lakedaimonian *perioikoi*, which were dependencies of Sparta, and Corinth's colonies on the west coast of Greece, which were founded in the seventh and sixth centuries BC, but remained always politically dependent on Corinth.[4] By the beginning of the fifth century BC most *poleis* probably were autonomous, and most of the city-states along the western coast of Asia Minor were autonomous after the battles of Salamis, Plataiai and Mykale. But at that time the very concept of *autonomia* may not yet have arisen, and by the time, from the middle of the fifth century, that *autonomia* became a key concept in Greek affairs,[5] more and more *poleis* were losing their independence. Many became members of the Delian or the Peloponnesian League, and both these leagues developed into empires, in which Athens and Sparta respectively reduced the members to dependent status.[6] And many *poleis* joined in federal states. In the hundred years between *c.*450 and 350 BC hundreds of city-states changed status from being independent states to being parts of a federal state (called *koinon* or *ethnos*) which normally comprised all the *poleis* in a region. In the middle of the fourth century BC we find such federal states in Boiotia, Phokis, Lokris, Thessaly, Epeiros, Aitolia, Akarnania, Achaia and Arkadia.[7] And finally the city-states on the west coast of Asia Minor went back to being under Persian rule as they had been before the Persian Wars; and by the King's Peace in 386 the Greeks were forced to recognise the sovereignty of the king of Persia over all the *poleis* of Asia Minor.[8]

There is no historical atlas with a map of Greece *c.*350 BC that shows which *poleis* were independent and which had lost their *autonomia* either by being dominated by one of the leading city-states or the king of Persia or by becoming part of a federal state. Such a map would reveal that the independent *polis* was already no longer the commonest type of state in Greece when Macedon became a major power under Philip II. What disappeared under Philip II was not the city-state but the hegemonial *polis* of the type of Athens or Sparta or Thebes. Those *poleis* were undeniably deprived of their status as major powers: the other cities hardly noticed the difference, whether they were dominated by Athens or fell beneath the sway of the king of Macedon or some other Hellenistic prince. The Greek view of the *polis* was that it was a community of citizens as to their political institutions: a *polis* was a self-governing community. But self-government does not necessarily imply independence.

In the sense of a self-governing community, the *polis* lived on through the Hellenistic Age and long into the Roman Imperial period.[9] But at the same time the concept of *autonomia* changed its meaning: it no longer implied full independence, but simply self-government. On the other hand, *autonomia* became a much more conspicuous concept in the relations between city-states after the King's Peace in 386 BC and in the relations between city-states and monarchies in the Hellenistic Age. *Autonomia* was with ever greater frequency bound up with *polis*. In the Hellenistic kingdoms all *poleis* were actually subordinate to the ruling monarch, but in different degrees. Many *poleis* were tribute-paying and so formally subordinate to the king, but many were formally free, independent states. The typical 'independent' *polis* was now a democracy (*demokratia*) that had its freedom (*eleutheria*) and self-government (*autonomia*) guaranteed by royal rescript published by the Hellenistic king in whose kingdom the city-state lay.[10] The history of the autonomous city-state did not end in the middle of the fourth century BC: on the contrary, that is when it began. In Roman times democracy was succeeded by oligarchy: the central political institution became the Council (*boule*) instead of the Assembly of the People (*ekklesia*), and a city-state was now ruled by a local aristocracy whose members occupied all the city's significant offices of state.[11] But the *polis* was still a self-governing community consisting of a city and its hinterland.

The 'decline and fall' of the Greek city-state culture occurred in late antiquity. The emperor Diocletian (AD 284–305) created a centralised bureaucracy, which set much narrower limits to what was left of city-state self-government.[12] And in the western part of the Roman Empire many cities sickened or completely disappeared as a result of the early medieval migrations. In the eastern half, by contrast, there were *poleis* that still had the characteristics of city-states in the fifth century AD, and even into the sixth. Here it was especially the Christian bishops who were hostile to the self-government of the cities:[13] the Church went on the offensive against the pagan political institutions and demanded that its members avoid the city square, the *agora*, which the pagan writers regarded as the heart of a city.[14] Corresponding to the nature of pagan religions, every *polis* had its own religious festivals and its own pantheon of gods: but now the pagan gods were abolished by a religion that did not permit local variations. But the decline and fall of the city-state was a long-drawn-out process, and the *polis* was still an important political institution under Justinian (AD 527–65): Prokopios recounts how an African town was raised to the status of a *polis* by imperial decree in 533. But after Justinian there are no more traces to be found of city-states in the political sense of the word.[15]

7

How *Poleis* Arose and Disappeared

(a) *poleis* arose either by an existing city changing its political status or by a new self-governing city being founded. In Greece most *poleis* arose by natural growth: it was, mostly, a long drawn-out and almost unnoticeable process, and with the sources we have, it is impossible to say exactly when the inhabitants of a city began to feel themselves to be citizens of a *polis*.

With the exception of regions of western Greece, most of the *poleis* in Greece arose during the Archaic period, many so early that *polis* had not yet become a key concept in political thought. The lack of source material is an insurmountable hindrance to our ever being able to trace the beginnings of the hundreds of city-states in Greece that our Classical sources characterise as *poleis* with a long history behind them.

However, many *poleis* had a foundation myth. It was typical of the Greeks that they did not conceive the emergence of a *polis* as the result of a continuous evolution, but believed that it had been created by the deliberate intervention of a named person (or god). The Thebans in the Classical period believed that their *polis* had been founded at the dawn of time by Kadmos, a brother of Europa whom Zeus had seduced in the shape of a bull;[1] and the Athenians believed it was Theseus who, a thousand years back, had founded Athens both as city and as state, having the whole of Attika as its territory.[2] Through their foundation myths the *poleis* of Greece proper came to resemble their colonies, which could regularly trace their foundation to a person, the person who had brought the first colonists and was regarded as a 'hero' after his death.[3]

It is striking that there is not a single source of the Classical period that talks of a new *polis* arising naturally. By that period there was a fully developed concept of a *polis* and a whole set of criteria for distinguishing a *polis* from a village:[4] only a *polis* could have a victor in the pan-Hellenic games;[5] only a *polis* could designate a citizen of a neighbouring city as its *proxenos* (a kind of consul to act on behalf of the citizens who were visitors in a neighbouring city);[6] only a *polis* could designate a *theorodokos* (a citizen whose duty it was to meet and house envoys (*theoroi*) sent, for example, from Delphi to announce the holding of the Pythian Games);[7] only a *polis* could declare war or make peace or join a federation or become a member of a federal state; only a *polis* could strike coins, etc.[8] Some of those characteristics must have implied the recognition by other *poleis* of a city as a *polis*.[9] In both the Hellenistic period and the Roman Imperial period a community could achieve the status of *polis* by royal rescript or imperial decree.[10] And the emperor could also deprive a community of its status as a *polis*.[11] What, then, was done in the Classical period? It was as late as the fifth and fourth centuries BC that the *polis* became the prevailing form of settlement and political organisation in the west Greek regions of Epeiros, Akarnania and Aitolia;[12] but even in the quite extensive sources we have for the history of western Greece in the Classical period there is still not a single example of an existing community at a given moment acquiring the status of a *polis*.[13]

The founding of a *polis* took place either by colonisation (*apoikismos*) or by coalescence (*synoikismos*). Colonisation implied emigration over a long distance of a group of people to a place where the colonists could settle. That is how Kyrene was founded as a colony from Thera *c.*630 BC.[14] Synoecism implied emigration from a group of closely set neighbouring settlements to a place in the vicinity or an unoccupied place where a new *polis* was founded or to an already existing *polis* whose population was powerfully increased by the immigration.[15] An example of the founding of a new city is Megalopolis, founded in 368 by the synoecism of a number of cities in southern Arkadia;[16] an example of immigration into an already existing *polis* is the synoecism in Boiotia by which a set of small unfortified neighbouring cities were incorporated by Thebes in 431 at the beginning of the Peloponnesian War.[17]

Most of the *poleis* outside Greece were colonies, but some had arisen naturally, typically by a local community turning itself into a Greek *polis*.[18] In Greece proper, on the contrary, a few *poleis* were founded as colonies,[19] others arose by synoecism,[20] but by far the majority arose by smaller communities growing and turning into *poleis*. In one or two cases colonisation was combined with synoecism: for example, the founding in 426 of Herakleia in the

region known as Oiteia at the mouth of the River Spercheios.[21]
Sometimes a colony had its population reinforced by the sending
of new colonists from Greece, as in the case of the (alleged) 60,000
colonists sent to Syracuse in 341 BC[22] Another known example of an
existing *polis* having its population increased by immigration from
neighbouring cities is the synoecism by which King Mausolos in
c.370 BC re-created Halikarnassos as his city of residence.[23]

(b) While many have written about when the *poleis* arose, their
demise is one of the neglected problems of Greek history.[24] Since a
polis was partly a city and partly a state, we can choose between two
forms of demise: (a) a *polis* could disappear as a state but continue
its existence as a city, or (b) a *polis* could disappear as a city by being
levelled to the ground and as a state by its population being killed
or reduced to slavery or forcibly transferred to another city. This
latter form of demise was often accompanied by the destruction
of the physical city itself and the dismantling of its walls. And
if you look at the sources, you encounter the following variants.
(1) The entire population of the city-state is put to death. (That
was the fate of Sybaris in 510 BC[25].) (2) All males are put to death,
but the women and children are sold into slavery (that form of
destruction is called in the sources *andrapodismos*, and notorious
examples are the Spartan destruction of Plataiai in 427 BC and the
crushing by Athens of the island of Melos in 415[26]). (3) Such males
as survived the conquest are sold as slaves along with the women
and children. (That form of *andrapodismos* was used by Philip II
to deal with the Olynthians in 348 BC and by Alexander the Great
to deal with the Thebans in 335[27].) (4) The whole population is
forcibly transferred to another city. (In 484 BC the tyrant Gelon
of Syracuse caused the whole population of Kamarina to move
to Syracuse, but Kamarina was refounded with new inhabitants
in 461. In 483 the population of Megara Hyblaia was moved to
Syracuse, and the deserted city was still in ruins when Thucydides
wrote his history at the end of the fifth century BC[28].) (5) The
population of a *polis* is forced to flee and settle in small villages
in the hinterland of the *polis*, a process described in the sources
as *dioikismos*. (When the Spartans conquered Mantinea in 385 BC,
they made the population move out to the four villages in which
they had originally lived, and when Philip II in 346 conquered
the Phokians in the Third Sacred War, twenty-two Phokian *poleis*

were turned into villages, which were allowed to have no more than fifty households each.[29]) (6) A *polis* disappears because its entire population emigrates. (In *c.*650 BC the entire population of Kolophon transferred their city from Ionia in Asia Minor to Siris in Italy; Kolophon was abandoned for some years, though it was soon populated again[30].) (7) The population of a *polis* takes part in a synoecism whereby another city is founded or consolidated. (The small unfortified Boiotian cities Skolos, Skaphai, Hysiai and Erythrai were joined up to Thebes in 431 BC at the beginning of the Peloponnesian War[31].) (8) A *polis* changes its status and becomes a village (*kome*) or a commune (*demos*) in the territory of another city-state. (Pallantion in Arkadia is known in Classical sources as a *polis*, but was a *kome* in the Roman period until in the second century AD it recovered its status as a *polis* by imperial decree.[32] Grynchai and Styra were in the fifth and fourth centuries BC little *poleis* on Euboia, both members of the Delian League; but in the fourth century they fell under the large *polis* of Eretria, and subsequently turn up in the sources as merely communes (*demoi*) in the territory of Eretria[33].) (9) A *polis* disappears as the result of a natural catastrophe. (A huge eathquake in the Corinthian Gulf in 373 BC caused a tidal wave that destroyed the city of Helike in Achaia[34].)

If one studies the rise of the city-states and their extinction together, one obtains a constantly changing picture of the world of the Greek *poleis*. New *poleis* arose in the two Greek periods of colonisation: in the Archaic Age hundreds of *poleis* were formed along the coasts of the Mediterranean and the Black Sea, and in the Hellenistic Age several hundred *poleis* were founded in the Persian Empire, covering the whole of the Near East from Asia Minor to the Indus. In Greece the number of *poleis* in the regions facing the Aegean declined, while new *poleis* arose in western Greece in Epeiros, Akarnania and Aitolia. On Euboia the number of *poleis* fell from more than twelve in the Archaic period to four in the fourth century BC,[35] and in Arkadia in 368 BC a number of *poleis* disappeared as a result of the synoecism that led to the founding of Megalopolis.[36] Other large *poleis* created by synoecism in the Hellenistic Age were Thessalonike in 316 BC and Demetrias in 294: in both cases a large number of little *poleis* vanished as a result.[37]

In all this kaleidoscopic picture, one thing stays constant: the Greeks maintained their city-state culture all through antiquity, and no one made the least attempt to assemble all the city-states into a territorial macro-state like the Greece that arose in the nineteenth century. Such an idea would have been as foreign to the ancient Greeks as abolishing slavery.[38] The rise of larger political units took the form of leagues of city-states, which soon broke up again, or federations, which were more stable in structure. A federal state usually comprised all the *poleis* in a region; and when the Greeks chose this solution, it was doubtless because a federal state permitted the retention of the *polis* as the essential political unit.[39] In particular regions small *poleis* were often swallowed up by larger ones, but the result of such unification was always a bigger *polis*, never a territorial state in the modern sense.

Of course, the biggest *poleis* might well expand to a size that transcended the city-state. The taking over of all Lakedaimon and Messenia turned Sparta into a *polis* of more than 8,000 km²; and Syracuse under Dionysios I (405–367 BC) dominated the whole of eastern Sicily, a territory of more than 10,000 km²; and Kyrene in Libya acquired a territory of more than 4,000 km². But in all three cases these small empires were built on one *polis* that had many smaller *poleis* in its territory as dependencies: even in this case the *polis* remained as the primary form of political organisation.

8

What is a *Polis*? An Investigation of the Concept of '*Polis*'

After our detailed investigation of the chronology of the Greek city-state culture and its expansion, it is time to return to the question: what *was* a *polis*? The answer depends on whether the questioner wants to look at the Greek *polis* with the eyes of a modern historian or to find out what the Greeks themselves thought a *polis* was.[1] I have chosen the second approach.[2] What follows is, therefore, about the Greeks' understanding of themselves, and in such an investigation the written sources must take centre-stage, and an attempt must be made to analyse the words and concepts that the Greeks used to describe the institution. We must begin, therefore, with the question: what does the word *polis* signify? What concept lies behind the word? And what society does it apply to?

The Greeks knew quite well that they used the word *polis* with more than one meaning, and the sources show that in the Archaic and Classical periods the word had two main senses: (1) settlement and (2) community.[3] As settlement a *polis* consisted of houses; as community it consisted of people:[4] one is a concrete physical sense, the other more abstract and personal. Moreover, the sources show that not every settlement or community was a *polis*. As settlement, a *polis* was primarily a large nucleated settlement, i.e. a city; as community it was an institutionalised political community, i.e. a state.[5]

A study of all the occurrences of the word *polis* in the Archaic and Classical sources—there are some 11,000[6]—reveals that both the topographical and the personal use of the word had different sub-meanings. (1) In the meaning of 'settlement' *polis* is used (a) synonymously with *akropolis*, a small, usually fortified settlement on an eminence (see 40); and (b) synonymously with *asty*, just meaning a town; or (c) synonymously with *ge* or *chora*, meaning a territory (*polis* plus hinterland). (2) In the meaning of 'community' *polis* is used (a) synonymously with *politai*, the adult male citizens; (b) synonymously with *ekklesia* or *demos*, as the city's assembly or some other of its political institutions; or (c) synonymously with *koinonia*, the political community in a more abstract sense.[7]

But not all these senses of *polis* are equally important and well attested. (1a) The original sense 'fortified place' (*akropolis*) is already rare in the Archaic and Classical periods, and is found mostly on inscriptions in certain traditional archaising formulas of publication.[8] It disappears altogether in the Hellenistic period; and in the Roman period only learned scholars knew that *polis* had once meant the same as *akropolis*.[9] (1b) *Polis* meaning a town is exceedingly common, and in some writers accounts for more than half of all occurrences.[10] (1c) Territory as the primary meaning of *polis* represents only a tiny percentage of all occurrences.[11] (2a–c) The three commonest uses of *polis* in the sense of political community or state are closely related, and are really only different aspects of the same meaning.[12] In (2a) and (2b) *polis* is used in a more concrete sense, in (2c) in a more abstract one, just as we nowadays use the word 'state' sometimes in the sense of a set of people, the body of citizens, sometimes of the power of the state, i.e. its political institutions, and sometimes of the state as an abstract political person.[13] The different meanings often overlap, especially when *polis* is used as a generic term.[14]

It is always stressed—quite rightly—that an ancient Greek city was inextricably linked to its hinterland,[15] and *chora* (the land) is also the word in our sources that is most frequently linked with *polis*.[16] But they can be opposed in some cases, in different variations according to whether *polis* is being used as city or as state, and according to whether *chora* is being used as hinterland or as territory. (a) When *polis* means a state (a city plus its hinterland), *chora* means territory, of which the city is a part; (b) but when *polis* means a city, *chora* means the hinterland as contrasted with the city. So (c) *polis* in the sense of state is used as a generic term for *chora* (hinterland) plus *polis* (city), and (d) *chora* in the sense of territory can be used as a generic term for *polis* (city) plus *chora* (hinterland).[17] This complex use of what linguists nowadays call participatory opposition[18] is illustrated in table 1. The Greek use of *polis* and *chora* as antonyms indicates a striking difference

TABLE 1

polis (state)		chora (territory)	
polis (city)	*chora* (hinterland)	*polis* (city)	*chora* (hinterland)

between the ancient Greek *polis* and a modern European state. The words for 'city' and 'country' occur in many modern languages as antonyms: City/country in English, Stadt/Land in German, cité/pays in French, by/land in Danish etc. In ancient Greek it was the word for 'city' (*polis*) that came to mean 'state',[19] whereas in modern European languages it is the word for 'country' that is used to mean 'state'. In ancient Greece a war was always between two *poleis*, never two *chorai*,[20] and the word *polis* was used in all the contexts where we would nowadays use the word 'state':[21] today it is always the word for the country that is used, never the city. The most plausible explanation of this difference is that the typical *polis* had only one city, which was also its political centre, whereas the countries that grew up in the Middle Ages had neither a political centre nor a capital city: the king and his court travelled from city to city and from castle to castle,[22] so that it was not possible to identify the power of the state with a specific locality in the state and the state could only be identified with the whole country, as aforesaid.

If we move from the meaning of the word to its referent, and consider all the places where it is used about Greek societies, we observe that *polis* in the sense of territory almost always means the territory of a city-state (city plus hinterland) and only exceptionally a whole region or other large territory. In the sense of state, *polis* almost always means a city-state, and almost never a federation of *poleis* or a monarchy or empire.[23] *Polis* used of large states occurs practically only when *polis* is being used as a generic term for a set of states of which most are city-states, though some can be what we call territorial states. In some 98 per cent of all occurrences, *polis* is used either in the sense of a settlement, for what we call a city, or in the sense of a political community, for what we call a state. The word often has both significations at once,[24] so the word 'city-state' is an extremely precise translation of *polis* and not an anachronistic mistranslation, as it has become fashionable to allege.[25]

So a *polis* was part city, part state. The word *polis* has two different meanings: when we hear that a river runs through a *polis*,[26] we do not notice that *polis* can also mean a state, and when an alliance is formed between a set of *poleis*, we do not notice that the alliance is between cities.[27] Nevertheless the two meanings are inextricably linked, because they always have the same referent: if *polis* is used meaning a city, it is not every city that is called a *polis*, but only a city that is known in other contexts as the political centre of a *polis* in the other sense, the sense of 'state'.[28] And contrariwise, if *polis* is used in the meaning of state, other sources always show that that state has a city as its political centre, a city called a *polis* in the sense of 'city'.[29] These two observations run counter to two prevailing views: that there were numerous *poleis* (in the sense of state) that did not have a city at their centre;[30] and, conversely, that there were *poleis* (in the sense of city) that were not the political centre of a state.[31] Study of all the named Greek states that are called *poleis* disproves both contentions, and underpins the thesis that every *polis*-city was the centre of a *polis*-state, and every *polis*-state had a *polis*-city as its political centre.

On the other hand, not every town or city was called a *polis*. Nowadays we distinguish between large cities (or towns)[32] and smaller villages. Correspondingly, the Greeks used *polis* or *asty* of what we—in a historical context—call towns or cities,[33] whereas the smaller settlement was called a *kome*.[34] Nor was every political community a city-state. In the larger *poleis* the citizens were divided into territorial and/or kinship-based political groupings.[35] The city-state of Eretria on Euboia was divided into some sixty territorial communes (*demoi*), but at the same time the citizen body was also divided into six kinship-based tribes (*phylai*).[36] *Demoi* and *phylai* were what we should call units of local politics, while a *polis* was a self-governing (but not necessarily independent) community.

The Greek perception of a *polis* as a community of citizens inhabiting a city has its reflection also in the names they gave their city-states. Nowadays we use place-names to serve as the names of states: the Greeks preferred to name their *poleis* with an *ethnikon*, an adjective used as a noun derived from the place-name, indicating the people rather than the land.[37] *Danmark* (Denmark) is the name of the state, and to match this toponym we have the adjective *dansker* (a Dane), which in the plural form *danskerne* (the Danes) signifies the people who live in that state. The largest city in Boiotia in antiquity was *Thebai* (Thebes), and derived from the toponym was the adjective *Thebaios* (Theban), which in the plural form *Thebaioi* (the Thebans) designated the citizens of that city-state and, in a more general sense, the city-state itself.[38] Nowadays it is Denmark (and not the Danes) that is a member of the United Nations: in antiquity it was the Thebans (and not Thebes) that was the leading state in the Boiotian Federation.[39] This difference in naming conventions highlights two differences between modern states and the city-states of antiquity. (a) In our conception of the state, the main weight is given to the territory of the state, its land, and so the toponym is the name of the state. The Greeks placed the main weight upon the people of the state, and so used the *ethnikon* as the name of the state.[40] (b) In our concept of 'state', a state is a land, not a city: the Greeks conceived of a state as a city and thought less about its territory, and that again goes with the fact that all political institutions were situated in the city (*polis* in the 'city' sense of the word), and that a high proportion of the population was in fact resident in the city.[41] Hence the name of a state (e.g. the Thebans) was derived from the place-name of the city (Thebes) and not from the place-name of its land. The only modern European states called by the name of a city and not a whole land are Andorra, Luxembourg, Monaco and San Marino—and they are, actually, city-states just like the Greek *polis*.

While an *ethnikon* like *Thebaioi*, plural, meant the city-state itself, it was used in the singular, *Thebaios*, by the citizens of a city-state as a kind of surname. The name of a Greek person consisted of a first name plus father's name in the genitive, but a citizen could have as a third element the *ethnikon* of his city-state, which he would use whenever his name had to be listed side by side with the names of citizens from other *poleis*. An Olympic victor in 368 had his name inscribed on the base of the statue erected to commemorate his victory. It reads thus: 'Aristion Theophilou Epidaurios', i.e. 'Aristion Theophilos' son from Epidauros'.[42] In the Classical period only adult male citizens could use their state's *ethnikon* as a surname, so when we meet an *ethnikon* derived from the name of a city, we can conclude that the said person was a citizen of the relevant city-state.[43] That is actually one of the characteristic features of the ancient Greek city-state culture. It is relatively common in the languages of some other cultures to use place-names and derivatives of place-names as personal names (though not much in English), but such names mostly designate the place where the person (or his ancestors) were born, e.g. Welsh, London or Selby. The Greeks were, as far as I know, the only people to use a person's 'extra' name as an indication of political status, and that naming habit shows how great an importance citizenship had in the city-state culture of ancient Greece.[44]

9

The *Polis* as City and State

I have argued above that the *polis* was both a nucleated settlement and a self-governing polity, and from page 1 I have cast this view in modern terms and spoken of the *polis* as both 'city' and 'state'. Are these two terms and the concepts behind them well chosen in a description of the Greek *polis*?

Even if we accept that the *polis* ideally was both a city and a state, i.e. a city-state, what happens if, combining the two aspects, we apply them to individual *poleis*? Athens was both a city and a state, and that goes for many other *poleis* too: Corinth, Megara, Syracuse. Few will doubt[1] that Melos was a state when it was attacked by Athens in 416,[2] but was its small urban centre really a city? And what about tiny *poleis* such as Koresia on Keos?[3] Conversely, no one will doubt that Miletos was a city, but was it a state in the long periods during which it was a dependency of Lydia, Persia, Athens, Persia again and then the Hellenistic kings?

(1) Polis *as city*   Even if it can be shown—as I think it can, see *infra*—that all *poleis* were cities in the political and administrative sense, it does not follow that they were cities in the demographic and economic sense as well. We cannot assume a priori that the legal aspect of a *polis* coincided with the urban aspect. The medieval and Early Modern European city is an obvious example. In Germany cities, i.e. *Städte*, were defined legally. There were altogether 3,000–4,000 *Städte* and the precise number could easily be ascertained in any given year since a *Stadt* was a *Stadt* thanks to special rights and privileges.[4] On the other hand, very few of these *Städte* were cities in the urban sense. Only 100–200 of them had a population of more than 1,000 people. The rest of them were villages.[5] Thus in Germany—and in many other European countries too—there was a gap between the political and the socio-economic aspect of most urban centres.

The townscape of ancient Greece was different. In the fourth century—as I shall argue in the next chapter—almost all *poleis* in the urban sense were walled settlements but *c*.15–20 per cent were quite small: the urban area covered *c*.5–15 ha, and the territory came to 25 km² max. Nevertheless, the presumption is that even most of these small *poleis* must have had a four-digit urban population. Consequently, close to 90 per cent of all *polis* centres were populous enough to meet the requirement of a population of more than 1,000 to count as a city in the urban sense,[6] and the majority of them were considerably larger and had several thousand inhabitants.[7]

In all *poleis* (in the sense of state) the largest nucleated settlement was the *polis* (in the sense of city), but especially in the larger city-states there were below *polis* level a number of second-order settlements, called *komai* or *demoi*; see *infra* 68. Very few of these villages had a four-digit population. The only large village we know of in Boiotia is the *kome* Askra where Hesiodos was born; it covered *c*.10 ha and may have had *c*.1,000 inhabitants.[8] Apart from Peiraieus, in fact a part of Athens itself, none of the few attested Attic deme centres can be shown to have had as many as 1,000 inhabitants in the Classical period.[9] Eretria on Euboia had more than fifty demes, but only one is known to have had a sizeable urban centre, viz. Dystos, probably a former *polis* and perhaps still a dependent *polis* in the fourth century.[10] Thus, with a few exceptions none of the second-order settlements could muster more than a few hundred inhabitants.

The conclusion is that in ancient Greece the two aspects of *polis* fit together much better than the two aspects of *Stadt* in Germany, where the concept of city (*Stadt*) legally defined includes twenty to forty times as many nucleated centres as would have been included if the criterion for inclusion had been the physical size of the city and its population.

(2) Polis *as State*   The other half of the issue is whether the *polis* was a state as well as a city.[11] There are, of course, important differences between *polis* and state. Compared with most modern states, the Greek *polis* was a Lilliput.[12] The small and middle-sized *poleis* were face-to-face societies.[13] In the modern nation-state, ethnic and national identity is an essential aspect of political identity, and the nation-state is often held up as a model of the best form of state. In the *polis*, political identity was something entirely dif-

Chapter 9

ferent from ethnic or national identity. The citizens of a *polis* shared their ethnic identity (language, culture, history, religion) with the citizens of other city-states within the region, whereas their sense of political identity (including patriotism) was centred on the *polis* itself and separated any *polis* from all its neighbours.[14] Also, the Renaissance and Baroque concept of the sovereign as a supreme legislator who himself stands above the law is foreign to the ancient Greeks, who invariably emphasised the supremacy of the laws and held that a *polis* ruled by an absolute monarch was a tyranny, a perverted form of community which in its extreme form had ceased to be a *polis*.[15]

But there are essential similarities too, which in my opinion justify the view that the *polis* was indeed a type of state. The three basic elements of state and *polis* are (1) a defined territory; (2) a defined people, identified with the citizens in a political context and with the inhabitants in a judicial context; (3) a system of political institutions in possession of the sole right to define and enforce a legal order within the territory over the population.[16] The main difference concerns priorities: a state is principally a territory, a *polis* was first of all a people.[17] Furthermore, in the *polis* self-help was allowed against certain types of criminal, and, by and large, apprehension and prosecution of criminals were left to individuals and not usually performed by state officials. In this respect the *polis* resembles the European states of the seventeenth and eighteenth centuries, whereas the absolute monopoly on the legitimate use of force became the prerogative of state officials in the course of the nineteenth century.[18] Furthermore, both the state and the *polis* are not just the sum of the three elements: territory, people and government; both are also conceived as an abstract public power above ruler and ruled.[19]

Finally, there is the traditional requirement that a community must be independent in order to count as a state, whereas—as argued *supra*, 48—independence, in Classical sources called *autonomia*, was not an essential aspect of the *polis*. Some *poleis* were independent, some were dependencies (*poleis hypekooi*). But even here the difference between state and *polis* is not as essential as is often believed.

If the most essential characteristics of a state are a defined territory, a juridically defined population, and a sovereign legislature, then member states of federations are essentially states.[20] Consequently, like the ancient concept of *polis*, the modern concept of state is hierarchical. But while the dependent *polis* existed in a great variation of types in ancient Greece, the state hierarchy in the modern world has until recently been kept at two fairly distinct levels: independent states and member states of federations. In recent years, however, the two-tier hierarchy seems to have broken down and intermediate forms to be developing, as with many *poleis* in ancient Greece: the members of the EU are no longer sovereign states; nor are they member states of a federation. A new fluent concept of state is developing, one in which sovereignty and independence are concepts that have to be either redefined or dissociated from the concept of state. A new parallel between the concepts of *polis* and state is emerging, one which did not exist a few decades ago, but one which might be of importance in our re-evaluation of the concept of state in the years to come.

10

Polis as City

All our written sources show that socially and economically a *polis* was a city plus its hinterland, and that politically it was a kind of state. Each of these aspects must be treated now in greater detail. We begin with *polis* as city. An important difference between *polis* as city and *polis* as state can be clearly seen if we attempt to answer the questions: Who lived in a *polis*? And who were members of a *polis*? Although the Greeks had a tendency to settle in cities, it is a fact that in ancient Greek there is no word that means the people living in a city as against the people living in the countryside. The word *polites* meant a 'citizen' in the political sense of the word, and signified the adult male citizen irrespective of where he lived.[1] The word *asty* (city) was used as a synonym of *polis* in the sense of a place,[2] but its derivation *astos* (man from the *asty*) is never used to mean 'city-dweller'.[3] Like *polites*, *astos* is used of a citizen only in the political meaning.[4] The adjective *agroikos* often means someone who lives in the country, and then can have the derivative meaning of 'simple, uneducated person'.[5] But its antonym *asteios* means only an educated person, never just simply one who lives in a city,[6] even though it is easy to discern what the basis of the distinction is. Perhaps the reason is that the relationship between city population and country population in a Greek city-state differed from what we know in our own culture; see 67–8.

11

The Settlement Pattern of the Ancient Greek City-States

In modern studies of historical settlement patterns it is customary to distinguish between nucleated settlement and dispersed settlement, and between three different forms of settlement: (1) cities (large nucleated settlements), (2) villages (smaller nucleated settlements), and (3) farmsteads (isolated dispersed settlements). In all studies of ancient Greece nucleated settlement in cities and villages is contrasted with dispersed settlement on farmsteads.[1]

Until the 1970s the prevalent view was that the Greeks lived in nucleated settlements, whether cities or villages, and that isolated settlement was so rare as scarcely to be evidenced at all.[2] But in the most recent generation a number of archaeological surveys in several different regions have been conducted, and large stretches of a city-state's territory investigated in search of traces of settlement,[3] and such surveys have caused an ongoing revision of the view of the historians, especially in two regards: (1) traces have been found of the part of the population that lived in the countryside and not in the city, and (2) many of those who lived in the countryside lived on isolated farmsteads and not in nucleated settlements.[4]

Archaeologists in their analysis of settlement patterns in the civilisation of ancient Greece use a fixed terminology for the three types of settlement: cities, villages and farmsteads. Discussion of the terminology the Greeks themselves used is avoided or dealt with in a brief historical section. But if we shift focus from the archaeological sources to the written ones and ask how the Greeks themselves conceived of their settlement pattern, quite a different picture emerges, both of the distinction between nucleated and dispersed settlement and of the conception of three different forms of settlement.[5] In the three-pronged hierarchy of settlements the Greeks had a fully developed terminology for the cities: *polis*, *polisma* and *asty*.[6] For

villages the Greeks sometimes used the word *kome*, which is simply
a word for village but is astonishingly rare in our sources,[7] sometimes the word *demos*, which really means a set of people but can
signify the citizen body of a municipality,[8] and in rare contexts is
used of its population centre.[9] For non-nucleated isolated settlements the Greeks had no fixed terminology at all, only a number
of words which in the appropriate context could signify what we
mean by a farmstead.[10]

However, the Greeks distinguished explicitly settlement in a city
(*polis*) from settlement in the country (*chora*), and they seem never
to have been interested in whether settlement in the country was
in villages or on isolated farmsteads.[11] They were much more interested in political structures than in forms of settlement, so they
contrasted the people who lived in the *polis* with the people who
lived in the *chora*, whether in villages or on isolated farmsteads; and
almost all their attention was directed to the *polis*. Living in *komai*
(villages) without any real city centre was regarded in the Classical
period as an outmoded form of settlement going back to the pre-
polis age; and in the Classical period such settlement patterns were
found mainly on the edges of the Greek world.[12]

We know very little about the villages that in the Archaic and
Classical periods lay in the territory of a city-state outside the city
itself. Excavations and archaeological surveys of the hinterland of
cities have greatly enlarged the number we now have knowledge
of. But even if we add the new archaeologically discovered villages
to those already known from the written sources, there are still
in many regions an astonishingly large number of *poleis* and an
astonishingly small number of villages. In, for example, Arkadia,
Triphylia, western Lokris, Phokis, eastern Lokris, in the Chalkidike
and on Lesbos there were, it seems, more *poleis* than villages.[13] In
Boiotia a third of all the settlements were *poleis*.[14] Attika was an
exception in having only one *polis* but 139 'demes', most of which
had a village as their centre of settlement. So there were two kinds
of region in Greece: some had a small number of big *poleis*, each
with a large number of villages in its territory; others had a large
number of small *poleis*, many of them having no village at all in
their territory. In Greece proper this latter pattern seems to have
been the commonest; and that is undoubtedly very different from
what we know of Greece in the nineteenth and twentieth centuries
in which a five-figure number of villages corresponds to a small

number of cities. The settlement pattern of Greece in the Archaic and Classical periods is, however, characteristic of many city-state cultures: it can be seen, for example, in the Sumerian city-state culture, which was similarly characterised by a large number of cities and a small number of villages.[15]

What conclusions can we draw from the sources we have? On the one hand, there can be no doubt that the Greeks had a skewed picture of their own settlement pattern: they concentrated attention on the *polis* and had no particular interest in the *komai* or in the isolated farmsteads that lay in a territory. From the Archaic and Classical sources we know of 447 cities that are called *poleis* as against no more than thirty named villages called *komai*.[16] About half of all *poleis* are explicitly classified as *poleis* in the sources; but there must have been many times more villages than the places in the sources called *komai*. We cannot explain this difference by saying that the *poleis* naturally attracted all the attention of our sources, whereas they did not have the same interest in naming *komai*. Greek historiography was mostly about wars, and we hear, for example, of the battles fought in Boiotia in the vicinity of cities: Plataiai in 479 BC, Tanagra in 457, Koroneia in 447 and 394, Chaironeia in 338. But just as many battles were fought in the vicinity of villages: Keressos *c.*525 BC, Oinophyta in 457, Delion in 424, Tegyra in 375, and Leuktra in 371; yet, while all the cities are explicitly described as *poleis* in our sources, none of the villages is ever called a *kome*.[17]

On the other hand, there ought to be no doubt that most of the population lived in the city within the city walls. That perception is contrary to the belief of most ancient historians,[18] but it is underpinned by archaeological evidence. The new archaeological surveys coincide with an increasing interest amongst ancient historians in the territory and settlement pattern of the city-state: the focus has shifted from the city to the hinterland, and from the written to the archaeological sources.[19] The archaeological surveys have given us invaluable new knowledge of the settlements that were outside the *polis* in its sense of city. Therefore they are adduced by historians who want to underline the importance of the hinterland as against the centre. But historians often forget to read the conclusions of the published surveys, so here we shall summarise the results of two of the best-published surveys, both focused on the division of the population between city and country.

The island of Keos south of Attika was divided between four

city-states. The most north-westerly of them was called Koresia,
with a territory of no more than 15 km² and a walled city centre
which in the fourth century BC covered c.18 ha, of which c.6–8
was a built-up area. We possess a roster of the citizens who were
liable for military service, inscribed c.300 BC on a marble *stele*. If
we apply a population model that seems to fit the populations in
the Mediterranean in Classical antiquity, we can conclude that the
city-state of Koresia in the fourth century had a total population of
c.1,000–1,300 persons. Now the whole of the territory of Koresia
was covered by an American survey in 1983–4 which showed that
within that territory there was not a single village or hamlet in
the fourth century BC, and very little trace of isolated farmsteads.
Virtually the entire population must have lived inside the city walls.
Many of them were, of course, farmers; and they went out daily to
their fields outside the city and home again each evening to their
dwelling in the city. The archaeologists guess that between 60 and
90 per cent of the population of that city-state lived in the 6–8 ha
built-up area inside the city wall, which gives a population density
of c.100–200 per ha.[20]

   As for villages, we find a rather different population pattern in
the Peloponnese. Southern Argolis was divided between two city-
states, Hermione and Halieis. Hermione had a territory of 275 km²
and a walled city centre of 22.5 ha, of which about 17 ha was a built-
up area. Halieis had a territory of c.75 km² and a walled city centre of
c.18 ha, of which c.15 ha was a built-up area. Stanford University
in 1972–82 conducted one of the most comprehensive and best
published surveys, which covered intensively c.15 per cent of the
350 km² and extensively a much larger area. In addition to the two
sizeable cities, traces were found of about ten villages and about
a hundred isolated farmsteads. In the two cities the houses were
pretty small and very closely packed. The archaeologists guessed
at a population density in the fourth century of c.250 persons per
ha in the built-up parts of the cities, but 125 per ha in the less
densely populated villages (which had no walls) and a household
size of at least five persons on the isolated farmsteads. Putting all
this together, it is apparent that the two city centres together had a
population of c.8,000 people, while c.4,500 people in all lived in the
villages or on the isolated farmsteads.[21]

   These two surveys of the territory of one and two city-states
respectively can be supplemented by a general view of the division

between city and country populations in an entire region. In Boiotia in the fourth century BC there were in all about twenty-five city-states. Much the largest was Thebes, whose city centre covered *c.*350 ha; the two smallest had city centres of only 3–5 ha.[22] If you add up the whole area of the twenty-five city centres, i.e. the area surrounded by walls, it comes to *c.*1,050 ha, of which Thebes accounts for a third. If we reckon, on a cautious estimate, that only a bit more than half of those 1,050 ha was a built-up area, and if we reckon on a population density of a bit less than that in the Argolid, i.e. 225 persons per ha of built-up area, we arrive at *c.*120,000 Boiotians living in the cities. On the basis of evidence about the strength of the army of the Boiotian Federation, and some other sources, the entire population of Boiotia can be calculated as between 150,000 and 200,000 people.[23] So it can be presumed that somewhere between 60 and 80 per cent of the population of Boiotia lived within the walls in the built-up parts of the cities.

Other investigations lead to the same result,[24] and all the evidence we have today shows that a large city population and a much smaller population on the land is characteristic of small and middle-sized *poleis*.[25] But if we go to the biggest *poleis* like Athens and Sparta, there can be no doubt that the majority of *their* populations lived in the territory, not the city. Thucydides states expressly that more than half the Athenians lived outside Athens in 431, when many of them fled into the walled city at the beginning of the Pelo-ponnesian War.[26] And in the fourth century about a third of the Athenians were still living within the long walls that surrounded Athens and Peiraieus.[27] A big survey of central Lakedaimon north of Sparta also testifies to a more densely populated countryside, and the presumption is that only between a quarter and a third of the population of the region lived in Sparta proper, mainly the Sparti-ates themselves and their families.[28] So while most of the population in the small city-states lived in the cities within the walls, most of the population in the big city-states was settled in the hinterland. So we can propose the following formula to apply to all the *poleis* altogether: in the ancient Greek *poleis* the degree of urbanisation was in inverse proportion to the size of the *polis*—the smaller the *polis* the more people lived in the city within the walls, the bigger the *polis* the more of its people lived in the hinterland.[29] This rule applies especially to the Classical period; as far as we can see, the picture changes in Hellenistic and Roman times, when settlement in villages becomes more usual and a real alternative to settlement within the *polis* itself. In surveys the number of villages rises in the Hellenistic period, and in the written sources—both inscriptions and literary sources—there is also a much larger number of settlements explicitly classified as *komai*, especially in the eastern part of the Greek world.[30]

12

The Size and Population of the Cities

The areas of cities are not a thing in which historians show much interest. They prefer to estimate the size of cities by the number of inhabitants. There can, indeed, be no doubt that knowledge of population size is much more important than knowledge of how large an area the city covered: the problem is only that in the case of ancient cities we have next to no knowledge of their population size and are consequently reduced to making guesses about a city's population size from what we know about its area.

In the Classical period almost all *poleis* had walls, and of many of the walls enough survives for us to be able to calculate with complete or fair certainty the area enclosed by them. For 232 of the 1,035 *poleis* in the Polis Centre's Inventory we can calculate the city's area, and the figures work out as shown in table 2.[1] These figures must, of course, be read with caution, for the area of the city walls is not always an adequate criterion of the size of the city. Many cities had a large open area within the walls, where the population from the countryside could take refuge in case of war.[2] Within the city there might be a separately walled *akropolis* which was mostly but not always kept free of habitation;[3] and large areas could be reserved for the city's marketplace and temples and sports centres, etc. On the other hand, there were cities with whole habitation quarters lying in suburbs outside the city walls.[4] Table 2 includes only those cities whose walls enclosed the entire city: in numerous cases we have evidence that the city had a fortified *akropolis* but no wall round the city itself, and all cities of that kind are excluded.[5] But the table does show that almost all *poleis* had an area of more than 5 ha; the average size is 65 ha and the median 40 ha.

In the literary sources we have only one single calculation that gives evidence for the size of a city's population: Thucydides tells how in spring 431 BC the city of Plataiai was fallen upon by a Theban army of 300–400 men introduced by traitors through a

TABLE 2

0–4 ha	10
5–9 ha	33
10–19 ha	38
20–49 ha	68
50–99 ha	44
100–49 ha	16
150+ ha	23
TOTAL	232

city gate in the middle of the night. The Plataians succeeded in repelling the Thebans, and it emerges from Thucydides' account that the Plataians outnumbered the Thebans and the traitors all put together. A total of, say, 500 adult male Plataians corresponds to a total population of not less than 2,000 inhabitants in a city whose walls encompassed an area of 10 ha.[6]

But the remains of ancient Greek cities can get us much further, especially remains of the cities built on the so-called Hippodamian plan, where two sets of straight parallel streets crossed each other at right angles, and each block of houses had between six and twelve individual plots. When such cities are excavated, one can often determine the number of houses, and if one can work out the average size of a household, one gets an approximate figure for how many people lived in the city: it is not particularly precise, but not so terribly bad either, and as historians of antiquity, we are always shooting with a shotgun rather than a rifle. We have far too few sources to hit the bull's-eye, but the sources often allow us to set, in a given case, a minimum and maximum, and that often gives an adequate degree of precision to the historical analysis we are trying to undertake. I call it the 'shot-gun method', and that is what we have to employ in the present case.[7]

As said already, we often know how many hectares a city wall enclosed. If we can work out the percentage of the area used for habitation and the number of inhabitants per hectare, we can make a plausible guess as to the population. Take, for example, the city of Priene in Ionia in Asia Minor. It was built on the side of a hill. Its walls encompassed an area of 37 ha, and excavations have shown that the inhabited area was *c*.15 ha. The dwellings were terrace-houses, and there were *c*.480 in all; each house contained one household.[8] Now we do not actually know how big a Greek household was, but combining a population profile that seems to fit ancient societies with what we know about the Greek *oikos*, five to six persons seems to be the most likely average.[9] Priene will thus have had between 2,250 and 3,000 inhabitants, living on a site of 15 ha, which gives a population density of *c.*150–200 persons per ha. The figures for Priene correspond to the figures we have for other excavated cities, e.g. Olynthos in the Chalkidike, which seems to have had some 700 houses in all in the quarters on the hills, and probably a population of 3,500 to 4,200 living within the city wall, which enclosed an area of 35 ha, of which some 31 ha seem to have been used for habitation.[10]

Of course, we have to correct our calculations in cases where we know of specific circumstances. Priene was on a hillside, and so the inhabited area comprised a smaller fraction of the whole area of the city than in many other places. In Olynthos the houses built in the new city are the largest found in any Classical city, and, accordingly, the density of population is the lowest attested in any city before the Hellenistic period. On the other hand, in the fourth century BC Olynthos had a big inhabited quarter outside the walls, so we can calculate that its total population will have been somewhat larger than 4,000—but how much larger we cannot say.[11] But the figures for Priene and Olynthos and twenty-six other cities known from excavation or survey[12] roughly correspond to the figures for Plataiai.

Where we have no precise figures, we must use the average as calculated for the excavated cities. So we can reckon that inhabited areas accounted for about two-thirds of the area in the smallest *poleis*—i.e. those with a walled area of 9 ha max.—about half of the area enclosed by walls in small and middle-sized *poleis* with a walled area of 10–150 ha, and about a third in very large *poleis*,[13] and that the population density was 150–200 persons per ha.[14] If we combine the minima, we shall usually be firing short with our shotgun, and if we choose the maxima, we may run the risk of overshooting.

If we apply this method to the 232 *poleis* whose areas we know, and if we conjecture that these 232 *poleis* from all over the Greek city-state world are representative of the ancient Greek *polis* as a whole, we can conclude that there were a very small number of *poleis* whose population could only rate a few hundred inhabitants, all those, in fact, whose walls encircled an area of at most 4 ha. In the next group (areas of 5–9 ha), most must have had about 500–1,000 inhabitants. Over 80 per cent of all *poleis*, however, had a population of more than 1,000, and at least 10 per cent had a population of more than 10,000. It is the archaeological digs and surveys that enable us to draw this picture, and the numbers given here are much larger than those with which most other ancient historians reckon. It is still the prevailing view that most of the population lived in the country,[15] and that very few *poleis* had a population in five figures. The Polis Centre's Inventory shows that in small *poleis* the majority of the inhabitants lived within their city walls, whereas in larger *poleis* the urban population seems to have constituted about half of the total population, and only in the very large *poleis* did the majority of the population live in the countryside, either dispersed or in villages. So far more *poleis* than is usually allowed had populations in four and five figures.

13

The Demography of the Greek City-State Culture

The abundant information about the sizes of walled *poleis* is the best evidence we possess if we want to assess the total number of Greeks in the age of Alexander the Great, both the Greeks settled in the homeland and those settled in all the colonies and Hellenised communities.[1]

The total area enclosed by all 232 walls comes to 15,628 ha, and that is a minimum. On the assumption that the 232 walled cities are representative of all the *c.*1,000 *poleis* in existence in the fourth century, the grand total of walled urban space in the late Classical Hellenic world is 67,360 ha. But is it legitimate just to add up the urban space of all the 232 walled *poleis* and to presume that they are representative of the *c.*1,000 *poleis*? Cities with walls enclosing more than 100 ha seem to be better represented among the 232 *poleis* than small cities with an urban centre covering less than 10 ha. Instead of the rough summing up of all walled *poleis*, we must connect the information we have about measurable defence circuits with the information we have about the size of the territory of these *poleis*, and here I shall use the five categories we applied in the Copenhagen Inventory of *poleis*: (1) 25 km² max., (2) 25–100 km², (3) 100–200 km², (4) 200–500 km², and (5) 500 km² min. Of the 1,035 *poleis* it is possible to place 636 in one or, at least, in one or two of these five categories. For a full survey, see *CPCInv.* 71. For the present investigation I shall use the slightly simplified version shown in table 3.[2] The size of the territory is known or, at least, roughly estimated for 194 of the 232 *poleis* which have sufficient remains of their defence circuits to allow us to measure the area enclosed by the walls. The relation between the size of the territory and the size of the urban centre is as shown in table 4. We have 636 *poleis* for which we can calculate the size of the territory

TABLE 3

Category	Attested *poleis*
1	93 = 15 per cent
1 or 2	109 = 17 per cent
2	198 = 31 per cent
3	100 = 16 per cent
4	69 = 11 per cent
5	67 = 10 per cent
TOTAL	636 = 100 per cent

TABLE 4

Category	*Poleis*	Total area	Average
1	13	100 ha	8 ha
1 or 2	17	351 ha	21 ha
2	56	1,514 ha	27 ha
3	33	1,601 ha	49 ha
4	37	3,810 ha	103 ha
5	38	6,918 ha	182 ha
?	38	1,332 ha	
TOTAL	232	15,626 ha	

and 232 *poleis* for which we know the size of the urban centre. For 194 *poleis* we possess both types of information. But what about all the other *poleis*? Is it legitimate to extrapolate from the evidence set out above and calculate first the urban population and then the total population of the Hellenic world? Both the 636 *poleis* and the 232 *poleis* are spread out over the entire area inhabited by the Greeks in the Archaic and Classical periods: France, Sicily, Italy, western Greece, the Peloponnese, central Greece, Thessaly, the Aegean islands, Macedonia, Thrace, the Pontic region, Asia Minor, and Libya. They are attested in all regions of the Greek world,[3] but it must be kept in mind that the colonial areas are underrepresented; see *infra* 84. It is also problematical to treat the evidence as synchronic, but in my opinion it is admissible. Some walls are Archaic, some were built in the fifth century, but most of the information we have concerns the fourth century. Many of the defence circuits were built or repaired in that century, and many

TABLE 5

Category	Attested *poleis*	All *poleis*
1	93 = 15 per cent	150
1 or 2	109 = 17 per cent	170
2	198 = 31 per cent	310
3	100 = 16 per cent	160
4	69 = 11 per cent	110
5	67 = 10 per cent	100
TOTAL	636 = 100 per cent	1,000

TABLE 6

Category	*Poleis*	Total area
1	150	1,200 ha
1 or 2	170	3,570 ha
2	310	8,370 ha
3	160	7,840 ha
4	110	11,330 ha
5	100	18,200 ha
TOTAL	1,000	50,510 ha

walls of the Archaic or early Classical period were still in use in the late Classical period. If we focus on the fourth century, it should be possible to present a synchronic picture.

Of the 1,035 *poleis* included in the Copenhagen Inventory, 862 were certainly or presumably in existence *c*.400.[4] On the other hand, there are many *poleis* which have not left sufficient traces in our sources to become an entry in the Inventory. If we assume that the number of *poleis* in the fourth century totalled *c*.1,000, we cannot be far out in our reckoning, and, on this assumption, we can construct table 5. If, within each category, we multiply the average size of the urban space by the calculated number of *poleis* in that category, the areas enclosed by walls add up to the totals shown in table 6. If we take half the space to be used for habitation in small and middle-sized *poleis*,[5] as against one-third in large *poleis*, and assume a population density of 150 persons per ha, we get a total of close to 3.5 million people living in the *c*.1,000 cities, as shown in table 7.

TABLE 7

Category	*Poleis*	Total area	Urban population
1	150	1,200 ha	90,000 (50%×150)
1 or 2	170	3,570 ha	267,750 ——
2	310	8,370 ha	627,750 ——
3	160	7,840 ha	588,000 ——
4	110	11,330 ha	849,750 ——
5	100	18,200 ha	910,000 (33.3%×150)
TOTAL	1,000	50,510 ha	3,333,250

The final step is to relate the urban population to the population settled in the territory. Here I rely on those surveys which not only map out a settlement pattern but also attempt to assess the population settled in the surveyed area. These surveys seem to agree that a majority of the population lived behind the walls in small and middle-sized *poleis*, whereas a majority lived in the hinterland in the large *poleis*, viz. those with a territory of 500 km² or more.[6] For this final calculation I assume the following distribution between town and hinterland. For *poleis* category 1–3 (territory up to 200 km²) I assume that two-thirds of the population lived in the urban centre. For *poleis* category 4 (territory of 200–500 km²) I assume that the population was equally divided between town and hinterland, and for the *poleis* category 5 I assume that two-thirds were settled in the hinterland.[7] On these assumptions the average population of a *polis* in each of the five categories was as shown in table 8, and the total population of the Hellenic world was as shown in table 9.

Thus, my first overall conclusion is that, if we apply this method consistently to the entire Greek world, there were close to 7 million ancient Greeks in the second half of the fourth century. But some variations in the settlement pattern must be taken into account. I have treated the Greek world in the second half of the fourth century as a world of *poleis*, a world in which the total population was settled in *c*.1,000 *poleis*, each consisting of an urban centre and a hinterland. In every region (Arkadia, Achaia, Phokis, Thessaly etc.) every person belonged to a *polis* in which he or she was either a citizen, a foreigner or a slave. In the second half of the fourth century BC, such a settlement pattern prevailed in the Greek homeland up to and including Akarnania, Aitolia and Thessaly.

TABLE 8

Category	Urban centre	Territory	TOTAL
1	600	300	900
1 or 2	1,575	790	2,365
2	2,025	1,010	3,035
3	3,675	1,840	5,515
4	7,725	7,725	15,450
5	9,100	18,200	27,300

TABLE 9

Category	Urban centre	Territory	TOTAL
1	90,000	45,000	135,000
1 or 2	267,750	133,875	401,625
2	627,750	313,875	941,625
3	588,000	294,000	882,000
4	849,750	849,750	1,699,500
5	910,000	1,820,000	2,730,000
TOTAL	3,333,250	3,533,875	6,789,750

Settlement in *poleis* goes for the Aegean islands too, and for the west coast of Asia Minor (Troas, Aiolis, Ionia). In the northern part of the Greek homeland, however, and in the colonial world, the settlement pattern and the political organisation of the regions were different. In the regions of Epeiros and Macedonia, there were some *poleis*, some of them Greek colonies, but the majority of the population was settled either in villages or dispersed.[8] The population of the colonial world too was different from the pattern in the Greek homeland. Most of the Greek colonies were small Hellenic 'islands' separated by large stretches of land inhabited by an indigenous population. In Sicily, for example, there was a substantial inland population of Elymians, Sikanians and Sikels in addition to the Hellenic population in the *poleis*, most of which were situated along the coasts. But since the purpose of this investigation is to assess the number of ancient Greeks, the indigenous population of the various regions is excluded from my calculations, except when it had been Hellenised in the fourth century and now lived in what had become Greek *poleis*. Close to half the Sicilian *poleis*, most of them fairly small, were in fact indigenous communities which, in the second half of the fourth century, had become sufficiently Hellenised to count as Hellenic *poleis*.[9] Therefore the method I use can be applied to Sicily and to most of the other colonial regions as well: Spain and France, southern Italy, Illyria, Thrace, the Pontic, the Hellespont, Karia, Lykia, the south coast of Asia Minor, Syria, Egypt and Libya.[10]

So, the really problematic regions are Epeiros and Macedonia. For these my estimates are definitely much too low, and to reach the total number of Greeks—including Epeirotes and Macedonians, another half a million or rather more have to be added to the result I have obtained.[11]

To conclude, if we include Epeiros and Macedonia, the total population of the Greek world comes to 7.5 million, and that is a minimum figure.[12] If we change one or more of the variables, we can reach 8 or 9 or perhaps even 10 million.[13]

A cautious total of 7.5 million ancient Greeks and a possible total of 8–10 million is a much higher figure than supposed nowadays by those historians who try to address the problem.[14]

These findings are of the utmost importance for our understanding of Greek history; so, summing up, let me repeat that to reach them I have had to make four assumptions: (1) that it is admissible to extrapolate from the 232 attested walled cities and the 636 assessed territories to the altogether 1,000 *poleis* which constituted the Hellenic city-state culture in the fourth century; (2) that the percentages 50 per cent versus 33 per cent inhabited space inside the walls of small to middle-sized versus large *poleis* respectively stand up to scrutiny; (3) that the average of 150 persons per hectare of inhabited space is realistic or, rather, minimalistic; (4) that the urban population constituted about two-thirds of the population in small *poleis* (200 km² max.), half in middle-sized *poleis* (200–500 km²), and one-third in large *poleis* (over 500 km²).

Because published landscape surveys are still few and far between, the most problematic assumption is the relation between the urban and the rural population. Most ancient historians assume that the great majority of the population was settled in the hinterland, dispersed or in small villages, and that the urban population constituted a small fraction only of the total population.[15] The Polis Centre's investigations indicate that, in small and middle-sized *poleis* the majority of the population lived in the urban centre and a minority only in the hinterland.[16]

Now, for the sake of the argument, let us accept the prevailing view and assume that the urban population constituted no more than 10 per cent max. of the total population.[17] In that case the population settled in the hinterland of all the *poleis* was more than 30 million persons, and we get a total population of 35 million ancient Greeks—provided, of course, that the other assumptions stand up to scrutiny, as I think they do. To have a total of 35 million ancient Greeks in the fourth century BC is out of the question. So our investigations show, in any case, that the degree of urbanisation of ancient Greece must have been much higher than assumed by many ancient historians. There can be little doubt that in small and middle-sized *poleis* the majority of the population lived behind the walls, but many of them were farmers who every morning walked to their fields and back again to the town in the evening. They were Weberian *Ackerbürger*.[18]

Another startling result of this investigation is the distribution of this total of at least 7.5 million ancient Greeks. We claim that the typical *polis*, the *Normalpolis* in German terminology, had a small territory, often of less than 100 km² and a population that numbered a few thousand inhabitants altogether. That is indeed true: the Polis Centre's investigations have shown that about 80 per cent of all *poleis* had a territory of at most 200 km².[19]

On the other hand, the present investigation, based on the Polis Centre's Inventory, shows that these 80 per cent of all *poleis* seem to have accommodated no more than 35 per cent of the entire population.[20] Next, some 10 per cent of all *poleis* had a territory of 200–500 km², and they seem to have accommodated about 25 per cent of the entire population. Finally, some 10 per cent of all *poleis*, *c.*100 altogether, had a territory of more than 500 km², and they may have accommodated about 40 per cent of the entire population.

Poleis with a territory of more than 500 km² had an urban centre that, on average, covered close to 200 ha, with an urban population of, on average, 9,000 and a total population of *c.*27,000, of whom some 7,500 would be adult males.[21] In the fourth century there seem to have been about 100 such *poleis*, and about half of them seem to have had an adult male citizen population of 10,000 persons or more. So if we measure the typical *polis* by size of population rather than by size of territory, the conclusion is that the typical large *polis* either was or was close to being a *myriandros polis*, a *polis* with 10,000 adult male citizens.[22] Thus the *myriandros polis* was not—as is often assumed—an exceptionally large ideal *polis*;[23] it was the normal large *polis* which accounted for, I guess, something like a twelfth of all *poleis* inhabited by about a third of all the ancient Greeks.

As my last shot from the shotgun, I will show what happens if we break down the totals into *poleis* in the Greek homeland as against *poleis* founded as colonies outside the Greek homeland plus indigenous communities in the colonial areas which by the late Classical period had become Hellenised so that they now counted as Hellenic *poleis*. I shall here define the Greek homeland in the late fourth century as being mainland Greece from Epeiros to Thessaly, the islands in the Aegean including Crete and Rhodes, plus the West coast of Asia Minor from Troas to Ionia.[24]

On this definition of the Greek homeland, we can see that 40 per cent of all *poleis* were colonies lying outside the Greek homeland.[25] If for the 636 *poleis* with known size of territory we calculate the population following the same method as above, we get a population of 4 million in the homeland versus 3 million in the colonies and Hellenised communities.[26] But we must take into account that the colonies are underrepresented among these 636 *poleis*: no fewer than 449 (=71 per cent) lay in the Greek homeland, while 187 (29 per cent) were colonies and Hellenised communities outside the Greek homeland.[27] For this reason, and because the colonies were, on average, larger than the *poleis* in the Greek homeland,[28] it can be presumed that the colonies would count for a larger percentage of the total population if we had all the evidence at our disposal. Conversely, the populations of Epeiros and Macedonia are grossly underrepresented in an investigation based on walled urban centres. Thus, on balance it seems fair to say that in the second half of the fourth century BC probably as many as 40 per cent of all the ancient Greeks lived outside the Greek homeland, in colonies or Hellenised communities.[29]

14

The Economy of the Cities: Max Weber's 'Ideal Type'

In all our analysis up to now we have distinguished between cities and villages, and have usually described them as settlements of a certain size surrounded by walls. But that is not enough. If one is to understand the ancient Greek city-state and put it in its world-historical setting, one must also describe its structure and function, and begin with the quite fundamental question: what is a city? Scholars still discuss the question of what a city is and what consti-tutes the difference between a city and a village; but to all intents and purposes, all of them still focus on the criteria that the Austrian sociologist Max Weber proposed in 1921 in his article 'Die Stadt'.[1] According to Max Weber, a city is a nucleated settlement in which the houses lie so close together as to be often wall-to-wall, and where the number of inhabitants is such that they can no longer all know each other as people can in a village. In the economic field the city is characterised by division of labour, so that the city-dwellers buy a substantial part of what they need in the city market, and these goods are produced by the people in the city and its hinter-land for the purpose of being sold in the market. With urbanisation man gives up the subsistence economy (in which each household produces everything it needs).[2]

On the basis of economic criteria, one can distinguish between two types of city, consumer cities and producer cities. In consumer cities the economy is directed to satisfying the interests of the con-sumers, and the consumers are consequently the ruling class of the city—a monarch and his court, a bureaucracy, a class of landown-ers who live in the city. In producer cities it is the craftsmen and traders who form the ruling class. Seen as a political community, the city has a territory and has local self-government with the fol-lowing characteristics: (1) the city is protected by walls; (2) it has a market; (3) it has its own laws administered in its own courts; (4) it has its own political institutions; and (5) it is autonomous, or possesses at least local autonomy. As to the relationship between city and hinterland, Max Weber distinguishes the city of antiquity, where a large proportion of the citizens were farmers living in the city but going out daily to work in their fields in the hinterland (*Ackerbürger*), and the city of the Middle Ages where there was a far sharper distinction between the population on the land, who were farmers, and the population in the city, who were dominated by craftsmen and tradesmen.[3]

What happens if one compares Weber's 'ideal type' description of the city[4] with our latest accounts of the ancient Greek *polis* in the Archaic and Classical periods? As far as I can see, there is in six regards a clash between Weber's model and the orthodoxy prevailing among ancient historians.

(1) In contrast to the close connection between the urbanistic and political aspects in the ancient and medieval city, it has become customary for ancient historians to dissociate *polis* as city from *polis* as state.[5]

(2) The Greek *polis* is almost always described as a 'face-to-face' society, whereas Weber insists that settlements where everybody knows everybody else are villages rather than cities.[6]

(3) Weber's description of the ancient city-state as a consumer city is increasingly thrown into doubt by the historians, who emphasise the importance of production and trade in the ancient Greek *polis*.[7]

(4) Weber regards *Ackerbürger* as a characteristic of the ancient city, whereas modern historians assert that a settlement where landowners and farmers form a sizeable part of the population is not a city at all in the proper sense of the word.[8]

(5) The prevailing orthodoxy is that the economy of the city-state was a subsistence economy,[9] whereas Weber's model insists that the inhabitants of a city obtained a significant part of their needs in the city market, and that those goods were partly produced by the city's own population but partly imported from other cities.

(6) City walls are in Weber's model one of the characteristic signs of a city, whereas ancient historians today insist that the building of city walls came late in the history of the city-state and that some *poleis* had none.[10]

If the ancient historians are right, Weber's 'ideal type' applies to only a score of all the 1,000 *poleis*: namely cities like Akragas, Argos, Athens, Corinth, Kyrene, Miletos, Syracuse, Thebes and a few others. In that case the model can be cast aside as useless.[11] On the other hand, it cannot be excluded that perhaps it is the ancient historians who have drawn a skewed or even simply erroneous picture of the ancient Greek *polis*, so that Weber's 'ideal type' description ought still to be maintained as the best model so far on offer.[12] Let us go back over the six points.

(1) *The* polis *as city-state* The dissociation of the urban and political aspects of the *polis* rests on three assumptios: (a) some *poleis* had no city centre at all;[13] (b) the city centre occurring in some *poleis* does not justify being called 'city' in the functional sense of the word[14]—only the very largest *poleis* like Athens, Corinth, Thebes and a few others can be described as cities in the proper sense; and (c) both in Greece proper and in the colonies the *polis* as a state arose in the second half of the eighth century BC, whereas urbanisation proceeded so slowly that we can speak of 'cities' only from the end of the sixth.[15]

(a) Sparta is almost always quoted as an example of a *polis* without any city centre. It is correct that there was no city wall round Sparta in the Classical period: it consisted in fact of four villages.[16] However, the villages were quite close together and covered an area of 3–4 km². With some 40,000 members of the Spartan families living in the four villages, there was a population density of at least 100 persons per ha,[17] so Sparta must be regarded as a significant city in respect of both population and economy. It is what is called a 'conurbation', a city created by the coming together of close neighbouring villages. Also, we know that the Greeks themselves regarded Sparta as a *polis* in the sense of 'city': that it shown with all desirable clarity in a number of sources in which the terms *asty*, *polisma* and *polis* in the sense of 'city' are applied quite naturally to Sparta.[18]

A complete analysis of all the source material only strengthens the unbreakable connection between city and state in the ancient Greek city-state culture. The Polis Centre's investigations reveal that in Archaic and Classical times what is called *polis* in the meaning 'city' is known to have been the centre of a *polis* in the meaning 'state': of the 1,035 *poleis* in the Inventory of the Polis Centre, 447 are explicitly attested as *poleis* in the sense of 'city'. Of those, sixty-three must be left out of account because we have absolutely no evidence as to their political status in the Archaic and Classical periods. Of the remaining 384, there is no reason to doubt that 364 were *poleis* in the political sense; in the remaining twenty cases their political status can be disputed, but there is just a single one of these cases in which we can with certainty *dis*-sociate the political from the urban aspect: in his little treatise on the economy of the *polis* Xenophon proposes that a *polis* ought to be founded in the mining district of Attika where the mining slaves can live.[19]

Our investigations support also the complementary proposition, that in the Classical period every *polis* in the political sense has a *polis* in the sense of 'city' as its administrative and economic centre: of the 1,035 *poleis*, 287 are explicitly called *polis* in the political sense. Of those, 204 are known to have had a walled city centre that can be dated at the latest to the second half of the fourth century BC. For another twenty-four *poleis* a city centre is attested either archaeologically (Elis) or in the written sources (Aitna) or both (Sparta). Of the remaining fifty-nine *poleis*, the locality of twenty-three has not yet been identified, and thirty-four have not yet been examined. So there are only two *poleis* where no city centre has been found although they have been investigated by the archaeologists: Epitalion in Triphylia and Delphi in Phokis. It is still on the cards that Epitalion's city centre may turn up, but it is undeniably striking that still no trace has been found of a city centre at Delphi.

Another investigation gives the same result: of the 287 *poleis* that are called *polis* in the political sense, 243 are also referred to in the written sources as *polis* in the sense of 'city'—including Delphi. Of the remaining forty-four, thirty-one have a city centre confirmed by archaeology, twenty-six of them with city walls. Of the remaining thirteen *poleis*, the locality of six has not yet been identified, and six have not yet been examined. The last is Epitalion.[20]

(b) The best-known assertion that the ancient Greek *polis* does not deserve to be called 'city' in the urban sense is found in Moses Finley's book *The Ancient Greeks*, in which he stated—and repeated many years later—that many *poleis* simply were not cities but only 'civic centres' where the population was settled. Thus, when Sparta in 385 BC destroyed Mantinea and moved the population out into its four original villages, it was not a 'city' that it destroyed but only a settlement where a population of landowners chose to live protected by the walls of the city separately from their lands, living a life-style known in Homer 'which had nothing else to do with city-life'.[21] After forty years Finley's view is repeated and accepted in the latest large-scale account of the lack of urbanisation in the city-state culture of ancient Greece and the whole Mediterranean world before the rise of industrialisation in the eighteenth and nineteenth centuries.[22] But in 385 BC Mantinea *was* a city centre with at least 7,000 and possibly more than 10,000 inhabitants. It is inconceivable that the majority of them were landowners living off the income of their estates. Before the Industrial Revolution much the largest part of all mankind must have been producers mainly occupied in securing food for themselves. Many of the citizens of Mantinea must have been *Ackerbürger* in the Weberian sense: farmers, but living in the city, and many must have been traders and craftsmen. *Rentiers* cannot possibly have accounted for more than a tiny fraction of the city's population, and the city-dwellers must have acquired their necessities by purchase in the market.[23]

(c) In the early Archaic period there may have been *poleis* in the political sense whose nucleated centres appeared only *c*.500 BC or later; but they are not easy to find.[24] The territories of most city-states have not been surveyed well enough for us to say that there was no city centre, or that the city centre that has been discovered cannot have been older than 500 BC.[25] And, on the other side, where we have a city centre that can only have been built after 500, we lack the epigraphic or literary evidence to tell us whether it was already a *polis* in the political sense in the seventh and sixth centuries, i.e. *before* the community got itself a city centre. There has not yet been found a single unassailable example of a society specifically called a *polis* in the Archaic period whose city centre demonstrably belongs to a later period. It may well be that in Greece in the seventh century there were only, say, between 100 and 200 settlements large enough to be called *poleis* in the sense of 'city', but it may equally well be the case that at that period there were in the whole of Greece no more than 100–200 *poleis* in the political sense either: we do not know and may never know.

(2) *The* polis *as a face-to-face society*   According to Max Weber, one of the differences between a city and a village is that its population is too large for everyone to know everyone else. At first sight that opinion appears to be in conflict with the demand of Plato and

Aristotle that a *polis* must never be bigger than for everone to be able to know everyone else,[26] and with the description of the *polis* by modern historians as a 'face-to-face' society.[27] But the difference between the two standpoints is diminished if one takes into account that Plato and Aristotle were thinking only of the citizen body of the ideal *polis*—that is, adult male citizens with a given property rating—whereas Weber's point applies to all the inhabitants of a city, of whom at most a quarter were full citizens. Some *poleis*, however, were so small that all the inhabitants could have known each other; and in such cases a settlement on Weber's model would have been a village rather than a city.[28]

(3) *The* polis *as a consumer city*   The distinction consumer city versus producer city was taken over by Weber from Werner Sombart. In a consumer city (city plus hinterland) most of the population lives out on the land, cultivates the soil, and provides the food base for the modest fraction of the population that lives within the city. Most of the city-dwellers are landowners, who are parasitic upon the much larger country population by demanding taxes and rents from the farmers, and they use those resources as payment for the food supplies which the farmers bring into the city and sell in the market. So there is a sort of trade between city and hinterland, but it is to a large extent a closed system. There is only a small sector of producers and traders in a 'consumer city', and foreign trade plays only an insignificant role in the economy.[29]

Werner Sombart applied his model to the cities of the Middle Ages and modern times down to the rise of industrialism. Max Weber extended his range of reference to include antiquity.[30] Here, as elsewhere, Finley trod in Weber's footsteps,[31] and the majority of ancient historians still use the consumer city as the preferred model for describing the city-state cultures of antiquity.[32] My view is that we should return to Sombart's standpoint and leave antiquity out.

The typical Greek city-state—i.e. the *c.*80 per cent of all *poleis* that had a territory of at most 200 km²—was not a 'consumer city' in Sombart's sense. The majority of the population did *not* live out in the country but in the city proper. There was no distinction between city population and country population, because a large proportion of a city's population were farmers who tilled their fields in the hinterland of the city; and the majority of the city population were *not* landowners paying for what they needed with rents and taxes, but farmers and craftsmen who to a not insignificant extent produced for a market where traders organised the exchange of goods.[33]

So the typical *polis* was not a 'consumer city', but what of the great *poleis*, the 10 per cent that had a territory of more than 500 km² and where most of the population lived in the hinterland? One of them fits Sombart's consumer city perfectly, namely Sparta.[34] In *c*.500 BC there lived in the city of Sparta *c*.8,000 Spartan full citizens and their families.[35] The Spartans were neither farmers nor craftsmen: they were professional soldiers. Out in the countryside in Lakedaimon and Messenia the land was cultivated by helots, farmers tied to their masters, who were required to hand over a part of their crops annually to the Spartans. In the relation between helots and Spartans we can see a distinction between a larger population of farmers on the land, exploited by a much smaller population of consumers in the urban centre. Sparta had only a small sector of producers and traders, and it was a closed society whose external trade was reduced to a minimum.[36]

The other giant amongst the city-states was Athens, and Athens was in economic as in other respects the exact opposite of Sparta. Attika had a territory of 2,500 km², far too large for it to have been possible for the majority of the population to live in the city of Athens plus its harbour Peiraieus. We know that from Thucydides, who says that the majority of the Athenians were living outside the walls when the Peloponnesian War broke out in 431 BC. In Athens we encounter once again the distinction between a smaller city population and a larger country population; but even here there were *Ackerbürger*,[37] and our sources also show that the majority of Athenian citizens were not consumers and did not get their daily bread by exploiting the country population. Athens was poor in agricultural land, yet in the 4th century BC had to feed a population of some 200,000 people.[38] They had to import masses of grain from the Black Sea, Egypt, Libya, Sicily and the Po Valley.[39] One of the most pessimistic estimates of the grain imports of Athens concludes that in a normal year the Athenians had to import about half of all the grain they needed;[40] by my calculations imports would have been a good deal larger than that even in normal years, and much larger in famine years, of which there were several. Grain was the principal item in the diet of an Athenian: if we have a situation where the Athenian in the street had to get half his requirement of grain by purchase in the market, we are a very long way from a subsistence economy. We have, on the contrary, a market economy based on significant outside trade. In the whole of the half-year sailing season from March to October, trading vessels sailed every day in and out of the Peiraieus, each with a cargo of 80–100 tons. The trade of Athens was not 'local trade' based on the sale of necessities by farmers to city-dwellers who payed with the resources they had extracted from the farmers in taxes, etc.; it was overseas trade, financed by the export of Athens' own products, first and foremost the silver from the mines of Laurion in southern Attika.[41]

Athens must have had an enormous foreign trade, and this emerges from our sources. The most important is a passage from a forensic speech in 400 BC. The speaker, Andokides, declares that in the year 402/1 BC he took on the contract for the harbour dues of 2 per cent on all imported and exported goods; i.e. he guaranteed this sum to the state and recouped from what actually came in. The proceeds of the contract was 36 silver talents, and Andokides allows that he made a little profit on the transaction.[42] So the whole of Athens' import and export trade, including transit trade, that year (which was one of the worst in the history of Athens) must have been worth more than 1,800 talents, which equals 11 million drachmas. A drachma was a day's wage for a daily worker, so 1,800 talents correspond to day-wages for 30,000 people, a whole year's wages for every single citizen of Athens. Part of that huge trade may have been transit trade; but that does not alter the fact that Athens had a foreign export–import trade on a scale that is impossible to reconcile with Sombart's consumer city.

Besides the 'consumer city' and the 'producer city' Weber operates with a third type: the 'trading city' (*Gewerbestadt*); he describes the Hansa cities as examples of such cities.[43] If we are to apply Weber's typology to the classical *poleis*, it is in this category that Athens belongs: it was not a 'consumer city' but rather a 'trading city' in line with Venice and Genoa.

But that is not the whole truth. We must not forget that 'consumer city', 'producer city' and 'trading city' are ideal types, and many actual historical societies have elements of all three types.[44] Like other trading cities, Athens had a consumer ideology. In the famous Funeral Oration for the city's fallen that Perikles delivered in 430 BC, he claims that Athens is the one city in Greece where one can buy things imported from all over the world. He does not claim that Athens' own products are so marvellous that they can be exported all over the world. And his point is echoed in other sources, which express the viewpoint that stress is always laid on imports, never on exports.[45] From a purely ideological point of view, therefore, Weber is right, and Athens *was* a 'consumer city', but not in Werner Sombart's sense of the term.[46]

(handwritten margin note: IDEOLOGY OF CONSUMPTION)

(4) *Ackerbürger*   In ancient Greece, as in all ancient societies, most of the population had to spend most of its time obtaining food. The majority of a city-state's population may have lived inside the walls, but they worked in the fields as farmers or herdsmen or on the sea as fishermen. The farmers went out every morning to their fields and back again in the evening, and the fishermen sailed out and back likewise. Most *poleis* lay on the coast, and in some of them fishermen comprised the majority of the population,[47] but landworkers were doubtless the major population group in the large and medium-sized *poleis*, and consequently the ones that historians have been interested in.[48]

It is undoubtedly true that a large part of the population of a *polis* were 'city-farmers' and that was possible because the great majority of city-states were so small. If the territory of a city-state was a circle with the city in the middle, a territory of 200 km² would have had a radius of 8 km. People could well walk 5–10 km every day (or ride a donkey) to go to and from work. That is something many modern historians find difficult to conceive but to which they need to acclimatise themselves: in ancient times people's daily mobility was much greater than is normally allowed, and it seemed entirely natural for farmers to go out of the city daily to their plots and back again.[49] From amongst all the relevant sources I will cite just one: the seven Theban exiles in 379 BC who succeeded in smuggling themselves into the city by mingling with the farmers going home in the evening from their fields.[50]

(handwritten margin note: 1–2 hr? walk)

Weber calls the 'city-farmers' *Ackerbürger*, and uses the term *Ackerbürgerstädte* to describe cities in which city-farmers predominate. He sees *Ackerbürger* as a criterion of ancient city-states and as one of the most important differences between the ancient and the medieval city.[51] He may be right, if by the Medieval city we are thinking of the north Italian city states where there was a sharp division between city (*città*) and hinterland (*contado*). But north of the Alps there were many cities like those of ancient Greece, which had city-farmers as a group connecting city and hinterland.[52]

Werner Sombart called them *Landstädte*: he did not regard them
as cities in the proper sense, and excluded them from his division
into consumer cities and producer cities.[53] On that point Weber is
unclear. In his discussion of the relation between *Stadtwirtschaft*
and *Landwirtschaft* he finds no difficulty in combining the concepts of 'city' and 'city-farmer' and argues that many *Ackerbürger*
produced for the city's market.[54] But when he is contrasting the
ancient city with that of the Middle Ages, he claims, first, that
virtually all the inhabitants of the ancient city were *Ackerbürger*
(which is an exaggeration), and next, that the city population being
largely *Ackerbürger* points to a subsistence economy (in which he is
in contradiction with his own previous admission that *Ackerbürger*
produced for the market).[55] In the rest of his article, however, he
takes it for granted that the Greek *poleis* were cities (*Städte*), and
consequently he must have thought that they corresponded to his
ideal type and fulfilled the inescapable necessity that the inhabitants of a city must obtain a large part of what they need in the city's
market. But by extrapolating from Weber's specific account of the
relation between *Ackerbürger* and the subsistence economy, Finley,
and historians after him, have taken the appearance of *Ackerbürger*
as fuel for the claim that the typical ancient Greek *polis* was not a
city in the proper sense.[56]

(5) *Subsistence economy in the city-state*   Weber conceived of the
ancient Greek *poleis* as cities, and in his description under ideal
types he emphasises market trading as the most important aspect
of the economy of a city. On this point his view was not adopted
by Finley or by recent historians following in Finley's footsteps.
The ruling orthodoxy is that the typical *polis* had a 'subsistence
economy' in which every unit produced for its own consumption;
there was limited trade between city and hinterland, and virtually
no long-distance trade. Athens, Miletos, Syracuse and a few other
giants among the city-states are quoted as the exceptions that prove
the rule.[57]

Not only what is said above about the 'consumer city', but also
many of our sources, tell against that primitivist historical picture.
Plato sees division of labour and trade as the most important driv-
ing forces leading to the foundation of cities; Xenophon paints the
same picture; and Aristotle declares that the most indispensable of
all magistrates[58] in a city are the inspectors of markets (*agoranomoi*);

these latter are found in every single *polis*, because trade in the city market (*agora*) is an important aspect of the life of a city.[59] Many city-farmers must have produced a surplus of country products which they brought to market and exchanged for other goods produced by other inhabitants. Some specialised in one or two items which they took to market and exchanged not just for other items but for the agricultural products they did not produce themselves. In one of Aristophanes' comedies we meet a countryman coming to the city with his wine in order to buy flour.[60] The sources show that imported grain was a necessity of life not just for Athens, the most populous of all *poleis*, and for Aigina, an island too small to feed its large population, but also for *poleis* like Teos, Ephesos and Samos in Ionia, Mytilene on Lesbos and little Anthedon in Boiotia.[61] During a grain shortage in Greece between 330 and 326 BC, Kyrene gave large amounts of grain to forty-two different *poleis*; and even city-states in Boiotia and Thessaly were amongst the beneficiaries.[62] Not just the big *poleis*, but also the medium and small ones seem to have fulfilled Weber's requirement that in a city the inhabitants have to get a significant part of their needs by purchase in the market.

(6) *City walls*   It is still widely held that a city wall was not part of what the Greeks understood as a necessity for a *polis*, and that many *poleis* in fact had no city walls. Investigation of the written sources and the surviving city walls paints a different picture. In the introduction to his History Thucydides sketches the development of communities in Greece from the earliest settlements to the Persian Wars, and one of his turning-points is the change from unfortified inland cities to fortified coastal ones. Thucydides sets the change in the period before the Trojan War. Correspondingly, Euripides tells how the wild Kyklopes live in caves and not, like Greeks, in a *polis* surrounded by walls.[63] It is true that Plato in the *Laws* prefers an unfortified city like Sparta, but Aristotle's comment on that was that it was an outdated point of view.[64] And since city walls are one of the most important characteristics of the cities described by Homer and the lyric poets of the Archaic Age,[65] we must conclude that Aristotle shared the view of Thucydides and regarded unwalled cities as a feature of pre-Homeric society.

Already in the Archaic period, then, walls were an important aspect of the Greek perception of what a *polis* was, and an overview of surviving walls only serves to strengthen that point. The locality of 166 of the 1,035 *poleis* in the Polis Centre's Inventory is not yet determined; of the remaining 869,[66] traces of city walls from the Archaic or Classical periods are preserved in 438, and another ninety are indicated in the literary sources as having walls.[67] We have evidence that some ancient walls have disappeared without trace,[68] and a survival ratio of 60 per cent shows that almost all *poleis* must have had a city wall or at least a wall protecting the city's *akropolis*. In the written sources, 222 *poleis* in all are referred to as walled in the Archaic and Classical periods, and only in nineteen cases is it expressly said that a city is unwalled; there are only four *poleis* of which we know positively that they did not have any wall at the end of the Classical period: namely, Delphi, Delos, Gortyn and Sparta.[69]

The conclusion of this whole investigation is that Weber's description of a city in terms of 'ideal type' fits the Classical *polis* much better than Finley and his followers thought. It was Finley who brought Weber into the debate about ancient history, but it was also Finley who maintained that Weber's model of the ancient city could not be used in a description of the typical *polis* and fitted only half a score of the biggest city-states. Finley stuck to the opinion that the ancient economy was a subsistence economy with limited local trade and insignificant external trade. He believed—as did all historians at that time—that most of the population were farmers living in the hinterland, and that most of the small population of the city itself were landowners, and that is the view still taken by most ancient historians.

The researches of the Polis Centre show that even small *poleis* can be described as cities in Weber's sense. The Classical *polis* was a self-governing but not necessarily independent society; its centre was a walled city, with houses wall to wall; and the medium and large city-states had a population of such a size that not all, but only the adult male citizens, could know one another. Only with that proviso is it right to say that the typical *polis* was a 'face-to-face' society. A sizeable proportion of the city-dwellers were farmers who went out daily to their plots in the hinterland or fishermen who likewise lived in the city and had their boats in the harbour, or craftsmen working within a system of division of labour. And the economic centre of the city was a market (*agora*) in which the city-dwellers bought or bartered a sizeable portion of what they needed. Both local trade and long-distance trade were an important item in the economy of a city. There may have been a small class of *rentiers* who did not themselves till the land they owned, but the *polis* was not a 'consumer city ' in Werner Sombart's sense. In that regard neither Sombart's model nor Weber's fits the evidence of the sources; but only the archaeological surveys of recent decades have enabled us to know that most of the population of a *polis* lived within the city, and that, consequently, there was no clear distinction between city-dwellers and country-dwellers.

15

Polis as City in the Archaic Period

In describing the *polis* in its 'city' meaning I have so far focused on the Classical period. I want now to return to the question how far back *polis* as 'city' can be traced, to set beside what we know of the origin of *polis* as 'state'. I begin with the written sources and consider the earliest evidence we have for the concept of *polis* as city.

In the Homeric poems all cities are provided with high walls and impressive towers, and inside the walls they have broad streets.[1] That picture may be a reminiscence of the cities of the Bronze Age, or be based on a vague knowledge of the big cities of the Near East; but it may reflect the cities of Greece proper that Homer's hearers lived in, say, in the seventh century BC; and that possibility is confirmed by other sources. In a lost—though much-cited—poem Alkaios of Lesbos says that a *polis* is not just a walled city but rather a community of men ready to defend their society: the antithetical way of putting it implies that other people did describe the *polis* as a walled city; and *polis* in that sense turns up in Archilochos of Paros. In Anakreon of Teos city walls are called the city's 'crown'. So as far back as our written sources go, the word *polis* is used both in the sense of city and in the sense of community; and the two meanings are actually contrasted in a poem of Tyrtaios.[2] The written sources thus show that the notion of *polis* as a walled city goes back to the seventh century BC, and perhaps further still.

If we turn from the written sources to the archaeological remains, at first sight we get a quite different impression of the chronology. Nowadays both archaeologists and historians conjecture that the *polis* in the sense of a political community arose long before people had cities at all. Ian Morris, for example, thinks that the boundary between the 'non-city period' and the 'city period' is to be drawn late in the sixth century BC, whereas the rise of the *polis* as a state has to be put *c.*700; so there were *c.*200 years before the rise of states was followed by the rise of cities. Similarly, Kolb believes that urbanisation in Greece cannot be dated earlier than the late sixth century BC.[3]

If we compare the written sources with the prevailing opinion as to when urbanisation took place, we have to conclude that the concept of *polis* in the sense of city arose between one and two hundred years before the cities that the concept refers to. That is not inconceivable, but it is, to put it mildly, odd. And we also have to conclude that the development of the meaning of the word *polis* went 'fortress–state–city' and not 'fortress–city–state' as one might have expected; and that also is odd.[4] To date *polis* in the meaning of state any later is excluded: that is shown by the sources, which give *c.*650 BC as the *terminus ante quem*.[5] If anything said so far has to be questioned, it must be the late dating of the rise of the *city* in Greece: and there is justification for that in the most recent archaeological evidence.

German excavations at Miletos in recent years have shown that the settlement was already in the seventh century a walled city with a population in, possibly, five figures.[6] It has long been known that Smyrna was a walled city in the eighth century BC and perhaps already in the ninth.[7] There is no reason to think that Miletos and Smyrna were the only cities on the coast of Asia Minor in the early Archaic period. The colony of Abdera had walls already in the seventh century.[8] The Swiss excavations at Eretria have unearthed a city centre that arose in the course of the eighth century, so that Eretria was already a considerable city by *c.*700 BC.[9] On the Greek mainland close-packed housing complexes have been found in Athens, Corinth and Argos, which *c.*700 BC were in process of combining into larger units.[10] And in Sicily the cities of Syracuse and Megara Hyblaia can be traced back to the eighth century, and Naxos became a city early in the seventh.[11]

Historians and archaeologists usually go on the principle that a close-knit group of settlements does not count as a city until it has developed a city centre.[12] But the Greeks themselves regarded such a group of small closely set villages as a city in the urban sense, a *polis kata komas oikoumene*, i.e. a *polis* consisting of villages.[13] Sparta is the example the sources quote. It was perhaps an old-fashioned kind of city, but it was a *polis* or *asty* all the same, and that kind of settlement ought to be called a city on the ground that a population in four or even five figures lived together in a small area with a population density which in Sparta's case may have exceeded 100 persons per hectare.[14]

Properly detailed archaeological investigation of the city centre has only been done for *c.*10 per cent of all the 1,035 *poleis* in the Polis Centre's Inventory,[15] and in many cases there is nothing or next to nothing found from the Archaic period even in *poleis* that in written sources are attested as having had a city centre in that period. The archaeological evidence is so sparse that perhaps one ought to avoid generalisations altogether;[16] but if you risk the leap, the evidence found in the course of the recent generation shows that the rise of cities in the ancient Greek city-state culture must be put back at least to the seventh century BC, and possibly early in that century. There is no ground for supposing an interval of 100 or 200 years between state formation and city formation: the two processes took place side by side, doubtless with constant interaction.

16

The Greek Conception of *Polis* as a City with a Hinterland

As shown above, a *polis* in the sense of 'city' was thought of as the centre of a *polis* in the sense 'state', and in most *poleis* in the sense of 'state' there was only one city called *polis*. It had a hinterland called *chora* or *ge*,[1] and a *polis* by the sea had a harbour, called *limen* or *epineion*.[2] Linked to the harbour there was often an *emporion*, a distinct market for the long-distance trade of the city-state.[3] Large cities situated inland could have a harbour-town, often treated as part of the city itself,[4] and sometimes connected to the city by walls.[5] In other cases the harbour-town had sufficient self-government to count as a dependent *polis*.[6]

Almost all *poleis* had a city wall that separated the city from its hinterland.[7] Larger *poleis* had villages within their hinterland. If the citizen body was subdivided into territorially based groups, many of those districts would have had a village as their central place; but in other cases the villages were just settlements with no political status.[8] Small *poleis* were often conquered by larger ones: if they were allowed to survive as dependencies with *polis* status, their city centre would still be a *polis*, and its hinterland a city-state territory inside the territory of the big city-state, and the big city-state became the centre of a hierarchical system of dependent city-states.[9]

In the sense of 'city' the *polis* was first and foremost a settlement and on the basis of excavations and surveys archaeologists nowadays distinguish two types, each with its own history of development: (A) a small settlement on an *akropolis* spreads out below the *akropolis* and grows into a city, and (B) a group of closely knit minor settlements coalesces into a city. A decisive moment in both cases is when the entire city gets surrounded by a wall.[10] In *poleis* of type (A) the *akropolis* itself was often walled and clearly distinct

from the city below.[11] The *akropolis* might go on being used for
settlement,[12] but was often reserved for temples and other public
buildings.[13] However, having an *akropolis* was not an absolute criterion of type (A). A *polis* of type (B) might have an *akropolis* as
one of the settlements that joined to form the city. Many cities had
two separate defence walls, one round the *akropolis* and the other
around the whole city.[14]

The first and most vital physical requirement for a city is water
supply; and a special type of monumental architecture in many
poleis was a spring-house or well-house where the inhabitants could
supplement the water they got from their own private wells.[15]

All common areas were public property and were used for walls,
streets, towers, harbours, temples, administrative buildings and
sports centres. The remainder of the city consisted of privately
owned lots built on with simple family dwellings.[16] Palaces were
unknown in the Archaic and Classical periods, even in *poleis* ruled
by tyrants: they turn up only in the Hellenistic period.[17]

The dwelling areas often had twisted streets and houses higgledy-
piggledy; but in the Classical period a sizeable number of *poleis*
acquired city plans with straight streets at right angles to each other.
The architect Hippodamos of Miletos used the rectangular plan in
laying out the Peiraieus in the middle of the fifth century BC, and
hence this kind of plan is called 'Hippodamian';[18] but it is in truth
much older. It can be traced right back to the colonies founded in
Sicily in the eighth century BC,[19] and from there it spread to Greece
proper and to the other colonies. Even more prominent than the
street network was the division of the rectangular blocks between
the streets into parcels of equal size (typically eight or ten or twelve
parcels per block) and the standardisation of the houses built on
those parcels. Only foundations are found in excavations, but we
may conclude that those houses must have been like the terrace-
houses of later times.[20] The degree of rationally organised planning
that the Hippodamian system testifies to is characteristically Greek,
and parallels the similarly rational organisation of their political
institutions and the division of the citizen body into groupings
such as demes, phratries, *hekatostyes* and so on.[21]

Besides being a settlement, a *polis* was also the centre for other
aspects of the city-state: (a) its political institutions, (b) its religious
ceremonies, (c) its defence, (d) its production and trade, (e) its
function in education and entertainment.[22]

(a) As the political centre of the city-state the *polis* housed all the central political institutions and the buildings they met in. Every *polis* appears to have had a *prytaneion* with a dining-room, where the principal magistrates of the city entertained to meals eminent guests and the recipients of the city's honours, like the victors in the pan-Hellenic games. Also in the *prytaneion* there would be an altar to the goddess Hestia, with a hearth with an eternal flame burning upon it as a symbol of the city's eternal life.[23]

Most *poleis* seem also to have had a Council-house (*bouleuterion*) as an independent structure, where the Council (*boule*) held its meetings,[24] and here and there in the city there would be offices (*archaia*) for the principal magistrates and boards of magistrates.[25] For unexplained reasons, separate court buildings (*dikasteria*) are not often mentioned in our sources, whereas we often hear of public buildings that were really meant for other purposes being used for the courts.[26] Only a few *poleis* had a special assembly place (*ekklesiasterion*);[27] assemblies of the people took place in the Archaic period in the market-place (*agora*),[28] and in the Classical and Hellenistic periods in the theatre.[29]

In the Archaic and Classical periods the political institutions were housed in modest buildings constructed of simple materials. Monumental political architecture appears only in the fourth century and the Hellenistic period.[30] In that period the *agora* was no longer the principal political centre of the city where public assemblies were held, but instead was the economic and social centre.[31]

(b) As a religious centre, the *polis* contained many sanctuaries,[32] the most important of which were adorned with monumental temples:[33] the sanctuary of Dionysos sometimes also had a theatre.[34] Until a generation ago it was the common opinion that almost all the important sacred buildings of a city-state lay within the walls, and the big temples were on the *akropolis*.[35] That opinion has now had to be significantly modified: the city was not necessarily the religious centre of the *polis* to the same extent as it was the political centre. Many of the most important shrines lay outside the city walls[36] or in the hinterland,[37] and often close to the boundaries of the city, perhaps as a marker of the city-state's territory.[38] Also, during the Classical period it became common to build temples in the middle of the inhabited area and no longer up on the *akropolis*.[39] Temples of Athena, Apollo and Aphrodite are typically found within the walls;

temples to Demeter, Hera and Zeus, on the other hand, could be in the hinterland.[40] Religious festivals for the gods were as a rule celebrated where the particular god had his shrine, whether within the city or in its territory, combined with a procession from city to shrine.[41]

(c) As a defence centre a *polis* was protected by walls, which often surrounded a large open space beyond the built-up area, to which the country population could flee for refuge if an enemy force invaded the territory of the city-state.[42] Many cities with an *akropolis* had double protecting walls, one round the *akropolis* and another surrounding the whole city. In the Classical period virtually all *poleis* had walls round either the whole city or its *akropolis*.[43] The exception was Sparta, which did not acquire walls until the Hellenistic period. A city wall was one of the characteristic signs of a *polis*, as in the Middle Ages, but there was a difference in the functions of walls: in the Middle Ages there was a sharper distinction between city and country, and the city gates were the boundary between the two zones, guarded night and day and locked at night. It was also common to demand tolls at the city gate on all the goods carried in and out of the city.[44] By contrast, in the ancient Greek *polis* the city wall served only military purposes, and no tolls were levied at the city gates.[45] In time of war, of course, the walls and gates were guarded,[46] but in peacetime anyone could pass through the gates in the daytime.[47] The gates were perhaps closed at night, but they were not guarded, and people could still enter and leave the city.[48] In the *polis* the walls were not seen as a barrier between city and country, but rather as a monument for the citizens to take pride in.[49]

(d) The economic centre of the *polis* was the market (*agora*)[50] and the harbour (*limen*),[51] and in the sources that give evidence about the economic conditions of the city-state those two are often referred to side by side.[52] Every *polis* had an *agora*,[53] which in the Archaic and Classical periods was just an open space marked with boundary stones (*horoi*).[54] Linked to the harbour, a city could also have an *emporion*, a market for external trade.[55] In the Homeric poems and in Archaic inscriptions the *agora* is named as the place for holding assemblies of the people.[56] In the Classical period the *agora* has become a market-place, and there is next to no trace of *agora* as an assembly-place.[57] When there were booths in the *agora*, they were of temporary construction and could be removed quickly.[58] On the other hand, the *agora* was often embellished with a covered hall, a *stoa*; and in the Hellenistic period it became regular to flank the *agora* with two or three *stoai*,[59] with shops in some of the spaces and administrative offices in others.[60]

(e) Lastly, the *polis* was the place where the schools and the sports centres lay. Before the Hellenistic period there were no public schools or educational institutions; but even small *poleis* had private schools for children.[61] More advanced private education of adults might be carried out in connection with the *gymnasia*, though the latter were principally sports centres.[62] In the Archaic and Classical periods *gymnasia* were outside the city wall,[63] but they gradually moved into the city,[64] and in the Hellenistic period they came to house the most important public institution of all, the *ephebeia*, which was the training ground of the young citizens for military and civil activities.[65]

City-organised entertainments were linked to the great religious festivals: the two most spectacular types were sports contests and theatre performances. Sports contests were held in a wrestling hall (*palaistra*)[66] or at a race-track (*stadion*)[67] or a horse-racing track (*hippodromos*);[68] plays were put on in the city's theatre.[69] In the Archaic and Classical periods sports centres[70] and theatres[71] were simple constructions that have left behind no trace, but in the fifth and especially the fourth centuries BC wooden benches and earthen floors gave way to more monumental constructions in stone; and alongside the city walls and the temples the theatres are the most monumental buildings that the ancient Greek city-state culture has left behind it.[72]

17

Polis as State

The concept of *polis* as a political community—what we call a 'state'—has different aspects, which are most clearly reflected in the different senses the word *polis* could have in a political context: (a) *polis* was used occasionally to mean a city plus its hinterland, and so meant a territory; (b) it was frequently used of the citizens and meant, in that context, the people of a state; and (c) it was with equal frequency used of the political institutions, e.g. the People's Assembly, or, more abstractly of the state itself and the way it was governed.

(a) *Territory*   The ancient Greek *polis* was a Lilliput, and that goes for the size of the territory and the size of the population. Of the 1,035 Archaic and Classical *poleis* in the Polis Centre's Inventory the locality of 166 is not yet known. But for 636 of the remaining of the 869 *poleis* it is possible to give an approximate idea of the size of their territories and place it in one of five categories: 25 km² or less, 25–100 km², 100–200 km², 200–500 km² and 500 km² or more.[1] Investigations show that 15 per cent of all *poleis* had a territory of at most 25 km², 60 per cent a territory of at most 100 km² and 80 per cent a territory of at most 200 km². Ten per cent at most had a territory of more than 500 km², and only thirteen *poleis* had more than 1,000 km².[2] As one would expect, the colonies had larger territories than the *poleis* in Greece proper. One of the tiniest of all city-states was the island of Belbina south of Attika, with a territory of 8 km². Aigina was a populous and prosperous *polis*, although its island covered only 85 km². Corinth had a hinterland of *c.*900 km²; Athens, which had subjected the whole of Attika, and Sparta, which had conquered Lakedaimon and Messenia, were exceptionally large, with territories of, respectively, 2,500 and 8,400 km².[3]

Almost all the *poleis* were small enough to be correctly described as city-states, i.e. a state consisting of a city plus its hinterland. If one reckons, tentatively, a city-state's hinterland as at most a day's walk from city to boundary, a radius of 30 km gives a territory of *c.*3,000 km². There seem to have been only four cities that went over that limit: Kyrene, Pantikapaion, Sparta and Syracuse; and all four were city-states that had other city-states situated in their territory as dependencies. They were not just city-states, but rather what one might call small city-state empires, in which each dependent city had a territory of at most a few hundred km².[4]

(b) *Population*　For the total number of ancient Greeks and their distribution in small and large *poleis*, see *supra* 83. When we seek more detailed information about the distribution of the total population into citizens, free foreigners and slaves, we encounter—once again—lack of sources: some are lost, but some never existed. The city-states often registered their citizens, and in some the full citizens were provided with tickets of lead or bronze as identity cards.[5] Free non-citizens were doubtless listed in so far as they had to pay an annual tax to the state they were in. But nobody ever counted how many slaves there were living in a *polis*. So what sources do we have?

In some cases we have (at least fragmentarily) citizen lists on stone. Some list only those liable for military service; some list all adult male citizens. Thus we can presume that in the early Hellenistic period there were 150 men liable for military service in the little *polis* of Koresia on Keos,[6] and that there were approximately 4,000 adult male full citizens in Eretria on Euboia: about 3,000 of their names are still preserved on a set of *stelai*,[7] and in view of the size of that state that constitutes the largest collection of prosopographical material we have from any *polis* whatsoever.

But most of our sources are statements by historians about the sizes of the armies that took part in the big battles. The figures they give are for the hoplites (the heavy-armed infantry) sent by each *polis*: figures for the cavalry and light-armed infantry are hardly ever given.[8] Using our 'shotgun-method' we can produce a rule of thumb that a city-state's corps of hoplites represented *c.*10 per cent of the whole citizen population, men, women and children.[9] So, in cases where the whole of a city's army was involved in the battle, we can get a notion of the number of citizens it had. In the Battle of Plataiai in 479 BC there were 3,000 hoplites from Megara, and 5,000 from Corinth, which corresponds to citizen populations of 30,000 and 50,000. It is yet more difficult to get a figure for size of population from information about a city-state's navy. Herodotos informs us how many ships each *polis* sent to Salamis in 480 BC. Most of the ships were triremes, each manned by *c.*180 rowers and about twenty other seamen and soldiers; but we do not know what proportion of the crew of a trireme were citizens—many of the rowers were doubtless slaves, and some were free non-citizens, but not necessarily people who lived in that city-state. The whole fleet of Aigina was seventy triremes, and should consequently have been manned by *c.*14,000 rowers, seamen and soldiers: that corresponds to a population of men, women and children of between 35,000 and 45,000.[10] If they all lived on Aigina (85 km²) we should get a population density of between 410 and 530 persons per km², and that is simply unimaginable.[11]

If our scattered sources are looked at together, it emerges that in the smallest *poleis* there will have been no more than, say, 300 adult male citizens. Medium-sized *poleis*, like Plataiai, had *c.*1,000 citizens, and big ones like Eretria had *c.*4,000–6,000; only the very big ones went above 10,000. Athens had 50,000–60,000 at the beginning of the Peloponnesian War, but only *c.*30,000 in the fourth century,[12] and Sparta had some 8,000 citizens at the time of the Persian Wars, but only *c.*1,200 at the beginning of the fourth century.[13]

We can add to our scanty demographic data about actual historical *poleis* the figures given in the sources for *poleis* in general or ideal *poleis*. In Plato's *Republic* the ideal *polis* has about 1,000 full citizens,[14] and in the *Laws* it is laid down that the colony of Magnesia is to have 5,040 households. Aristotle criticises the latter figure for being unrealistically high, if the citizens of Magnesia are to be freed from labour and devote themselves to participation in the political institutions.[15] So his own ideal *polis* must have had significantly fewer full citizens. But in both Plato's case and that of Aristotle we must take account of the fact that both are aristocratic in character, and that full citizens are only a part of all adult citizens; and the figure given as an ideal in other sources is also significantly larger, namely 10,000 citizens. The figure 10,000 is in Greek *myrioi*, and various sources say that a *myriandros polis*, i.e. one of 10,000 men, is the ideal size. That figure is first given in the ideal constitution written by Hippodamos of Miletos in the fifth century BC; but the city-state founded by the tyrant Hieron of Syracuse at the foot of Aitna was, it seems, planned as a city with 10,000 citizens, and in the constitution of Kyrene of *c.*322 BC the number of citizens is fixed at

10,000 men, all having a property of more than 2,000 drachmas.[16] A study of the remains of large urban centres indicates that, in the age of Alexander, there may in fact have been more than fifty *myriandroi poleis*. Thus, we have a plethora of small *poleis*, each with *c*.1,000 citizens, but also a significant number of very large *poleis*, each with ten times as many.[17]

As to the number of free non-citizens and that of slaves we are entirely in the dark. Every *polis* had plenty of both.[18] The citizens of a city-state probably knew how many non-citizens there were, because those permanently residing there usually had to do military service and pay taxes, and therefore were officially registered.[19] Slaves were employed as rowers in the fleet,[20] and a hoplite normally had an attendant slave to carry his armour.[21] But slaves were never allowed to bear arms and were not counted as part of the force. As far as we know, people did not have to pay tax on the slaves they owned, and consequently the slaves were never counted. The Greeks themselves did not know how many slaves there were in a city-state; but when they had to make a guess, it was often astronomical. According to Aristotle, there were supposed to have been 470,000 slaves on Aigina, an island of 85 km²![22] We can conclude that there were many slaves in the large *poleis*, but how many we have no idea. The various attempts to calculate the total population of Attika—and thereby the number of slaves—on the basis of the annual consumption of grain, are, in my opinion, unconvincing.[23] In discussions about the demography of the city-state modern historians add a conventional figure for free non-citizens and slaves to the number of citizens in a *polis*, but the convention is quite arbitrary, and the figure varies from 10 per cent to 50 per cent of the total population.[24]

(c) *Constitution*   The most general account we have of the *polis* as a political community is Aristotle's *Politics*, especially Books 1 and 3. He gives us a sharp-eyed analysis of the *polis* and its components, and at most points his description corresponds to the picture to be obtained from the other sources, both the Athenian sources and what we have for the rest of the ancient Greek city-state world.[25]

In Book 1 Aristotle produces a socio-economic description of the rise and development of the *polis* and its components. The smallest unit is the household (*oikia*); several households make a village (*kome*), and the city (*polis*) emerges by the joining together of several villages.[26] The diachronic perspective is more speculative than historical, but the three-tier structure of the *polis* is an inescapable fact, and in this context the 'atom' of the city-state is the household (*oikia*) consisting of man, wife, children and slave(s).[27]

In Book 3 Aristotle passes to analysis of the political structure of the *polis*. Now he argues that a *polis* is to be understood as a 'community' (*koinonia*) of citizens (*politai*) with regard to a constitution (*politeia*),[28] meaning the city's political institutions and how they are organised. In this analysis it is no longer the household (*oikia*) that is the 'atom' of the city-state but the adult male citizen.

Polis as a society in the socio-economic sense we have already considered: now I concentrate on the *polis* as a community of citizens in respect of their political institutions, in Greek a *koinonia politon politeias*.[29]

The word 'community' (*koinonia*) shows that for Aristotle the *polis* is not primarily a settlement but a society: it is a community of *politai*, i.e. adult male citizens, excluding women, children, slaves and all free non-citizens.[30] The insistence that only full citizens are members of the *polis* shows that *polis* in its political sense is kept apart from *polis* in its urban sense: as city, the *polis* includes women, children, slaves and free non-citizens, but from *polis* as state they are all excluded.

The third element in Aristotle's definition concerns the sphere of activity that the citizens have in common: that is, the *politeia*. The word *politeia* actually means 'citizenship' in the abstract, i.e. being a citizen of a *polis*; and that meaning is confirmed in hundreds of city decrees in which one or more named persons are granted citizenship in a given *polis*.[31] But from this basic meaning two other senses developed: (1) in a concrete sense the word *politeia* could mean the whole citizen body;[32] and (2) in an abstract sense it came to mean the political structure of the citizen body, and in that sense it can be translated by words like 'form of government' or 'constitution':[33] a modern political scientist might prefer 'political system'. In Aristotelian terms the 'citizen body' is the *matter* that makes the *polis*, while the 'constitution' is the *form* that the *polis* has.[34]

Apart from this philosophical singularity, Aristotle's analysis of *polis*, *polites* and *politeia* is quite in line with our other sources, Athenian and non-Athenian, and the use in the sources of *polis*, *polites* and *politeia* as three connected fundamental terms shows that the very heart of the *polis* concept was the citizen body understood as the participants in the city's political institutions.[35]

If we ask for a more precise definition of what *politeia* covers, we shall find that it is 'the structure of the political organs (*archai*) of the *polis* and in particular that organ that is in charge of the whole'.[36] But the structure of political organs varies from *polis* to *polis*. According to whether the supreme organ is a monarch or a minority of the citizens or a majority of them, we can distinguish three types of constitution: rule of the one, rule of the few, rule of the people.[37] In a monarchy power is wielded by a king (*basileus*) or a despot (*tyrannos*); in the rule of the few (*oligarchia* or *aristokratia*) it is wielded by a ruling class of wealthy men or aristocrats who monopolise the right to fill all the important offices of state; under a rule of the people (*demokratia* or *politeia*) it is the 'little people' (*demos*), the majority in fact, of the less wealthy citizens who exercise power through a People's Assembly in which all citizens have the right to speak and vote irrespective of their property status.

This fundamental division into three of the types of constitution is found in all our sources, in the literature[38] and equally in the documents on stone.[39] But if there are three forms of *politeia*, and if *politeia* is the very structure of the *polis*, did the Greeks consequently believe that there were three different forms of *polis*? To answer that question, we must go from *politeia* in the sense of 'constitution' to *politeia* in the sense of 'citizenship'. In the ancient Greek city-state culture 'citizenship' was what it has become again in the modern world: a person's juridically defined, inherited, membership of a state, in virtue of which that citizen enjoys a number of political, social and economic privileges in that state which a non-citizen living in the state is deprived of or can enjoy only to a limited extent. In most cases a given person can only have citizenship in one state.[40] In the Middle Ages and in Early Modern times 'citizenship' applied only to (some of) those who lived in the cities, and in the full political sense was found only in city-states in, for example, Italy, Switzerland and south Germany; but since the French Revolution citizenship has once again expanded into a political concept that includes all the native inhabitants of the state, and not just the city-dwellers.[41]

In Greece the corresponding terms *politeia* for the citizen body and *polites* for the citizen were used when stress was placed on political rights,[42] whereas *astos* (masculine)[43] and *aste* (feminine)[44] were used when what was referred to was the inherited membership of the citizen body. And as a general rule, you could only be *polites* in one *polis*.[45]

Aristotle's treatment of the concept of citizenship is fully in line with the dichotomy expressed in the terminology: in practice a citizen is defined as a person born of citizens (*astoi*);[46] but functionally a citizen is defined as a person (*polites*) who takes a part in the running of a *polis* by exercising his political rights.[47] In a democracy the two definitions coincide, because all native-born citizens have the right to take part in political decision making and the running of their *polis*. In oligarchies the functional definition applies only to that fraction of the native-born citizens who have a given property qualification. Since a *polis* is a community of citizens from which non-citizens are excluded, the *polis par excellence* is the democratic city-state.[48] Oligarchies, and especially monarchies, cannot be *poleis* in the same sense, because not just non-citizens and slaves but even native-born citizens are excluded from participation in the political institutions that are the centre of what makes a *polis*. In an oligarchy full political rights depend on a property qualification,[49] and in a monarchy the monarch is the *only* citizen in the political meaning of the word:[50] absolute monarchy was in Greek eyes 'tyranny',[51] and one can with a certain justification say that a city-state ruled by a tyrant is in principle not a *polis* at all.[52] In the fourth century and the early Hellenistic period there is a tendency to see *demokratia* as a constitution that a *polis must* have.[53] Aristotle, indeed, does not share that viewpoint, but he says that more or less all contemporary *poleis* are oligarchies or democracies, and democracy has become the commonest type of constitution.[54] An overview of all known city-state constitutions in the fourth century BC gives a rather different picture: namely, fifty-nine democracies, forty-seven oligarchies and thirty-nine tyrannies. If these figures are representative, tyranny was much commoner than Aristotle allows, and there were still a good many oligarchies around.[55]

But, on the other hand, the overview shows that the same institutions were found in all *poleis* irrespective of their type of constitution. Most oligarchies had an Assembly of the People:[56] its competence was, of course, limited, but as a rule all citizens had access, and only seats on the Council and access to the top administrative posts were confined to the wealthiest citizens. Tyrants also summoned assemblies,[57] and a tyrant's power often rested on his occupying the city-state's top administrative post and terrorising the city-state's political institutions into doing his bidding by means of his clique of followers or his bodyguard.[58]

(d) *Organs of government*   The ancient Greek *polis* was one of the most totally institutionalised societies in world history, and even in oligarchies and tyrannies there were a large number of administrative posts filled by ordinary citizens. Most *poleis* had the same set of institutions: an Assembly (*ekklesia*), a Council (*boule*), sometimes a Senate (*gerousia*), courts of law (*dikasteria*) and magistrates (*archai*), either elected or picked by lot. It was the way in which power was divided between the institutions, and the limited access to some of them, that distinguished one type of constitution from another.

A typical example is the constitution we call the 'moderate oligarchy' of Kyrene. It was founded in 322 BC or immediately after, and inscribed on a marble *stele* which was found when Kyrene was excavated in the 1920s. It is the oldest surviving written constitution in the world, and in outline it lays down the following provisions. Citizenship belongs to all persons born of citizens in Kyrene and the *poleis* founded by Kyrene. Political rights are confined to 10,000 citizens over 30 years of age with a property of at least 2,000 drachmas. Amongst the political institutions the following are referred to: (1) an Assembly of the People in which all 10,000 can meet; (2) a Council of 500 men over 50 years of age chosen by lot for two years at a time; (3) a Senate of 101 men over 50 serving for life, chosen by the Assembly; and (4) boards of magistrates, the most important being the board of five *strategoi* chosen by the Assembly to serve alongside the Egyptian ruler, Ptolemy, who is perpetual *strategos*. Crimes punishable by death must be judged by the Senate, the Council and 1,500 jurors chosen by lot from the 10,000.[59]

If we turn from the institutions to their competence, we can best get a picture by surveying the tasks that, according to our sources, were performed by the *polis*, i.e. where the *polis* appears as the acting subject.[60] First of all, the *polis* legislates and passes laws, or naturalises foreigners, or bestows honours on foreigners. In the administration of justice it passes sentences, or inflicts punishments, or arrests somebody, or brings an action on behalf of a citizen, or shelters a refugee, or appoints a panel of jurors. In financial matters it strikes coins, or accepts as legal tender coins struck by other *poleis*, or collects revenue, or defrays expenses, or takes up a loan, or pays interest on a loan, or enters into a contract, or owes money, or pays a fine, or buys landed property, or pledges some property. In religious matters it organises a festival, or makes sacrifices to a god, or makes a dedication to a god, or consults an oracle. In foreign policy it sends out envoys and representatives, or enters into an alliance, or goes to war, or sends out an army, or buries the citizens killed in war, or makes peace, or defects from a league or a ruler, or founds a colony.

Alternatively, one can take a look at the decisions that were taken in councils and assemblies and put into practice by the magistrates and dealt with in the courts. Some of the laws and decrees that have come down to us are about the political machinery itself: rules about meetings of Assembly and Council, about election or choosing by lot of magistrates and so on. Other laws concern the working of the legal system, and fall under what we nowadays call criminal law, law of inheritance and family law. In many such laws most of the provisions are about the administration of justice. On the other hand, there are very few laws about production and trade and the whole economic sector. Such provisions as do concern the economy are mainly about taxes and customs, the taking up and paying back of loans from the sanctuaries and how to secure the city's grain supply. Laws about foreign policy include declarations of war, peace treaties and alliances, mobilisation of army and navy, and upkeep of the fortifications. There are comprehensive laws about the organisation and financing of the great religious festivals, and long tables of all the festivals that have to be celebrated during the year, listed month by month. Finally, there are a huge number of grants of citizenship and honourary decrees for citizens and non-citizens. They survive in great numbers because they were often inscribed on marble *stelai* and displayed publicly.[61]

Below the *niveau* of the *polis* there was in every *polis* a network of subdivisions of the citizen body. Especially in the larger *poleis* the citizens were divided into smaller units, some territorial, others based on personal relationships.[62] The territorial ones were often communes (*demoi*)[63] or villages (*komai*)'[64] the ones based on personal ties were tribes (*phylai*),[65] brotherhoods (*phratriai*),[66] or clans (*gene*), and so on.[67] The kinships on which these units were supposedly based were fictive, and in the period covered by our sources the groupings were only administrative divisions, though they sometimes retained the old kinship-based names such as 'tribe' or 'brotherhood'; sometimes, however, they acquired entirely new titles that reveal their artificiality, such as *pentekostyes* (groups of fifty) or *hekatostyes* (groups of a hundred).[68]

Having established the concept of the dependent *polis*, and having disposed of independence as the essential criterion for distinguishing a *polis* from a municipality, we have to address the question: if many *poleis* were dependencies, what was then the difference between a dependent *polis* and a civic subdivision, such as a *demos*, a *kome*, a *phratria*, a *phyle*, etc.? Like a *polis* (dependent or independent), a civic subdivision could have its own sanctuaries, including a theatre, its own cults and its own festivals. It had its own Assembly, in which laws (*nomoi*) and decrees (*psephismata*) could be passed and taxes and liturgies imposed; there were separate local magistrates and a local court.[69] But in contradistinction to a *polis* (dependent or independent) a civic subdivision had no *prytaneion*, no *bouleuterion* and no *boule*; its members were citizens of the *polis* of which the civic subdivision was a part, and were not citizens of the civic subdivision as such; a local Assembly had no right to pass citizen decrees and proxeny decrees; a local court could impose fines but was not empowered to pass a sentence of death or exile, and no civic subdivision seems to have had a prison (*desmoterion*). A civic subdivision did not strike its own coins, and it had no right to enter into relations with foreign states. The members of a civic subdivision could form a unit of the army of the *polis*, but would not operate as a separate army.[70]

All these matters that the *polis* concerned itself with show that the city-state was not only a political community, but a religious, economic and social organisation as well. From a modern standpoint it is tempting to see the political institutions as a framework within which the *polis* ran its defence and religion and social and economic affairs; but such an analysis would not coincide with the ideals and self-perception of the Greeks themselves. They saw politics as a value in itself, and participation in the political institutions as an end in itself, not just as a means to some other ends. Aristotle defines man as a *zoon politikon*, a 'political animal'—or a '*polis* animal'[71]— and the purpose of human life was precisely to take a share in the establishment and distribution of the values of the society.[72] The nub of the *polis* was its political institutions, and through them the city-state regulated the various sectors that were important for the maintenance and furtherance of the society.[73]

18

Army

The main duty of a citizen was to defend his *polis* and if necessary give his life for his fatherland (*patris*).[1] Every *polis* had its own army; armies put in the field by federal states or leagues of states consisted of contingents supplied by each individual *polis*.[2] Here, as in all respects, the *polis* was the basic unit in the Greek city-state culture.[3] The principal feature of an army comprised the hoplites, the heavy-armed infantry, who fought in close formation (called a *phalanx*) supported by squadrons of cavalry and light-armed soldiers.[4] Citizen soldiers had to pay for their own armour,[5] and there was in that way a link between military service and the class structure: the upper class served in the cavalry or else, along with the middle class, as hoplites, whereas the lower class were light-armed troops in the army or marines or rowers in the navy.[6] The backbone of the hoplite army was made up of middle-class citizens; many of them were peasants,[7] but many craftsmen and tradesmen also had to serve as hoplites.

The connection between citizens and hoplites was in some *poleis* so close that political rights were reserved for those who served as hoplites in the army. In some *poleis* full citizenship altogether was reserved for those on active service, so that veterans lost their political rights when they left the army, apparently at age 60.[8] Aristotle says that the type of constitution was rare, but had been commoner in olden times, and was then regarded as a form of democracy.[9] Ancient Sparta seems to have been a *polis* of that type,[10] and Sparta is described as a democracy in a document of the seventh century BC, the only one we have surviving that has anything about the nature of the Spartan constitution.[11] It is still widely held that the development of the hoplite *phalanx* as the nub of the army grew with the development of the *polis* as a type of state, and that fighting in close formation went hand in hand with the development of an Assembly of the People, which was actually an assembly of the hoplites.[12]

In the Classical democratic *polis* political rights were granted to
all native-born citizens, so that not only the hoplites but also the
light-armed and the rowers had access to the political institutions.
By 500 BC or perhaps earlier there had grown up a clear distinction
between citizens and 'metics' (free non-citizens), but metics in the
middle class were obliged to perform hoplite service just as citizens
did.[13] The link between hoplites and citizens thus disappeared in
the course of the Classical period, and another distinction of the
army from the citizen body opened up whereby it became more and
more common to supplement the citizen army with mercenaries or
simply replace it with mercenaries altogether.[14]

19

Religion

Ever since the ground-breaking book of Fustel de Coulanges, *La Cité antique*, of 1864, many ancient historians have declared that religion was the most important aspect of the society of the ancient Greek *polis*:[1] (1) the institutions of the *polis* were the framework of Greek religion;[2] (2) in the *polis* there was no distinction between the sacred and the profane;[3] and (3) religion was at the centre of everything with which the *polis* concerned itself.[4] I believe that this holistic conception of the *polis* is skewed, and it is the second and third points with which I disagree.

(1) With one small addition I can accept the first point: the *polis* *came to be* the framework of Greek religion.[5] The Greek pantheon and the temples and worship of the gods were not invented by the *polis*; they were much older and were adopted by the *polis*, but not at one go. It is often alleged that the *polis* arose in the early Archaic Age as a result of the communal co-operation that was required to build the monumental temples and organise the great religious festivals.[6] But in the Archaic period some temples were financed and built by private persons and not by a *polis*,[7] whereas the *polis* always counts as the builder in the sources we have for the Classical period and later. Many priestly offices went by inheritance in leading families, and only in the Classical period did the *polis* take over the filling of priesthoods by election or sortition from among all citizens.[8] Private cults confined to particular families or clans are also referred to in the early sources.[9] The control of religion by the city-state and the link between *polis* and religion were weakest in early times, and became ever more prominent in the course of the city-state's long history.

(2) As for a distinction between the sacred and the profane, we meet it everywhere in the sources. It could be a matter of life and death for a citizen if the olive-tree he had felled turned out to be one of the sacred olive-trees.[10] When you went through the wall that

surrounded a sanctuary, you were on holy ground.[11] There were numerous religious festival days when many activities were forbidden or at least were supposed to be avoided.[12] If the *polis* was in need of funds, it could often borrow money from the temple treasures that belonged to the gods, but the economies of the temples and the state were distinct, and the *polis* always had to repay the loan.[13] In ancient Greece the boundary between sacred and profane was as easy—or as hard—to draw as it was in the Middle Ages and still is to this day: the two spheres have always overlapped, and always will.[14] Religion was undeniably a powerful element in the life of the city-state: most activities—for example, meals—began with a ritual (as they have right to the time of our grandparents). But religion was only one aspect of all the things that the *polis* concerned itself with, and not necessarily the central one. Both a campaign and an Assembly of the People opened with a sacrifice to the gods[15] (in the Middle Ages accompanied by a prayer): both rituals were important, but they did not *transform* either the campaign or the Assembly meeting into a religious activity on a par with, say, the religious festival for one of the Olympic gods.

(3) Both as a political and as a military organisation the *polis* was a male society, and women were excluded from participation.[16] The wives of citizens had citizen status and passed that status on to their children, but they were not citizens in the functional sense; they were *astai* but not *politai*.[17] When it came to religion, however, the relationships were different: women did take part in almost all the rites and festivals of the city-state.[18] There were some cults from which women were excluded,[19] but others in which only women could participate, like the *thesmophoria*.[20] Most goddesses had female and not male priests in charge of their cults.[21] In religion women were officially recognised as an indispensable element in the community.[22]

Aristotle counts four types of official in a *polis*, and one of them is priests (*hiereis*) and persons who oversee the temples and the temple treasuries.[23] In the bigger *poleis* the functions of priest and overseer were separate: priests and priestesses performed the offerings and rites at the religious festivals, and at Athens they did not have the status of magistrates (*archai*). The temples and the treasuries were administered by magistrates who were not priests.[24] It was mostly in the small city-states that the two functions were carried out by the same person.[25] In the big ones there were separate boards of temple inspectors who administered the shrines and their temple treasures and religious festivals—but not the rites performed at the festivals. In an article on *polis* religion Walter Burkert draws attention to the fact that among the magistrates of the *polis* there were no *manteis* (soothsayers) or *kathartai* (purifiers), people who in other cultures turn up as specialists at every sacrifice and at every crisis, especially war. In the *polis* they were marginalised and played no official role.[26]

A shrine was inviolable and often functioned as a place of refuge.[27] A person who sought asylum in a temple and sat at the altar of the god was protected against seizure not just by his enemies but equally by the magistrates of the state. Even if he had committed a crime, he could not be touched: the power of the *polis* to punish stopped at the threshold of the temple.[28] But if the magistrates in spite of that did profane the shrine and seize the person at the very altar of the god, there was no one except the god himself who could punish them.

These considerations illuminate two facts about Greek religion: it was an important part (though not necessarily the central part) of what the *polis* was concerned with; on the other hand, there was no institutionalised or organised sphere of religion distinct from or opposed to the sphere of the *polis*. The *polis* had nothing like the medieval distinction between the different spheres of power that could be in conflict with one another: King and Church.

The central feature of the religion of the *polis* consisted in prayers and sacrifices performed by priests at all the religious festivals organised by the magistrates of the city-state at public cost and attended by all the inhabitants of the city, including women and children and even, in certain cases, slaves.[29] The festivals were the most spectacular part of Greek religion, but there were also private religious ceremonies carried out by individuals or non-state organisations.[30] In an inscription from Halikarnassos a priestess is instructed to perform both private and public sacrifices, including a monthly sacrifice on behalf of the *polis* for which the city pays her a drachma.[31] And nowadays, when we find in the excavation of shrines hundreds of thousands of votive gifts to the god, their inscriptions show that some were donated by the *polis*, but most were donated by private persons.[32]

Instead of the holistic idea of religion as the factor uniting everything the *polis* concerned itself with, I support the view that the side of religion that did belong to the sphere of the *polis* was a *mélange* of ceremonies and rites which (a) were used by the *polis*, (b) were administered by the *polis*, and (c) were invented by the *polis*.[33]

(a) Every activity that took place in the *polis* began with a ritual— thus an Assembly of the People at Athens was preceded by a prayer, a curse and a sacrifice.[34]

(b) The officers of the *polis* organised the big religious festivals that were paid for by the *polis* and attended by all inhabitants (not just the citizens).

(c) As the *polis* developed, new cults were created, directly related to the political institutions. Most *poleis* had a special protecting deity (some had several),[35] and many of the symbols of a city-state were connected with its protecting deity. The annual religious festivals for the protecting deity were amongst the grandest, and the coins of the city-state were often stamped with the picture of that deity.[36] In the Council-house worship was paid to Zeus Boulaios or Athena Boulaia, 'the giver of counsel',[37] and even abstract political concepts could have divine status and be worshipped: in Athens the democracy was hypostatised as the goddess Demokratia, and the Board of the *Strategoi* paid annual offerings to the goddess;[38] and we know of a corresponding Democracy personified at Knidos in Karia.[39]

The divinisation of the *polis* itself is not known before the Hellenistic period. The first known example is a statue from Antioch *c.*300 BC represented as a manifestation of the goddess Tyche ('fate') with a 'mural crown' and her right foot on the river-god Orontes;[40] and the nearest we get in Archaic and Classical times to worship of the *polis* as such is that of the goddess Hestia, which in most cities was carried out in the *prytaneion* of the *polis*, and on the altar of Hestia there burned a perpetual flame symbolising the continuance of the city-state.[41]

20
State and Society

The traditional and still prevailing view about the ancient Greek city-state is that the *polis* was a fusion of state and society and controlled the behaviour of its citizens in every department of life: religion, family, upbringing, education, housing, production and trade. In a *polis* the citizens did not distinguish between state and society, between, on the one hand, a public sphere in which the state determines and upholds a rule of law within a territory over a body of citizens and, on the other hand, a private sphere in which everyone can live as he pleases as long as he keeps to the law.[1]

This view fits perfectly the ideal states described in Plato's *Republic* and *Laws* and in the seventh and eighth books of Aristotle's *Politics*. The *Laws*, especially, is often—and rightly—quoted as a dreadful example of a society where everything is regulated by the state down to the smallest detail.[2] But those utopias were written precisely to show contemporaries how a *polis ought* to be governed. In all those treatises Plato and Aristotle are at one in subjecting all existing *poleis* to merciless criticism: the philosophers were quite clear how far it was from ideal to actuality.[3] If we turn from philosophy to history, we shall perceive that it is not possible to say how far the ancient Greek *polis* was a fusion of state and society or recognised a sphere of society in which the citizens could live as they chose.

The traditional view works perfectly for Sparta. In the Spartan *polis* upbringing and education were a public matter; marriage and family life were regulated by the state; there was strict control of production and trade; and all citizens from the age of 20 to 60 were forced to live in a military community.[4] The Spartan political system was equated with life in a barracks,[5] and obedience to the laws and the authorities was emphasised as a Spartan's prime duty.[6] So the coalescence of state and society in Sparta corresponds neatly to the fact that Sparta was to all intents the only *polis* that found favour in the eyes of the philosophers.[7]

But the democrats of Athens championed the opposite view: they found the Spartan way of life incompatible with the democratic ideal.[8] They distinguished between a public and a private sphere.[9] The public sphere was the *polis* sphere, and it was first and foremost a political sphere; but the *polis* did not regulate the conduct of the citizens in all activities of life: upbringing, agriculture, craft, trade, and many other economic and social activities were only minimally regulated by law and only rarely debated in the Assembly.[10] As long as an Athenian kept the laws (and there were far fewer of them than in the modern state) he could do what he liked.[11] He also had freedom of expression, both private, to say and think what he chose, and also public, i.e. to have his say in the political assemblies.[12]

So we can conclude that *poleis* governed like Sparta practised a fusion of state and society, but *poleis* governed like Athens practised a separation of a public *polis* sphere from a private sphere in which every citizen could live as he liked as long as he kept the laws. For *poleis* as such, in general, no conclusion can be drawn. There is no doubt that Sparta and city-states with a similar social structure were *poleis* just as much as Athens and the city-states that were like Athens.[13] So the assertion that 'the ancient Greek *polis*' was a fusion of state and society is a false generalisation: it is true for Sparta but false for Athens, and it has a long history.

From the Renaissance until the beginning of the nineteenth century people were far more interested in Sparta than in Athens, and the sources that people relied on were principally Plato, Aristotle, Polybios and Plutarch. Not only was it thought that Sparta was the most important society in ancient Greece, but also that it was the typical ancient Greek city-state.[14] So the Spartan fusion of state and society was the yardstick by which the other Greek city-states were measured—even Athens.[15] But in the nineteenth century the study of ancient history was radically reformed, first in Germany and then in the rest of Europe, and now sources such as Herodotos, Thucydides, Xenophon and the Attic orators took centre-stage, and a serious start was made to bring the rapidly expanding mass of inscriptions into the interpretation of ancient Greek society. From the middle of the nineteenth century it was Athens rather than Sparta that people became most interested in, and it was especially George Grote's monumental *History of Greece* that set the new agenda.[16]

The prevailing opinion today is that both Athens and Sparta were exceptional city-states, both in size and in government.[17] It is also admitted that the Spartan way of life was an exception in the Classical Age,[18] whereas far more *poleis*, especially democratically governed *poleis*, seem to have been like Athens. In spite of which, when the question comes up about the relation between state and society, many still stick to the older view, that in Greece there was no such thing as a private sphere over against a public sphere, and that the *polis* was a type of society in which everything was determined politically and there was no personal freedom.[19]

21

Civil War (*Stasis*)

Ideally the city-state was a community of citizens who regarded the *polis* as their fatherland and were willing to sacrifice life and possessions for it.[1] But very few *poleis* were societies in harmony which lived up to the ideal. To judge from our sources, most *poleis* were split into two rival *poleis*,[2] one of the rich, who supported oligarchy, and one of the poor, who preferred democracy.[3] The rival parties could also be different ethnic groups living side by side in the same *polis*, a situation typical of *poleis* founded by colonists from several different city-states.[4] Or the community could be polarised around two rival groups of rich contending for power.[5] In all those cases the purpose of both groups was to control and, if necessary, reform the institutions of the city.[6] The result was almost constant political tension, which often led to civil war, in which every group was ready to work hand in hand with a like-minded group in a neighbouring city or in one of the powerful cities that led the shifting alliances of *poleis*. The members of both groups were therefore prepared to sacrifice the independence and autonomy of their city if, in return, they could keep or win power in the *polis*.[7]

Such a group was called a *stasis*, and the word was also used for the civil war itself that often resulted from the splitting of rival groups.[8] The word *stasis* actually means 'stance'; but it underwent shifts of meaning as follows: (1) stance, (2) standpoint, (3) group of people with the same standpoint, (4) in the plural: two or more groups with opposing standpoints, (5) the split between groups, and (6) civil war.[9] *Stasis* always means a group that wants to preserve or obtain power by deceit or violence,[10] i.e. a revolutionary group, never[11] a political group operating within the constitutional framework of the city-state, i.e. what we call a political party.[12]

If we assemble the sources for the Archaic and Classical periods we find evidence of 279 outbreaks of civil war in 122 different *poleis*;[13] and to this must be added the more general observation that many or all of the *poleis* in a region were plagued by *stasis*.[14] Given that our sources are so fragmentary, we must presume that most of the *poleis* in the Greek world were afflicted by civil war at least once in their history, and many lived constantly with civil war as their sword of Damocles. In Syracuse there were twenty-seven outbreaks of civil war in the period *c.*670–279 BC.[15]

From the frequent civil wars it can be concluded that for many citizens their loyalty to their group was stronger than that to their *polis*. This resulted in citizens betraying sometimes their country, sometimes its constitution; but of course there was talk of treason only if you belonged to the losing faction. That is why the Greek city-states had so many laws about treason,[16] and that is why so many Greeks were obliged to live in exile in other *poleis*, because their group had lost a civil war or was sent into exile to prevent a civil war.[17] Correspondingly, we frequently hear about reconciliation of conflicting groups and, in pursuance of reconciliation, amnesty for exiles.[18]

If one group called in a foreign *polis* to gain or keep power in their own *polis*, the result was a loss of the independence (*autonomia*) of that *polis*; but in compensation, the group held on to what was much more important: to be able through the state's political institutions to enforce their will in all the daily affairs of the citizens.[19] The city might have to pay tribute to the city that had helped the dissidents to power, and it might also have to supply military assistance; but usually the hegemonic city-state was a long way away and allowed the dependent city-state wide self-rule in by far the majority of spheres. Conversely, there could be advantages in being a dependent state under a hegemonic city-state: the smaller city got the big one as its protector and would be able more easily to defend itself against hostile neighbours. Political dependence would be a heavy burden only if the hegemonic *polis* put a garrison on the small city's *akropolis* or sent in magistrates to govern the dependent *polis*, or sent colonists to take over part of the citizens' land.[20]

For a *polis*, unity among its citizens was much more important than independence; and this is clearly reflected in the religion of the city-states. Independence was in ancient Greek *autonomia*, unity was *homonoia*: *autonomia* was never divinised and made the object of religious festivals, but *homonoia* was indeed personified and raised to the status of a goddess whom people worshipped, especially in the late Classical and Hellenistic periods.[21]

22

Relationships between *Poleis*

At the beginning of this book I stressed the interaction between all the Greek *poleis* that resulted from migrations, trade and various interstate social activities. I shall conclude with a short sketch of the relationships between the city-states in war and in peace.

Diplomatic ties between *poleis* were maintained not by a class of ambassadors but by envoys sent *ad hoc* when two or more city-states wanted to declare war or peace or enter into an alliance.[1] In the Classical and Hellenistic periods envoys were called *presbeis* or *presbytai*, i.e. old men,[2] and quite often only citizens over 50 could be chosen for the task;[3] for the cities wanted to have men of experience to carry out the negotiations. All official communication between city-states at war was carried on through heralds (*kerykes*).[4] The pan-Hellenic festivals and sporting contests were proclaimed a year in advance by special envoys (*theoroi*), who called upon the city-states all over the Greek world to take part in the festival and to respect a cessation of hostilities that protected the *polis* hosting the festival for the period when it was held.[5]

Apart from all these official envoys sent out by the city-states, there was a fine-meshed network of personal relationships between prominent persons in the different cities based on 'guest-friendship' (*xenia*): two friends (*xenoi*) from different *poleis* could promise to house and help each other when they were in the *polis* of either of them.[6] *Xenia* was gradually supplemented by a formal political institution called *proxenia*.[7] A *proxenos* was not a guest-friend (*xenos*) of the person he housed and helped, but acted *as* a guest-friend (*pro-xenos*).[8] The city-state of Eretria, for example, could pass a decree saying that a named citizen of the city-state of Taras should be *proxenos* for all the citizens of Eretria who found themselves in Taras.[9] The institution of *proxenia* is very like the consulate of more recent times, with one difference: that a *proxenos* never had official recognition in his own *polis* for the duties he undertook for the *polis* that had named him as its *proxenos*.

There were always city-states at war with one another, and for many *poleis* it was normal to be at war and exceptional when there was peace.[10] Only when Greece became a Roman province in 146 BC did things quieten down, and only in the Roman period did the ancient Greek city-state culture experience a long period of unbroken peace. They made good use of the Pax Romana, and the more peaceful relations are reflected in city architecture: after 146 BC the Greeks stopped building city walls, and existing walls were often allowed to decay, since there was no longer any need for them.[11]

Many wars were fought between neighbouring cities: Sparta and Argos, for example, were traditional enemies.[12] The greatest wars were fought between leagues of *poleis*, such as the Peloponnesian War between the Delian Naval League led by Athens and the Peloponnesian League led by Sparta. The Delian League had more than 330 *poleis* in it, and even some barbarian tribes;[13] the Peloponnesian League consisted of the city-states of the Peloponnese, except Argos and the Achaian cities, plus some of the city-states of central Greece.[14]

The endless wars resulted sometimes in the destruction of a *polis* and the annihilation of its inhabitants.[15] In the sources covering the Archaic and Classical periods we hear of forty-six *poleis* that suffered *andrapodismos*, which consisted typically in the males being slaughtered and the women and children sold into slavery; and of a further fifty-six *poleis* we learn that they were razed to the ground. In fifteen of those cases we know that the population was driven out, and in many of the forty-one others we can presume that the people were killed or sold as slaves, as in the forty-six attested cases of *andrapodismos*. Finally, there are some examples of the population being expelled without the city being razed to the ground. All in all, 121 *poleis* are known to have been destroyed in one way or another, and, if we think how few sources we have, that paints a very grim picture indeed of the fate that overtook many a *polis*.

There is, however, reason to think that the destruction of *poleis* was far from always as total as the sources give the impression of it being. Many of the cities that were razed to the ground and/or had their population suffer *andrapodismos* turn up only one or two generations later on in other sources as communities in full bloom, and in some cases we learn that a city was refounded and newly populated with many of its original inhabitants, who must thus have escaped the general *andrapodismos*.[16]

And by no means all defeated cities were destroyed. In many cases the conquered city just fell under the power of the victor and lost its status as a *polis*. For example, Mykenai, Tiryns, Orneai, Mideia and Hysiai, all minor city-states in the northern Argolid, were conquered by Argos in the period 468–416 BC and reduced to being communes in the city-state of Argos.[17] The conquest of smaller neighbours could also lead to the conquered *poleis* becoming dependent *poleis*: they kept some self-government and their status as *poleis*, but now only as 'dependent city-states' (*hypekooi poleis*). In the Archaic period the whole of Lakedaimon was conquered by Sparta, and members of many of the conquered communities acquired the status of *periokoi*: i.e. free persons who were not Spartan citizens but lived in small *poleis* as citizens who possessed local self-government but were subordinate to Sparta in foreign policy and with the duty to serve in the Spartan army.[18] Other examples are the city-states along the western coast of Asia Minor, which were conquered by King Kyros (558–530 BC), and had from then on to pay tribute to the king of Persia and follow him in war; but they went on being *poleis* with a degree of self-government, and the Persians interfered in their constitutions and their internal arrangements only if they tried to revolt.[19]

War could lead to alliances between city-states, and alliances could lead to wars. The Corinthian War of 395–386 BC came about as a result of an alliance of Athens, Thebes, Argos and Corinth directed against Sparta.[20] Larger and more permanent alliances took the form of leagues of *poleis* with a set of common institutions that controlled the finances of their members and their joint campaigns. The two biggest leagues were the Delian Naval League (478–404 BC)[21] and the Peloponnesian League (*c*.550–366).[22] Both leagues were hegemonic; i.e. the league was binary, with the leading *polis* (the *hegemon*) on one side and all the other *poleis* on the other, and the leading role of the *hegemon* was built into the structure of the league. Both leagues turned in the end into empires, and their members lost their autonomy and became subordinate states under Athens and Sparta.

Over the course of time almost all *poleis* became dependent states, and this led to a change in the character of the city-state—but not to its demise. City-states disappeared as independent counters in the game of international politics, but they persisted as self-governing communities. Dependent *poleis* were to be found in many different forms. The commonest (which I list here roughly in chronological order) were: (a) small *poleis* taken over by their larger neighbours;[23] (b) certain colonies that retained some dependence *vis-à-vis* their mother-city (*metropolis*);[24] (c) the city-states on the west coast of Asia Minor in the periods when they were under Persian rule;[25] (d) *poleis* that were members of a hegemonic federal state;[26] (e) the members of the Delian and Peloponnesian Leagues in the period when the leagues had developed into empires;[27] and (f) all the *poleis* in the Hellenistic and Roman periods that were dependent states under a Hellenistic monarch or a satrap or a Roman provincial governor.[28]

The world of the ancient Greek city-states was never a system of equal[29] independent[30] *poleis*, but a complicated hierarchy of *poleis*, some independent, some not, but all with a good deal of self-government, in internal affairs at least.[31] In the Hellenistic period practically all *poleis* had become dependent states,[32] and thus the *polis* was combined with other types of society, of which some were above and some below the *niveau* of the *polis*. The most important political unit bigger than the *polis* was the federal state, and over time by far the larger number of *poleis* in Greece proper turned into members of some federal state. So in the Hellenistic period there were two great powers in Greece: the Achaian League, which came to include all the *poleis* of the Peloponnese, and the Aitolian League, which embraced most of the *poleis* in central Greece.[33]

A typical example of the hierarchical structure of the city-state world is the Boiotian Federation as it was organised in the period 447–386 BC.[34] The federation had a common Council, common magistrates and an army in common. The only independent *polis* was Thebes, which, in addition to being the leader of the federation,[35] had kept its own status in international politics and the right to make treaties with other *poleis*.[36] Under Thebes was a set of *poleis*, e.g. Thespiai, which as members of the federation sent magistrates and councillors to the institutions of the federation and a force of soldiers to the federal army.[37] There were eleven such *poleis* (until the destruction of Plataiai in 427/6 BC, after which there were only ten);[38] but under each of those *poleis* there were again a lot of little dependent *poleis* which were dependencies of the middle-sized ones; and each of them had its own territory: Chorsiai, Siphai, Eutresis and Thisbai were *poleis* dependent on Thespiai and in the territory of Thespiai.[39] Finally, in the hinterland of Thespiai there were some villages, of which one, at least, Askra, where Hesiod came from, had the status of a *kome* and not a *polis*.[40] Chorsiai, Siphai, Eutresis and Thisbai probably had the same institutions as other small *poleis*; what institutions Askra may have had we do not know.

The institutions of a federation dealt with foreign policy and treaties and minted coinage on behalf of the federation—which did not prevent some of its members from also coining their own money.[41] There was also a federal court of law.[42] In the Chalkidian Federation we hear that a citizen of one *polis* had the right to marry a citizen of another *polis* and to have full ownership of property in other *poleis* of the federation.[43] A further development led to a real 'citizenship of the federation', whereby every citizen in the federation had dual citizenship, in the federation as such and in the *polis* he belonged to.[44]

23

The Hellenistic *Polis*

In this book the main weight has been placed on the Archaic and Classical periods, when the *polis* was the exclusive society of adult male citizens to deal with their political institutions, when war between the city-states was the order of the day, and when the majority of the citizens preferred to live within the city's protecting walls.

In the course of the Hellenistic period the *polis* underwent a set of changes, which have already been noted in the relevant contexts, but not assembled as a whole. So to set the classical *polis* in relief, I will give a sketch of a *polis* from the second half of the second century BC, when Greece had become a part of the Roman Empire.

By then not just some but almost all *poleis* were dependent states. On the other hand, self-government (*autonomia*) remained an ideal and an expressly stated goal for a *polis*.[1] In the early Hellenistic period 323–146 BC democracy was the preferred type of constitution, and tyrannies and oligarchies were eclipsed;[2] but with the Roman domination oligarchy reappeared.[3] The political institutions of a city were the same as in the Classical period: Assembly of the People, Council, courts and magistrates (often functioning not as individuals but in boards).[4]

The *polis* in the political sense was not to the same extent as formerly an organisation of adult male citizens, and the Archaic character of the *polis* as a community of warriors—which had already waned in the Classical period—became even more attenuated in the Hellenistic period, when many *poleis* gave up having an army and a navy.[5] The place of women in the *polis* was no longer limited to the religious sphere: they were much more evident in the public sphere, although they never got the right to hold magistracies or take part in political assemblies.[6] Non-citizens also became to a greater degree part of the *polis*, and gradually they got the right to participate in the *ephebeia*, the most important social institution in the Hellenistic *polis*, whose primary function was the education of the young citizens.[7] *Ephebeia* is known from the fourth century BC, primarily as a sort of 'national service' in which young citizens were trained in weaponry; but in the Hellenistic period the training came to include a much wider cultural and social aspect,[8] and the institution came to play a central role in the Hellenisation of the Near East.[9]

The cults of the Olympic gods continued, but new ones were added. Some of these were of foreign deities like the Isis cult from Egypt,[10] but others were hypostatised ideas like 'Unity' (*Homonoia*),[11] or 'Fate' (*Tyche*).

The division of the citizen body into *phylai, demoi, phratriai* and so on continued, but no longer had the same significance.[12] To make up for this, there grew up a network of semi-public or quite private organisations, often related to the economy of the city.[13] The Rhodian *koina* is a case in point.[14]

Polis in the urban sense had also changed its character. Under the Pax Romana nobody built city walls any more, for they were no longer needed, and the existing ones were seldom repaired and were allowed to decay.[15] If the city was the residence of a prince or a governor, it usually contained a palace.[16] The buildings where the citizens and their magistrates met were much more monumental, especially the *bouleuterion*, where the Council met,[17] but also the theatre, where Assemblies of the People were held;[18] and the offices of the administrators that were often housed in the pillared halls (*stoai*) that now surrounded the market (*agora*).[19] Sports centres and educational buildings were now commonly built of stone as monumental architecture, and also the *gymnasium*,[20] which no longer lay on the outskirts but had been transferred to the midst of the city, where it was the home of the *ephebeia*.[21] The most important temples of a city were no longer all together on the *akropolis*, but were spread out in the habitation quarters.[22] More and more cities were built, or restored, on the grid plan,[23] but the houses were no longer as uniform in size and style as in the planned cities of the Classical period.[24] The social gap between rich and poor was more clearly apparent in the architecture.[25]

Outside the city in the city-state's territory there were now far more villages (*komai*),[26] and we must suppose that a larger part of the population lived in the territory, i.e. outside the walls. Perhaps it was the more peaceful situation under Roman control that resulted in the different pattern of settlement.

The federal states came to play an ever larger role,[27] but also across the federations the co-operation between city-states was intensified.[28] Many people became citizens of more than one city-state;[29] it became common to marry a woman from another city-state; there was legislation about all sorts of juridical and economic interaction between *poleis*; a vast number of treaties were passed between cities;[30] arbitration between *poleis* by third parties was invoked to solve conflicts;[31] and one can with some justification say that it was in the Hellenistic period that international law arose.

In the century after Alexander the Great's conquest of the Persian Empire, several hundred new *poleis* were founded in Asia.[32] Those Hellenistic colonies were governed by the Greek and Macedonian ruling class, but were kitted out with the typical institutions of the city-state: Council, courts, Assembly of the People, *gymnasium*, etc. But they were all dependent states under a Hellenistic monarch. Some were autonomous *poleis* governed by the city-state's own institutions; others were subject to royal administration.[33] By far the greater number of them were founded by the Seleukids, whose empire stretched from Asia Minor to India. The written language in all those city-states was Greek, and in most of them Greek was probably also the dominant spoken language.[34]

Over the course of several hundred years the Greek city-state culture underwent an expansion to the east, and here the typical *polis* was no longer a coastal city with market and harbour as its two social and economic centres. Most of the new *poleis* lay inland, some developed from garrison towns, others founded as administrative and economic centres.[35] Nevertheless, several of the new *poleis* were in the Mediterranean like the old ones, amongst them the two largest: Alexandria in the Nile delta and Antioch at the mouth of the river Orontes.[36]

III

CONCLUSION

24

The *Polis* Compared with Other City-State Cultures

What remains is to put the Greek city-state culture into perspective by comparing some essential aspects of the *polis* with what we know about similar characteristics in other city-state cultures.

Emergence   Unlike many other city-state cultures, the Greek *poleis* did not come into existence by the disintegration of a macro-state.[1] The *polis* belonged in the other category: it was a demographic and economic upsurge in the Geometric period that resulted in the simultaneous rise of cities and states and led to the formation of the *polis* as the specific Greek form of city-state and city-state culture.[2]

In Greece the interval between the demise of the Mycenean civilisation and the emergence of the *polis* in the late Geometric period spans more than three centuries. Accordingly, it is unlikely that the *polis* should be seen as a direct continuation of Mycenean civilisation.[3] But it cannot be precluded that the Bronze Age civilisations which preceded the *polis* were, at least to some extent, city-state cultures. In the New Palace Period Crete may have been divided between what were in fact five city-states.[4] And we now know that the Mycenean palaces were centres of proper towns: Thebes covered at least 19 ha, Pylos some 20 ha, and Mykenai has been estimated at 32 ha.[5] Each town seems to have controlled a territory of no more than ca. 1,000–2,000 km².[6] They were not *poleis* but probably monarchically governed city-states, and a similar status can be presumed for Tiryns, Athens, and other Mycenean centres. If so, ancient Greece is yet another example of a region of which at least a part was organised as a city-state culture twice in history.[7]

Alternatively, the *polis* may have emerged in connection with the colonisation in the eighth century, in particular the colonisation of Sicily and southern Italy. Colonisation of a foreign territory must have favoured nucleated settlement in towns and furthered the formation of political institutions which were to be responsible for the organisation of the new community. According to this model, the *polis*—both as a town and as a polity—emerged first in the colonies and only later in the homeland.[8] Examples of city-states emerging in consequence of colonisation are the Viking city-states in Ireland, the Mzâb city-states in North Africa, the Philistine city-states in the Near East, and the Aztec city-states in Mesoamerica.[9]

City-state cultures often appear in clusters: there were four in Mesoamerica, five in West Africa, and at least nine in Mesopotamia and the Fertile Crescent: the Sumerian, Assyrian, Anatolian, Syrian, Palestinian, Phoenician, Neo-Hittite, Neo-Babylonian and Philistine.[10] The Greek city-state culture bordered on the Phoenician in Sicily, and the two city-state cultures virtually overlapped in Cyprus. The Greek city-state culture could perhaps be seen as a Western extension of all the city-state cultures we find in the Near East, and in that case the origin of the *polis* may be found in Cyprus, and acculturation may be seen as a concomitant factor in the formation of the *polis*.[11]

Disappearance   The Greek city-states disappeared as slowly and imperceptibly as they emerged. They did not come to an end abruptly by the city-state region being conquered by a neighbouring macro-state. The Macedonians allowed the Greek *poleis* to persist. In fact, the Macedonian towns were themselves transformed into *poleis* with all the institutions we know from the older Greek *poleis*.[12] The Romans too kept the *poleis* as dependent polities, and what caused the demise of the Greek city-state culture was the transformation of Rome from a city-state empire into a bureaucratically governed organisation and the contemporary spread of Christianity. The *polis* with its polytheistic cults and festivals was a pagan institution in which good Christians could not participate.[13]

A similar development is attested in other parts of the world: in Mesoamerica, for example, the Aztecs subdued the Mixtec and Zapotec city-state cultures but allowed the city-states to persist as dependencies, and in the first period the Spanish conquistadores too governed the region through the existing network of city-states. It seems to have taken several generations for the former Aztec Empire to be transformed into a bureaucratically governed Spanish colony. Again, in West Africa the Kotoko became part of the Bornu Empire *c.*1600, but their city-states continued to exist as dependencies until the region was taken over by the colonial powers in the 1890s.[14]

Size   One essential characteristic of a city-state is its small size. All city-states were micro-states, and that goes for the size of the territory as well as for the size of the population. What characterises the proper city-state is the close interaction between its inhabitants, and that presupposes a restricted population settled in a small territory. Small and middle-sized city-states were face-to-face societies, and when a city-state became so big that not even its adult male members could know one another any longer, the community began to lose its character of being a city-state.[15]

As regards the size of the territory, almost all the *poleis* were small enough to be proper city-states. Even very large *poleis* such as Athens and Thebes came within the suggested norm of *c.*3,000 km² max.[16] Only Sparta, Syracuse, Kyrene and perhaps Pantikapaion exceeded the limit, but in all four cases the large *polis* was organised as a small city-state empire consisting of one dominant *polis* in control of a number of smaller *poleis* within its territory.[17]

The size of the population too matches what we meet in most other city-state cultures. Most *poleis* had a population in four digits. A fair number of large *poleis* had a five-digit population. Athens is probably the only *polis* with a six-digit population, and thus the only *polis* which, according to Aristotle, was too big to be a proper *polis*.[18] Parallels can be found in other city-state cultures. Old Oyo in West Africa and Tenochtitlan in Mexico were also over-sized city-states with, probably, a six-digit population figure, and both lay among a large number of other much smaller city-states.[19] Rome became an oversized city-state in the course of the fourth century.[20] Venice too got a six-digit population in the late Middle Ages and came to possess a territory of 35,000 km². In many respects Venice became a small country-state and no longer a city-state, but—like Rome—it kept a political structure and organisation which betray its origin as a city-state.[21]

Urbanisation   The fundamental characteristic of a city-state culture is that each state in the region consists of a city with its immediate hinterland.[22] Agrarian micro-states without an urban centre cannot be described as city-states. They lack all the social and economic ramifications that follow from having an urban centre in which a large part of the population live closely together. Most micro-states have been city-states, but some agrarian micro-states are known: e.g. Schwyz, Uri and Unterwalden in 1291 when they formed the Swiss confederacy.[23] The investigation of the thirty-seven attested city-state cultures shows that almost all the member states of all the city-state cultures were centred on a city which was the political, military, religious, economic and social centre of the state and accommodated a substantial proportion, often the majority, of its population.[24]

The ancient Greek *polis* conforms to this model: every *polis*-state seems to have been centred on a *polis*-town, which normally was the only substantial nucleated centre within the city-state, other nucleated centres being just villages. Conversely, every *polis*-town was the political centre of a *polis*-state.[25] Furthermore, the number of second-order settlements was small, and in several regions the *poleis* outnumbered the villages.[26] Only large *poleis* like Athens or Eretria had a substantial number of second-order settlements in their territory.

A similar settlement pattern is found in other city-state cultures. In Sumer, 'by 2500 B.C. it looks as though 80% of the population resided in substantial cities of more than 40 ha'. In the Mixtec city-state culture, 'The capital city was by far the largest, and sometimes the only, community within the city-state and served as the city-state's primary economic, political, and religious centre.' In the valley of Mexico the urban population of the city-states constituted some 40–75 per cent of the total population. In north Italy in the fourteenth century, *c.*25–30 per cent of the population lived in cities.[27] In all city-state cultures the urban population constituted a much higher percentage of the total population than the *c.*10 per cent or less which was the norm in most macro-states.

The importance of the urban centre is reflected too in the language. In ancient Greek, as in many other languages, the terms for city (*polis*) and country (*chora*) formed a pair of antonyms,[28] and as in many other city-state cultures, it was the word for city that came to denote the political community, i.e. the state,[29] whereas in most macro-states it has been the word for country that has been used for the state too. Similarly, the name of the *polis*-state was derived from the name of the *polis*-town, just as in most other city-state cultures the names of the city-states were identical with the names of the urban centres of these states.[30] In the Greek city-state culture the toponym was used to denote the state as well as the town, but in most cases the name of the state is an ethnic derived from the name of its *polis*-town.[31]

Economy   By and large a low degree of urbanisation goes with a high degree of subsistence economy, and, conversely, urbanisation is linked to a market economy based on trade. The size of the urban populations in city-state cultures necessitated a large-scale trade in foodstuffs alone. Much came from the town's immediate hinterland, including that brought to town by city-farmers (*Ackerbürger*), but much of the trade in grain or rice or maize was long-distance. The recognition of trade as a crucial factor of the Greek *polis* has for some time been obscured by a dominant primitivistic interpretation of the economy of the ancient world. But the Greek and Roman city-states appear in a new perspective when seen in connection with all the other city-state cultures.[32]

A large number of the major Italian city-states were important trading communities, and so were the Dutch and the south German city-states. Assur was a transit centre for the trade in tin and textiles brought to Anatolia and exchanged for gold and silver. Contracts, accounts and other documents testify to an advanced and highly specialised trading economy as early as *c.*1900 BC.[33] The Phoenicians were famous merchants and artisans.[34] In Africa the Mzâb organised much of the trade across the Sahara.[35] Mecca and Medina lay along the caravan route from Palmyra to Aden.[36] The Niger delta city-states played a key role in the transatlantic slave trade.[37] The Swahili stone towns were centres for the trade with the Middle East and India in ivory, gold, slaves, gum, cotton and other goods.[38] In his description of one of the Malay city-states, a Portuguese said that 'Melaka has nothing of its own and everything of the world'.[39] Or listen to what Bernal Diaz wrote about the Aztec markets: 'On reaching the market-place . . . we were astounded at the great number of people and the quantities of merchandise . . . You could see every kind of merchandise to be found anywhere in New Spain.'[40] Such observations match Perikles' praise of Classical Athens: 'The magnitude of our city draws the produce of the world into our harbour, so that to the Athenian the fruits of other countries are as familiar a luxury as those of his own.'[41] A comparison of all the city-state cultures demonstrates the close connection between city-states and trade, and emphasises long-distance trade as one of the

handwritten marginalia: long distance trade C-S together

essential links which could hold together the separate city-states of a city-state culture.[42]

Statehood In earlier studies of city-states and systems of city-states, independence, often equated with autonomy, was put forward as *the* most important single characteristic of what constitutes a city-state.[43] The reason why independence was singled out as the defining criterion of the city-state was probably a tendency to think of the city-state in terms of European notions of statehood in the nineteenth and twentieth centuries: if the city-state is a type of state, and if independence is an essential criterion of a state, then a city-state must be independent. The problem with this syllogism lies in the second premiss. To make independence a corner-stone of the concept of state is today an anachronism and has been for a long time.[44] Member states of federations are not independent; nor do the members of the European Union enjoy independence any longer. But member states of a federation, as well as the members of the European Union, are states.[45]

A rigid application of independence as a *sine qua non* for being a city-state would cut most of the city-state cultures into halves, and place the dividing line in an awkward place, one which would be incomprehensible for the peoples in question, and from the modern historian's point of view it does not lead to a meaningful analysis either. We would have to delete the following city-states and city-state cultures from our investigation: the Syrian city-states when ruled by the Hittites or Egypt, as well as those dominated by Ebla (no. 2); the Palestinian city-states when under Hyksos or Egypt (no. 3); the Anatolian city-states in the Old Assyrian period (no. 5); the Phoenician city-states in the twelfth to eleventh centuries and again in the ninth and eighth centuries when they paid tribute to their Assyrian overlords (no. 6); the smaller Neo-Hittite city-states which were either dependent on Karkamis, the largest city-state in the region, or clients of the Assyrian Empire before they were conquered by the Assyrian kings and incorporated into Assyria (no. 7); the Neo-Babylonian city-states in the ninth and eighth centuries which paid tribute to the Assyrian kings before they became fully integrated into the Assyrian Empire (no. 8); the Philistine city-states for most of their existence (no. 9); the Lykian city-states which formed part of the satrapy of Lydia (no. 11); the Latin *civitates* after 338 BC (no. 13); the Viking city-states in Ireland when they had become dependencies under Irish kings (no. 15); the south German city-states which had no feudal overlord but were still under the Emperor (no. 17); the Dutch city-states after 1579 (no. 19); the emerging Chinese city-states under Shang and Western Zhou (no. 20); the city-states on the fringes of the Taklamakan desert, torn between Chinese and Mongolian domination (no. 21); Sriwijaya as a city-state culture (no. 22); some of the Malay *negeri* after *c.*1520, e.g. those under Aceh (no. 23); most of the Tai Müang (no. 24); the Swahili city-states under Portuguese and Omani domination (no. 27); the Yoruba city-states in the Oyo Empire (no. 29); the Fante city-states under the hegemony of Mankessim (no. 30); the Kotoko city-state under the Bornu Empire (no. 31); most of the Maya city-states for most of the Classical period (no. 34); the Mixtec city-states after *c.*1450, when they had been subjected to the Aztecs (no. 35); all the small city-states lying in the isthmus of Tehuantepec which came under the power of the one large hegemonic city-state in the region: Tehuantepec (no. 36); most of the Aztec city-states (no. 37).[46] The principal city-state culture in which independence seems to have been an essential criterion for being a city-state is the Italian.[47]

Similarly, the Greek *poleis* were not peer polities, but formed hierarchically organised systems of polities of which some were hegemonic, some independent and some dependencies. The dependent *polis*—the *hypekoos polis*—is the Greek version of the dependent city-state[48] which is found in the great majority of the so far identified city-state cultures.

A specific and very common form of dependent city-states is the federation in which a large number of city-states become members of a federation which is governed either by a separate federal government or by the largest of the city-states.[49] In the latter case the hegemonic city-state acquires a double status: it is both a member of the federation like the other city-states, but at the same time the seat and *de facto* leader of the federal government.

It is in fact the Polis Centre's introduction of the concept of the dependent city-state,[50] in Greece the dependent *polis*,[51] which has made it possible beyond reasonable doubt to identify the majority of the thirty-seven civilisations as city-state cultures composed of city-states. A rigid application of the concept of independence would reduce the whole investigation to one of the city-state cultures, viz. the Italian plus, perhaps, a few others.

Government and constitution   City-states seem to have had the most institutionalised and centralised forms of government in world history before the modern period. Most of them were monarchies,[52] but several were republics, i.e. states ruled by councils or assemblies in which decisions were made by vote after a debate. Such city-states were either oligarchies or democracies. Oligarchically ruled city-states are attested in three continents in a number of city-state cultures: in Europe the Italian city-states are an obvious example;[53] in Africa oligarchies are found among the Mzâb,[54] the Swahili,[55] the Yoruba,[56] and the Konso;[57] and some of the Malay city-states testify to Asian oligarchies,[58] whereas no oligarchy is to be found among the Mesoamerican city-states.

Democracies, on the other hand, are rare. There were plenty in the Greek city-state culture. In the age of Aristotle democracy was the most common form of constitution.[59] But not many traces of democracy can be found in other city-state cultures. It is still a moot point whether popular assemblies existed in some of the Sumerian city-states.[60] There can be no doubt that some kind of assembly played an important role in several cities, but there is no way of telling whether these assemblies were democratic or oligarchical in character.[61]

If the Roman *comitiae* in the early republic had the powers with which they are entrusted in Livius' narrative, it is perhaps possible to follow Machiavelli, Rousseau and many others in describing Rome as a democratically governed city-state in the first period after the expulsion of the kings.[62] In the earliest phase of the history of the Italian city-states we hear about decisions made in assemblies of citizens,[63] but in the heyday of the *città* the powers of such assemblies had been arrogated by councils and magistrates appointed by election or sortition. In the thirteenth century there was movement towards more popular government and extension of the franchise,[64] but apart from five turbulent years in the history of Florence (1378–82) it is hard to find examples of what we could call a democratically governed *città*. In the first edition of the *Encyclopaedia Britannica* Basle is called a democracy, but like the other cantons it was in fact a narrow oligarchy.[65] Thus, apart from ancient Greece, democracies are poorly attested in the European and Near Eastern city-state cultures, and not one unquestionable example of a democratically governed city-state can be found in any of the city-state cultures in Mesoamerica, Africa or East Asia.

To conclude, the republic has a strong tradition in city-state cultures, but mostly in the form of oligarchy or aristocracy, and well-attested democracies are found in the Greek city-state culture only. In this respect the *polis* was different from other city-state cultures.

Population   A distinction between free and unfree (slaves or sometimes serfs) is attested in all ancient city-state cultures and in almost all later city-state cultures outside Europe. But slaves existed in all contemporary macro-states too, and it is not a distinctive mark of a city-state culture that a part, sometimes a substantial part, of the population is unfree.

More important is the distinction between the privileged citizens and a population of free but unprivileged persons. Citizenship was an essential aspect of the Greek city-state culture. A *polis* was first of all a community of citizens (*politai*). Foreigners and slaves lived in the *polis* but were not members of the *polis*. As a political organisation the *polis* was controlled by the adult male citizens, who isolated themselves from the rest of the population when they discussed and made decisions about how the *polis* should be governed. Assemblies, Councils, courts and administrative boards manned by citizens existed in all *poleis*, even in tyrannies.[66] In this respect the Greek city-state culture resembled the other European city-state cultures: the Etruscan, Latin, Italian, German, Swiss and Dutch.[67] In all these city-state cultures citizenship was a citizen's juridically defined, inherited membership of a city-state in virtue of which he enjoyed a number of political, social and economic privileges which non-citizens were deprived of. In some of the African city-state cultures, e.g. the Hausa and Yoruba, we can find many aspects of citizenship like those found in the Greek city-state culture.[68] In several of the Near Eastern city-state cultures there are clear traces of citizenship as outlined above.[69] There are also traces of citizenship in the Chinese city-state culture,[70] but not in the Malay city-states.[71] Finally, a distinction between citizens and non-citizens seems to be completely absent from the Mesoamerican city-state cultures.[72] Thus citizenship, though very important in the *polis* and in other European city-state cultures, cannot be seen as a constitutive characteristic of a city-state culture.[73]

Of the inhabitants of a city-state—the free as well as the unfree—some lived in the city, and some in the countryside. The relation between the urban and the rural population differed from city-state culture to city-state culture. (A) In some city-state cultures all inhabitants—or at least all 'citizens'—had the same status and the same privileges irrespective of where they lived. (B) In other city-state cultures there was an opposition between a privileged urban population and a less privileged or sometimes even a servile population living in the countryside.[74] This opposition is often emphasised in studies comparing the Greek *polis* (type A) and the Italian *città* (type B), but the same opposition is found in many other city-state cultures. Thus the Hausa, the Aztec and the Nepalese city-state cultures were type (A),[75] whereas, for example, the Fante and the Chinese were type (B).[76] The equality in status between the urban and the rural population is particularly prominent in the Greek city-state culture where in small and middle-sized *poleis* there was no opposition at all, since a large part of the population were *Ackerbürger* who lived in the city but worked in its hinterland.[77]

To conclude: the two most important aspects of the *polis* were its small size and the unbreakable connection between town and state. With very few possible exceptions, every *polis*-town with its hinterland was a *polis*-state, and every *polis*-state was centred on a *polis*-town. Most of the other essential features follow from these two characteristics. The *polis* is the Greek version of the city-state, and the network of more than 1,000 *poleis* constitutes the largest city-state culture in world history, both geographically and demographically. I hope in this study to have demonstrated that many important aspects of the ancient Greek city-state culture are better understood when seen in relation to all the other city-state cultures.

Notes

Abbreviations

References to literary texts follow the abbreviations of the *Oxford Classical Dictionary*, 3rd edn., with the following exceptions: Diod. = Diodorus Siculus, Hellan. = Hellanicus, Heracl. Cret. = Heraclides Creticus, Theopomp. = Theopompus.

References to inscriptions follow the conventions of *Supplementum Epigraphicum Graecum Index 1986–1995* (Amsterdam, 1999) 677–88, with one addendum: RO = P. J. Rhodes and R. Osborne, *Greek Historical Inscriptions 403–323 B.C.* (Oxford, 2003).

Introduction

1. I define a city structurally as a densely built-up area settled with— at least—a four-digit number of inhabitants (*infra* ch. 9 n. 6) and functionally as a central place which performs a number of specialised tasks in relation to a hinterland (*infra* ch. 14 n. 12). Politically the inhabitants are organised sometimes as a municipality, sometimes as a polity. Like most anthropologists, archaeologists and historians I use the terms 'town' and 'city' about the same nucleated settlement (*30 CSC*: 25), but in different contexts: when an urban centre is seen as a cluster of houses, I tend to call it a town; when the emphasis is on the inhabitants and their social and political organisation, I call it a city. This distinction matches the distinction in French between *ville* and *cité*. Cf. Rousseau, *Du contrat social*, the note on p. 361 in the Pléiade edn.: 'Le vrai sens de ce mot c'est presque entierement effacé chez les modernes; la plupart prennent une ville pour une Cité et un bourgeois pour un Citoyen. Ils ne savent pas que les maisons font la ville mais que les Citoyens font la cité.' For the *polis* as a type of city, see 62. Smaller nucleated settlements I call villages, see *infra* 68–9.

2. I define a state as a given territory, a given people and an institutionalised central government with the sole right to establish and enforce a legal order within the territory over the population; see *infra* 7 with n. 3, 63–5 and Hansen (1998) 114–23.

3. The English term 'city-state' was probably coined in 1885 as a rendering of the German term *Stadtstaat* in connection with the translation into English of J. Bluntschli, *Allgemeine Staatslehre*, 6th edn. (Berlin, 1886), 63 = *Theory of the State* (London, 1885), 60. The German term

Stadtstaat was probably coined in 1842 as a rendering of the Danish term *Bystat* (*by*=town; cf. Derby) in connection with the translation into German of J. N. Madvig, *Blik på Oldtidens Statsforfatninger med Hensyn til Monarkiet og en omfattende Statsorganisme* (Copenhagen, 1840) = *Blicke auf die Staatsverfassung des Altertums, mit Rücksicht auf die Entwicklung der Monarchie und eines umfassenden Staatsorganismus*, in *Archiv für Geschichte, Statistik, Kunde der Verwaltung und Landesrechte der Herzogthümer Schleswig, Holstein und Lauenburg* (Kiel, 1842), 42. The French term *cité-État* and the Italian term *città-stato* are both derived from *Stadtstaat* and/or *city-state*, and neither is attested earlier than the twentieth century (Hansen (1998) 15–16). The terms *Bystat* and *Stadtstaat* were first applied to Rome in the republican period, and only later transferred to descriptions of, primarily, the ancient Greek *polis* and the medieval Italian *città*. It was only from *c.*1950, in consequence of the new understanding of urbanism as a global phenomenon, that the concept of city-state, *Stadtstaat*, etc. has spread to Mesoamerican, African and Asian civilisations (*30 CSC*: 604 with nn. 32–4).

4. Four recommendable exceptions are Ruschenbusch's investigation of the number of *poleis* (1985), Gehrke's *Jenseits von Athen und Sparta* (1986), Bertrand's *Cités et royaumes du monde grec: espace et politique* (1992), and Brock and Hodkinson (eds.), *Alternatives to Athens* (2000).

5. The investigations conducted by the Copenhagen Polis Centre have been published in two series: (1) *Acts of the Copenhagen Polis Centre* = *CPCActs* 1–7 (contributions to the seven international symposia which the Centre organised; the Acts series is published by the Royal Danish Academy); and (2) *Papers from the Copenhagen Polis Centre* = *CPCPapers* 1–7 (articles written by scholars who have collaborated with the Centre; the Papers series is published by Steiner Verlag as *Historia*, Einzelschriften 87, 95, 108, 117, 138, 162, 180). For a comprehensive list of the Polis Centre's publications, see *infra* 191–3.

6. Published in *A Comparative Study of Thirty City-State Cultures* (= *30 CSC*) and *A Comparative Study of Six City-State Cultures* (= *6 CSC*).

Chapter 1: Cities, States, City-States and City-State Cultures

1. This chapter is a revised and much-abbreviated version of my Introduction and Conclusion in *30 CSC*: 11–34 and 597–623, and my Introduction in *6 CSC*: 7–21. In the present survey notes and references have been kept to a minimum. Full documentation can be found in the two books listed above.

2. Mellaart (1967; 1975); Mieroop (1997) 26. On the difference between a town and a village, see *infra* 67–9 and 89–90.

3. This heuristic concept of state is used in anthropology, sociology,

archaeology and history, and it is applied world-wide to civilisations of all periods. A much narrower historical concept of state is commonly found in jurisprudence and political science: the state is not only a government empowered to enforce a legal system within a territory over a population; it is also an *abstraction*, i.e. a continuous public power above both ruler and ruled, and a community must have a *sovereign* government and must be in possession of *full external sovereignty* in order to be a state. In this form the concept of state emerged in Europe. It can be traced back to the mid-seventeenth century and it flourished in the nineteenth and twentieth centuries. It can be used world-wide only after the mid-twentieth century. On the difference between these two concepts of state, see *30 CSC*: 12–14. On the various elements of the concept of state, see Hansen (1998) 35–51.

4. Southall (1998) 16 describes Çatal Höyük as a city-state, which I find unlikely (*30 CSC*: 15, 605), see Mithen (2003) 95.
5. Arnold (1997) 211–30.
6. Forde (1964); *6 CSC*: 26–7.
7. Olsen (1989).
8. *30 CSC*: 16–17; *6 CSC*: 12–16.
9. *30 CSC*: 531–2.
10. Ibid. 17–19.
11. See the survey *infra* 17–23.
12. *30 CSC*: 16. The term 'country-state' was, in fact, suggested by Henry Sidgwick *c*.1900, followed by Finer (1997) 6–7, both rejecting the term 'territorial state' as a misnomer in this context.
13. *30 CSC*: 611–12.
14. J. Miller (1984); *30 CSC*: 612.
15. *30 CSC*: 612–13.
16. Montesquieu, *De l'esprit des lois*, Book 9, chs. 1–3.
17. Elazar (1994), p. xv; *30 CSC*: 612–13.
18. Hansen (1998) 46–7, 121.
19. It is impossible to be precise, because every state has its own definition of what a town or city is. In Denmark a settlement with more than 200 inhabitants counts as a town/city (*by*), while in India the requirement is 5,000 inhabitants.
20. Bairoch (1988) 137. The ratio 90 : 10 is based on the assumption that an urban centre must have 5,000 inhabitants to count as a city. 80 : 20 is my guesstimate of the proportion if we accept 1,000 as the minimum population.
21. M. Trolle Larsen (1976).
22. Hicks (1969) 42–3; *30 CSC*: 614–15.

Chapter 2: A Sketch of the Thirty-seven Identified City-State Cultures

1. J. J. Glassner in *30 CSC*: 34–53; Å. Westenholz in *6 CSC*: 23–42.
2. I. Thuesen in *30 CSC*: 55–65.
3. J. Strange in *30 CSC*: 57–76.
4. M. Trolle Larsen in *30 CSC*: 77–87.
5. Barjamovic (2005).
6. H. G. Niemeyer in *30 CSC*: 89–115.
7. I. Thuesen in *6 CSC*: 43–55.
8. M. Trolle Larsen in *30 CSC*: 117–27.
9. J. Strange in *30 CSC*: 129–39.
10. M. H. Hansen in *30 CSC*: 141–87; *infra* 31–146.
11. M. H. Hansen and T. Marksteiner in *6 CSC*: 8–10 and 57–72.
12. M. Torelli in *30 CSC*: 189–208.
13. T. J. Cornell in *30 CSC*: 209–28, cf. 614.
14. J. Bæk Simonsen in *30 CSC*: 241–9.
15. P. Holm in *30 CSC*: 251–62.
16. S. R. Epstein in *30 CSC*: 277–93; M. H. Hansen in *6 CSC*: 17–18, cf. *supra* 17 with n. 12.
17. P. Johanek in *30 CSC*: 295–319.
18. B. Forsén in *6 CSC*: 91–105.
19. M. Stercken in *30 CSC*: 321–42.
20. M. Prak in *30 CSC*: 343–58.
21. M. E. Lewis in *30 CSC*: 359–73.
22. N. Di Cosmo in *30 CSC*: 393–407.
23. P.-Y. Manguin in *30 CSC*: 409–16.
24. A. Reid in *30 CSC*: 417–29.
25. R. A. O'Connor in *30 CSC*: 431–43.
26. G. Toffin in *6 CSC*: 107–23.
27. F. Jaabiri and B. Yahia in *30 CSC*: 445–62.
28. P. Sinclair and T. Håkansson in *30 CSC*: 463–82.
29. R. Griffeth in *30 CSC*: 483–506.
30. J. D. Y. Peel in *30 CSC*: 507–17.
31. R. A. Kea in *30 CSC*: 519–30.
32. M. H. Hansen in *30 CSC*: 531–2; see *supra* 10–11.
33. K. I. Princewill in *30 CSC*: 533–45.
34. Hallpike (1972); cf. Holder and Peatrik (2004) 13 n. 9.
35. N. Grube in *30 CSC*: 547–65.
36. M. D. Lind in *30 CSC*: 567–80.
37. M. R. Oudijk in *6 CSC*: 73–90.
38. M. E. Smith in *30 CSC*: 581–95.

Chapter 3: 'Country-States' versus City-State Cultures

1. Burke (1986) 142; Trigger (1993) 8; Yoffee (1997) 256; the description of macro-states as territorial states is avoided in Yoffee (2005).
2. *Supra* 14 with n. 12.
3. See *supra* 11–12.
4. The following (24–8) is based on *30 CSC*: 609–11 and *6 CSC*: 12–17.
5. Postgate (1992) 43–5; Kuhrt (1995) 74.
6. Gat (2002).
7. *6 CSC*: 16–17.

Introduction to Part II

1. This second part of the book is a revised and much-enlarged version of my chapter about the Hellenic city-state culture in *30 CSC*: 141–88. The focus is on the Archaic and Classical *polis* (*c.*750–323). The Hellenistic and Roman periods are discussed in the section about the chronology of the *polis* (48–50) but are covered only sporadically in the systematic part. A short survey of the main differences between the Classical and the Hellenistic *polis* has been added as an epilogue in ch. 23.
2. Hansen (1998) 17–34.
3. Of the 1,035 city-states included in the Polis Centre's Inventory of Archaic and Classical *poleis*, 604 were situated in 'Hellas' (see *infra* 84), 442 in the regions from Epeiros to Thessaly and on the Aegean islands (*CPCInv.* nos. 86–527), whereas 162 were situated along the west coast of Asia Minor in the regions Troas, Aiolis and Ionia (*CPCInv.* nos. 765–869) and on the islands of Crete and Rhodos (*CPCInv.* nos. 944–1000).
4. Of the 1,035 *poleis*, 408 were colonies founded in the Archaic and Classical periods or Hellenised communities in the colonial regions, 85 in the western Mediterranean (*CPCInv.* nos. 1–85), 220 along the coasts of Thrace, Propontis and the Pontos (*CPCInv.* nos. 545–764), 74 in Karia and Lykia (*CPCInv.* nos. 870–943), and 29 along the southern coast of Asia Minor, on Cyprus, and in Syria, Egypt and Libya (*CPCInv.* nos. 1001–29). There were 17 *poleis* in Macedonia (*CPCInv.* nos. 528–44) and 6 are unlocated (*CPCInv.* nos. 1030–5).
5. Tscherikower (1927) lists 298 Greek *poleis* founded in the Hellenistic period, almost all within the borders of the former Persian Empire; cf. G. M. Cohen (1995). To the *c.*1,300 attested *poleis* must be added an unknown number of *poleis* which cannot be traced in the sources. Thus, *c.*1,500 *poleis* altogether seems to be a realistic figure for the Greek city-state culture as a whole.
6. See index 10 in *CPCInv.* 1328–37. Of the 1,035 city-states in *CPCInv.* a total of 268 are classified as *polis* type C, which means that the sources

we possess are too scanty to show beyond reasonable doubt that the community was a *polis*. Conversely, there must have been a number of *poleis* for which we have so few sources that they now appear in the Inventory as non-*polis* communities.

7. M. E. Smith in *30 CSC*: 591–3.
8. Mieroop (1997) 6.
9. Hansen (2006*b*) and *infra* 82. Millar (1993) 254.
10. Migeotte (2002) 7.

Chapter 4: The Unity of the City-State Culture of Ancient Greece

1. The standard edition is still that of Müller in *Geographi Graeci Minores*, i (1855), 15–96.
2. Flensted-Jensen and Hansen (1996) 137–53.
3. 'The continuous part of Hellas' begins at Acheron (Ps.-Skylax 33) and ends at Peneios (Ps.-Skylax 65).
4. Hdt. 3.139.1; Thuc. 7.80.2; Xen. *An.* 7.1.29; Pl. *Cri.* 53a.
5. Pl. *Phd.* 109b; Hdt. 8.144.2.
6. Hekataios classifies Therme in Macedonia as a *polis* inhabited by Thracian Hellenes, as opposed to Chalestre, which is a *polis* of Thracians (fr. 146). Thus, the distinction between Hellenic and non-Hellenic *poleis* can be traced back to *c.*500, but note that the adjective 'barbarian' is not attested in the preserved fragments of Hekataios.
7. Pl. *Phd.* 109b; cf. Arist. *Pol.* 1271^{b}34–5.
8. Ps.-Skylax 34, 35, 36, 46, 61, 63, 64.
9. Ehrenberg (1973) 36.
10. Flensted-Jensen and Hansen (1996) 143–6. There are 162 occurrences of *limen* altogether; cf. Hansen (2006*a*) n. 140.
11. Thus, a five-digit number of new colonists were sent to Syracuse in 339 (Diod. 16.82.5; Talbert (1974) 30).
12. Graham (1964) 71–217. Some *poleis* remained dependent on their *metropolis*; see *infra* 48.
13. Syracuse was founded in 733 by colonists from Corinth, but became itself the *metropolis* of three other Hellenic colonies: Akrai (founded in 663), Kasmenai (founded in 643) and Kamarina (founded in 598); Thuc. 6.5.2–3; cf. Di Vita (1956).
14. Seibert (1979). At the Olympic Games in 324 Alexander the Great proclaimed that all exiles were free to return to their *polis*; Diod. 17.109.1; 18.8; Tod, *GHI* 201–2; cf. *RO* 101.
15. A free foreigner is in Greek a *xenos*, in plural *xenoi*. In some *poleis*, including Athens, foreigners who lived in a *polis* or stayed for a longer period were called *metoikoi*, in singular *metoikos* (Whitehead (1977) 6–10). According to Aristotle (*Pol.* 1326^{a}18–20), every *polis* accommodated a significant number of *xenoi* and *metoikoi*. See Gauthier (1988).

16. Parke (1933); Griffith (1934); Bettalli (1995); McKechnie (1989) 79–100.

17. During the last decades of the twentieth century the generally accepted view was that trade and long distance trade in particular was of little importance for the economy of the *polis*. The orthodoxy was preached by Moses Finley and his followers, e.g. Hopkins (1983) pp. x–xiv. But in recent years the pendulum of history has been swinging in the opposite direction; cf. Parkins (1998); Cartledge (1996); Garnsey (1999) 29–33; Migeotte (2002) 99–143. Already before the swing of the pendulum I ventured to emphasise the enormous importance of long-distance trade for the economy of Athens in the Classical period (Isager and Hansen (1975) 50–2); see *infra* 91–2 and 141–2.

18. *F.Delphes* II 84; *Revue de philologie et d'histoire anciennes*, 44 (1920): 274; Poulsen (1924) 43.

19. The number of spectators is a guesstimate based on the size of the Olympic stadion which, in the fourth century, seems to have accommodated *c.*45,000 persons altogether; cf. Yalouris and Yalouris (1995) 15.

20. 'Barbarian speaking' Karians are mentioned as early as in Homer *Il.* 2.867, but the opposition between Hellenes and barbarians became prominent in Greek thought only after the Persian Wars (Thuc. 1.6.6; Eur. *Iph. Aul.* 1400, quoted by Aristotle at *Pol.* 1252^{b}8–9): 'it is proper that Greeks should rule barbarians'; cf. Pl. *Menex.* 245d–e; Isoc. 5.124; Pl. *Pol.* 262d, where the population of the world is subdivided into Hellenes and barbarians. E. Hall (1989); Cartledge (1993) 36–62.

21. Emphasised by Herodotos in connection with the colonisation of Miletos (1.146.2–3). The prevalence of Italic dress ornaments in the earliest colonial graves of Pithekoussai strongly suggests mixed marriages; see Coldstream (1993). Graham, however, argues that mixed marriages were exceptional (1980–1), and that the Greek male colonists were usually accompanied by Greek women.

22. Momigliano (1977) 12–14. Cf. Hdt. 2.154.2. One exception was Timesitheos of Trapezunt, who knew the language of the Mossynoikeans and was the interpreter used by Xenophon in 400 (*An.* 5.4.2–4). According to Arr. *Anab.* 6.30.3, Peukestas was the only Macedonian general and governor who cared to learn Persian. For other exceptions, see J. M. Hall (2002) 114 n. 121.

23. Strabo claims that *Magna Graecia* in his age had become completely barbarised, except Taras, Rhegion and Neapolis. For Poseidonia, see Aristoxenos fr. 124, Wehrli. See also Hdt. 4.108.2 about the Gelonoi in Skythia and Arr. *Anab.* 1.26.4 about the Pamphylians in Side.

24. J. M. Hall (1997) 40–51; Fowler (1998) 9–14.

25. Hippoc. *Aer.* 12–24; Pl. *Resp.* 435e; Arist. *Pol.* 1327^{b}17–32.

26. Hainsworth (1968); Morpurgo Davies (1987). For a more pessimistic view, see J. M. Hall (1997) 172–4 and (2002) 116.
27. Indicated by Hdt. 1.58.1; Thuc. 1.3.4; Xanthos (*FGrHist*. 765) fr. 16; Poseidippos fr. 30.3, *PCG*.
28. Speeches to the army are held by, e.g., an Arkadian (6.1.30), a Lakedaimonian (3.2.1), and a Lydian who speaks Boiotian (3.1.26). Interpreters are mentioned at 1.2.17 and 5.4.4–5.
29. Pl. *Ap*. 17d; cf. Morpurgo Davies (1987) 12.
30. Hainsworth (1982) 865.
31. Palmer (1980) 174–93; but cf. Ste Croix (1981) 16, which refers to *Act. Apost*. 14.11.
32. Burkert (1985) 114–18.
33. Morgan (1993).
34. Schachter (2000); Kearns (1996*a*) 1300.
35. Pl. *Symp*. 182b; Hdt. 8.26.2–3. Sansone (1988) 6. For a more cautious statement of this view, see Pleket (1996).
36. Robert (1967) 14–32; Nielsen (2002) 203–10.
37. Moretti (1959).
38. Glotz (1928) 34; Giovannini (1971) 87; von Lübtow (1972) 108; Mossé and Schnapp-Gourbeillon (1990) 119; Cartledge (1993) 4.
39. Arist. *Pol*. 1327^{b}20–33; cf. Hansen (1996*a*) 203–5.
40. Barbarian *poleis* are mentioned by Herodotos (e.g. Pteria in Kappadokia, 1.76.2), Thucydides (e.g. the Etruscan *poleis*, 6.88.6), Xenophon (e.g. the *poleis* in Phrygia, *Hell*. 4.1.1), and Ps.-Skylax (e.g. Rome and eight Libyrnian *poleis*, 5, 21). For the exceptional use of *polis* in Aischylos' tragedy *The Persians* referring to the Persian Empire (213, 511–12, 715, 781), see Hansen (1998) 125–6.
41. Hdt. 4.59; cf. Hansen (2000) 180–2.

Chapter 5: The Rise of the Ancient Greek City-State Culture

1. Rostovtzeff (1926) 50; Gauthier (1993); Millar (1993); Davies (1984); Gruen (1993); Ward-Perkins (1998); Ma (1999) 150–74.
2. *Kn As* 1517.12; cf. Thumb and Scherer (1959) 335 §337 13a; Morpurgo Davies (1963) 262.
3. Frisk (1970) 576–7; Monier-Williams (1899) 635: 'púr, f. a rampart, wall, stronghold, fortress, castle, city, town.' See also Strunk (1970) 2.
4. It is misleading when Benveniste (1973) 298 claims: 'we have thus here an old Indo-European term, which in Greek, and only in Greek, has taken on the sense of 'town, city', then 'state'.' In Sanskrit *púr* certainly developed the meaning 'town', 'city', and since some of these cities were actually centres of states I would not preclude that the word may have taken on the sense of 'state' or 'political community'

as well. In Lithuanian *pilis* has developed 'palace' and not 'town' as its secondary meaning.

5. Thuc. 4.26.2, cf. 4.3.2–3. Hansen (1996c) 35.
6. Phokylides fr. 4, Diehl: 'a small *polis*, well settled on the top of a hill, is better than stupid Ninive'; Thuc. 2.15.6; see Hansen (1998) 35.
7. Hayden (1988) 16–17; Nowicki (1992). Note, however, Lang (1996) 41 suggesting that all post-Mycenean city walls in the Greek homeland date from the mid-eighth century or later.
8. e.g. the walls at Zagora which date from the second half of the eighth century; see Cambitoglou (1981).
9. Snodgrass (1991) 8; Camp (2000) 48–9.
10. On similarities and differences between *polis* and state, see Hansen (1998) 117–20 or the revised French edn. (2001) 171–7, esp. no. 13 on p. 174.
11. e.g. Snodgrass (1980) 28–32 and (1985) 263–5.
12. Cherry (1986) 21; Hansen in *6 CSC*: 7. Traditionally the New Palace Period is dated c.1600–1375, but the termination is here dated back 150 years in conformity with the Greenland ice core chronology which shows that the eruption of Thera took place 1647 ± 5 years.
13. Drögemüller (1970) 487–92; van Effenterre (1985) 27–8 *et passim*.
14. Archilochos fr. 228, West; *polis* in the sense of community of citizens (*astoi*): fr. 13.2, in the sense of town: fr. 49.7.
15. Tyrtaios fr. 4.4, West; *polis* in the sense of town: fr. 10.3; in the sense of community: of citizens at fr. 4.8, 12.28 (*demotas andras*) and fr. 4.5 and 9 (*demou plethos*).
16. Meiggs–Lewis, *GHI* 2.1–2, now dated c.650 BC; *Nomima* 1.81, 650–600 BC; Koerner (1993) no. 90.
17. The distinction between citizens and non-citizens is attested, e.g., in Drakon's law on Homicide (Meiggs–Lewis, *GHI* 86.28–9, c.624 BC) and in a law from Gortyn (*I.Cret.* IV 4.13; *Nomima* 1.1, late seventh century BC).
18. Finley (1956) 35; Austin and Vidal Naquet (1977) 40.
19. Murray (1993) 63; Morris (1986) 100–4; Raaflaub (1993) 46–59 and (1997a). However, Schmidt (2004) 1350 shows that in Homer the meaning of town (*stadt*) prevails and is much more common (1358–76) than the meaning of community (*Stadtgemeinde*) (1376–7).
20. Lord (1962) 188–93; Bennet (1997) 513.
21. It is striking that, emphasising the Iron Age aspects of the poems, Morris and Powell (1997) make no mention of 'Homeric' palaces and temples. For palaces we must go back to Wace (1962).
22. *Il.* 6.242 ff. (palace of Priam); *Od.* 1.365 (palace of Odysseus); *Od.* 3.387 ff. (palace of Nestor); *Od.* 4.20 ff. (palace of Menelaos); *Od.* 7.81 ff. (palace of Alkinoos).

23. *Il.* 1.39; 5.446; 7.83 (temple of Apollo in Troy); *Il.* 6.297–300 (temple of Athena in Troy); *Od.* 6.10 (temples of the gods in Scheria).
24. Wace (1962) 490; Pöhlmann (1992) 191–2. Both the Mycenean remains and the Homeric 'Halls' (*domata*) are so magnificent that the traditional designation of them as 'palaces' seems well chosen. For an attempt to reconcile the Homeric 'palaces' with remains of Iron Age residences, see Ainian (1997) 363–8.
25. Hansen and Fischer-Hansen (1994) 25–30. I. Nielsen (1999) 72–6 upholds the traditional belief that a tyrant may have lived on the *akropolis* of his *polis*, and she interprets Building F on the west side of the Athenian *agora* as the residence of Peisistratos and his sons.
26. For some 'primitive temples' antedating 700 BC, see Lawrence (1996) 61–5. As the evidence stands, the earliest known 'monumental' temple is that of Apollo at Eretria, probably a *hekatompedon* of the late eighth century; see *CPCInv.* no. 370, p. 655.
27. Judiciously emphasised by Scully (1990) 2–3.
28. Greenhalgh (1973) 7–18; Ducrey (1986) 38–41.
29. Hope Simpson and Lazenby (1970) 153–71.
30. The most disturbing problem is lack of correspondence between Nestor's realm as described in *Il.* 2.591–602 and the evidence of the Linear B tablets found in the palace at Ano Englianos, discussed by Hope Simpson and Lazenby (1970) 155–6. McInerney (1999) 120–7 shows that the section on Phokis in The Catalogue of Ships reflects a mixture of Bronze Age sites and Iron Age sites.
31. B. Powell (1991) adducing as possible analogies (11–12), e.g. Wulfila's invention of Gothic script *c.* AD 400, see also B. Powell (1997). The epigraphic evidence, however, indicates that a much better analogy is, e.g., the Nordic runes. They were invented in the first century AD, but it took many centuries before they were used for longer texts.
32. Jensen (1980) 96–171, reviving and defending the position of Cauer (1923) 126.
33. For a very clear and succinct account of 'Homeric society', see Raaflaub (1993) 46–59 and (1997a).
34. See also the judicious and cautious approach in Baurain (1997) 403.
35. Snodgrass (1991) 7–9.
36. Hansen and Fischer-Hansen (1994) 30, 35–6, 42–4, 75, 81. It is still debated whether the large apsidal peripteral building excavated in Lefkandi (*c.*1000 BC) was a chieftain's house turned into a *heröon* when he died and was buried in the *megaron*; see Lawrence (1996) 62; Ainian (1997) 353–4; Thomas and Conant (1999) 85–114.
37. Graham (1982) 159.
38. Malkin (1987) 12 followed by Hansen (1994a) 15–16.
39. Reasonably reliable foundation dates of many of the western colonies,

not always matching the foundation dates reported by Thucydides at 6.2–6, are now established by archaeological evidence alone, and there is no reason to suspect a circular argument, i.e. that archaeologists base the chronology of proto-Corinthian pottery on Thucydides' foundation dates, whereas historians argue that Thucydides' dates are corroborated by the proto-Corinthian pottery found in the colonies; see van Compernolle (1992); Morris (1996).

40. Fischer-Hansen (1996) 334–51. De Angelis (2003) 43–5 estimates the population of Megara Hyblaia *c*.700 at 675 people, but admits that his estimate is a minimum.

41. See *supra* ch. 2 no. 15, the Irish Viking city-states. The Anglo-Saxon colonisation of England took place in the fifth century AD, long before there was any kind of state formation in the proper sense in Denmark and northern Germany.

42. Graham (1964) 7, 220, followed by Osborne (1998).

43. Morgan and Hall (1996).

44. Gschnitzer (1988) 291–3; Demand (1996*b*); Niemeyer in *30 CSC*: 109.

45. Malkin (1994).

46. Smyrna: *CPCInv*. no. 867, p. 1100, cf. 99 *infra*; Miletos: *CPCInv*. no. 854, p. 1087.

47. Snodgrass (1980) 32; (1991) 9.

48. Graham (1982) 159.

49. Camp (2000) 48–9.

50. Hansen, in *30 CSC*: 22; *6 CSC*: 7.

51. Morgan (2003).

52. Karia: Hornblower (1982); Lykia: Bryce (1986); *CPCInv*. 1138–40.

Chapter 6: The End of the City-State Culture in Ancient Greece

1. Thomas (1981) 40; Bengtson (1977) 286, 295; Green (1990) 53, 56, 80, 220; Cawkwell (1996) 98 and *passim*.

2. Cawkwell (1996) 98.

3. Hansen (1995*a*); (1996*d*); *CPCInv*. 92–3.

4. Graham (1964) 118–53; cf. *CPCInv*. 89 *Re* (4) and *infra* ch. 22 n. 24.

5. Ostwald (1982) 14–26.

6. Athens: Schuller (1974) 109–24; Hansen (1995*a*) 28–34. Sparta: Ste. Croix (1972) 96–101; Hansen (1995*a*) 35; *CPCInv*. 90 *Re* (8).

7. J. A. O. Larsen (1968); Beck (1997); *CPCInv*. 90 *Re* (7).

8. Xen. *Hell*. 5.1.31. Jehne (1994) 31–47; *CPCInv*. 91 *Re* (12).

9. This is today the prevailing view, see *supra* 39 with n. 1; but there are still quite a few who insist on independence as a necessary criterion and therefore prefer to let the history of the *poleis* end with Philip II's victory over the Greeks and Alexander the Great's conquest of the Persian Empire; see *supra* 48 with n. 1.

10. e.g. *OGIS* 229.9–16. Quass (1979); Davies (1984) 306; Gauthier (1993) 217–25; Ma (1999) 150–74.

11. Ward-Perkins (1998) 371–82; A. H. M. Jones (1964) 712–66.

12. A. H. M. Jones (1940) 85. One example is Menander Rhetor's treatise on how to praise a *polis*, composed *c.* AD 300. The urban aspects of the *polis* are emphasised; but when it comes to the political achievements and the constitution of the *polis*, Menander admits that there is no longer much to be said here, because all Roman *poleis* are now governed by one *polis*, sc. Rome! (360.10–16; 363.10–14).

13. Saradi-Mendelovici (1988) 374–7.

14. Lib. *Or.* 11.266; see Saradi-Mendelovici (1988) 384–8.

15. A. H. M. Jones (1940). For *polis*, *komopolis* and *kastron* denoting towns in the Byzantine period, see Haldon (1999) 1, 11–14.

Chapter 7: How Poleis *Arose and Disappeared*

1. Pherekydes (*FGrHist.* 3) fr. 41d; Paus. 9.5.2. Gantz (1993) 467–73; Schachter (1985).

2. Thuc. 2.15.1–2. Hornblower (1991) 259–64.

3. Leschhorn (1984); for Asia Minor, see Scheer (1993).

4. For the following indications of *polis* status see Hansen (1996c) 12–13 and 55–62, nos. 15, 16, 23, 34, 40, 41, and *CPCInv.* 88.

5. *CPCInv.* 107–10.

6. *CPCInv.* 98–102; Rhodes (1995) 103, 107.

7. *CPCInv.* 103–6.

8. *CPCInv.* 144–9.

9. The Peace of Nikias of 421 BC includes one clause (Thuc. 5.18.6) which amounts to the *re*-establishment of three *poleis*, but neither this treaty nor any other known treaty of the Archaic and Classical periods prescribes the creation of a new *polis*.

10. By royal rescript issued by Eumenes II of Pergamon (197–59 BC), Toriaion was made a *polis* and granted the right to have its own constitution (*politeia*) and laws (*nomoi*) and a *gymnasion* (*SEG* 47 1745.1–29). Pallantion was—once again—made a *polis* by Antoninus Pius (Paus. 8.43.1). See also Schuler (1998) 25.

11. Under Julianus (AD 361–3) Kaisareia in Kappadokia was struck off the list of *poleis* (Lib. *Or.* 16.14).

12. Aitolia: Funke (1997) 145–88; Akarnania: Gehrke (1994/5); Epeiros: Dakaris (1972).

13. The closest we get to an attestation of change of status in the Classical period is Limnaia in Arkarnania. Thuc. 2.80.8 describes Limnaia as an unfortified village (*ateichistos kome*), but in the fourth century BC the community was walled (Winter (1971) 98, 111), and it appointed

theorodokoi for *theoroi* from Epidauros in 356 (*IG* IV²1 95.8) and from Nemea *c.*330–315 BC (*SEG* 36 331.A.31–3).

14. Meiggs–Lewis, *GHI* 5; Chamoux (1953) 69–127.

15. The best—in fact the only—source we have for how such mass migrations were planned and implemented is Antigonos Monophthalmos' letter to Teos in 303 about the planned synoecism with the smaller *polis* of Lebedos (*Syll.*³ 344, trans. in Austin (1981) no. 40).

16. Diod. 15.94.1–3; Paus. 8.27.1–8. T. H. Nielsen (2002) 413–55.

17. *Hell. Oxy.* 20.3. Moggi (1976) 197–204; Demand (1990) 83–5.

18. The towns in Lykia became Hellenised in the late Classical and early Hellenistic periods, and from the third century onwards they appear as Hellenic *poleis* (Marksteiner and Hansen in 6 *CSC*: 8–10, 57–72).

19. In Aitolia both Chalkis (Thuc. 1.108.5) and Molykreion (Thuc. 3.102.2) were colonies founded by Corinth. Another example is Naupaktos in west Lokris which *c.*500–475 was reinforced by new colonists from Opountian Lokris (Meiggs–Lewis, *GHI* 20). Another is the island Astypalaia which was colonised by Epidauros (*Syll.*³ 357.2) and, perhaps, Megara (Ps.-Scymnus 551).

20. Survey in Moggi (1976).

21. Thuc. 3.92–3; Hornblower (1991) 501–8.

22. Plut. *Tim.* 23.4–6; cf. *supra* ch. 4 n. 11. The number is incredibly high, but a significant extension of Syracuse to the north during the fourth century BC is archaeologically attested; see Talbert (1974) 146–7.

23. Kallisthenes (*FGrHist* 124) fr. 25. Hornblower (1982) 78–105.

24. Two exceptions are McKechnie (1989) 34–78: 'Cities Founded or Destroyed in the Fourth Century' and Corvisier (1999).

25. Hdt. 6.21; Diod.12.9–10.

26. Plataiai: Thuc. 3.68.2; Dem. 59.103. Melos: Thuc. 5.116.4; Isoc. 12.100.

27. Olynthos: Diod. 16.53.3. Thebes: Din. 1.24; Arr. *Anab.* 1.9.9; Diod. 17.14.3.

28. Kamarina: Hdt. 7.156.2; Thuc. 6.5.3; Diod. 11.76.5. Megara Hyblaia: Hdt. 7.156.2; Thuc. 6.49.4.

29. Mantinea: Xen. *Hell.* 5.2.7. Phokis: Diod. 16.60.2.

30. Hdt. 1.14.4; Arist. fr. 601; Timaios (*FGrHist* 556) fr. 56. Demand (1990) 31–3.

31. *Hell. Oxy.* 20.3.

32. Xen. *Hell.* 7.5.5; Paus. 8.43.1.

33. Grynchai: *IG* I³ 270.V.22; *IG* XII.9 249B.361. Styra: Thuc. 7.57.4; *IG* XII.9 245A.36. Knoepfler (1997) 383–4, 402.

34. Diod. 15.48.1–49.4; Polyb. 2.41.7.

35. Knoepfler (1997) 352.

36. T. H. Nielsen (2002) 443–65.

37. Thessalonike: Strabo 7 fr. 24; Strabo 9.5.15; Plut. *Demetr.* 53.7.
38. At *Pol.* 1327^{b}32, however, Aristotle notes that the Hellenic race, if united under one constitution (*politeia*), would be strong enough to rule the world. But to have one *politeia* does not necessarily imply to be one *polis*. Aristotle may be thinking of a kind of alliance or federal constitution; cf. the collection of 158 Aristotelian *politeiai* which include several federations, e.g. the *politeia* of the Aitolians (fr. 476, Gigon), the Akarnanians (fr. 477), the Arkadians (frr. 487–8), the Boiotians (fr. 489), and the Thessalians (frr. 502–5). The most ambitious attempt to create a large political unit beyond *polis* level was the abortive plan, suggested by Thales *c.*545 BC, to unite all Ionian *poleis* and form one large political unit with its centre at Teos (Hdt. 1.170.3). For the utopian idea to unite a whole *ethnos*, see also Hdt. 5.3.1 (the Thracians) and Thuc. 2.97.6 (the Skythians).
39. Arist. *Pol.* 1261^{a}29 with Hansen (1999*a*).

Chapter 8: What is a Polis? *An Investigation of the Concept of* 'Polis'

1. Burke (1992) 45.
2. Hansen (1996*c*) 7–14. For a similar approach, see also Lévy (1990); Sakellariou (1989).
3. Arist. *Pol.* 1276^{a}17–27; Pl. *Def.* 415c; Kleanthes in Stob. *Flor.* 2.7; *Etym. Magn.* 680.1–4; see Hansen (1998) 17–20.
4. A *polis* consists of houses (Arist. *Oec.* 1343^{a}10), or of persons (Thuc. 7.77.7).
5. Settlement: Ps.-Skylax 33 *et passim*. State: Arist. *Pol.* 1274^{b}41, 1276^{b}1–3. In Hansen (1998) 52–97, 114–23, and (2002) I have argued that the *polis* (like other city-states) was a type of state, and not a 'stateless society' as argued by Berent (1996), (2000) and again in (2004).
6. Hansen (2000) 178–9; *CPCInv.* 12. *Polis* is in fact the most common noun in ancient Greek. It is no. 39 in a list of the 2,000 most common words in Greek and comes before *aner* (man), no. 42, and other common words such as *theos* (god), no. 65; cf. Toner (2004).
7. (1a): Phokylides fr. 4; Thuc. 2.15.6. (1b): Dem. 18.215–16; *IG* XII.2 4.7, 17. (1c): Hdt. 7.58.2; Din. 1.77; (2a): Arist. *Pol.* 1274^{b}41. (2b): *Syll.*^{3} 359.3–5; *SEG* 43 310.1–4. (2c): Pl. *Resp.* 371b; Arist. *Pol.* 1252^{a}1–7; *CID* II 4. See Hansen (1998) 20–5.
8. *IG* XII.1 677.13–19. Hansen (1996*c*) 34–6.
9. Plut. *Pelop.* 18.1; Paus. 1.26.6.
10. Sc. in Herodotos and (of course) in Aeneas Tacticus and Pseudo-Skylax. See Hansen (2000) 178–9.
11. Hansen (2001) 249–50 n. 239, an extended version of (1998) n. 239.
12. Compare Xen. *Hell.* 2.3.35 with Lys. 24.22–3 and Pl. *Cri.* 50c. Hansen (1998) 56–73.

13. Thuc. 8.72.1; Dem. 21.31–5; Arist. *Pol.* 1276ᵃ8–16. Hansen (2002) 22–5.
14. *IG* II² 43.78; *CID* II 4.I.14–15. Hansen (1997*b*).
15. Osborne (1987) 9 (quoting Louis Robert); Snodgrass (1990) 113; Wallace-Hadrill (1991) p. xv.
16. *Ge* is often used about the hinterland or the territory in the same sense as *chora*; cf. e.g. Thuc. 2.71.2 and 72.3.
17. (a) Arist. *Pol.* 1303ᵇ7–10; (b) Pl. *Leg.* 745b; (c) Aen. Tact. 15.9–10; (d) *Syll.*³ 147.3–7. Hansen (1997*c*) 17–20.
18. Or 'semantic marking', see Lyons (1977) 307–8. One example is the antonyms 'day' and 'night'. 'Day' can denote both the twenty-four hour period and the daytime as opposed to the night hours, whereas 'night' invariably means the dark hours between sunset and sunrise.
19. The same usage is found in many other city-state cultures: Yoruba: *Ilu* (town/state)—*ileto* (country); Hausa: *birni* (town/state)—*karkara* (country); China: *guo* (town/state)—*ye* (country); Indonesian languages: *negara* (town/state)—*desa* (country), Hansen in *30 CSC*: 16.
20. For the rare use of *chora* in the sense of 'country' or 'state' see e.g. Arist. *Pol.* 1327ᵃ32.
21. Hansen (2002) 24–5.
22. See e.g. *Magna Carta* sect. 8: 'That common pleas shall not follow the court of the lord king, but shall be assigned in some fixed place'; and *The Laud Chronicle* (1104): 'In this year [1103] at Christmas the king held his court at Westminster, and at Easter at Winchester, and at Whitsun again at Westminster.' For the medieval German empire, see *Westermann Großer Atlas zur Weltgeschichte* (9th edn. 1976), 62 III & IV.
23. *Polis* in the sense of 'territory': *I.Cret.* IV 144.9 (Gortyn); Xen. *Hell.* 5.4.49, Hansen (1996*c*) 36–8 and (1998) 22, 26, 31–2, 53–6. *Polis* in the sense of 'country' or 'region': Krateros (*FGrHist* 342) fr. 18 (Egypt); Eur. *Ion* 294 (Euboia) (cf. Harp. s.v. *Keioi*), Hansen (1998) 124–32. *Polis* in the sense of 'city' *passim*, Hansen (2000b). *Polis* in the sense of city-state *passim*, Hansen (2004b). *Polis* possibly used in the sense of federation (Arist. fr. 498, Rose, but see *CPCInv.* 35 n. 60). *Polis* in the sense of (large) monarchy, Diod. 7.16 (oracular response) or empire, Aesch. *Pers.* 511–12, Hansen (1998) 124–32.
24. Thuc. 2.9.1–2; *IG* II² 43, Hansen (1997b). As against some ten thousand attestations in archaic and classical sources of *polis* denoting a city and/or a city-state, there are about a score of occurrences of *polis* used about macro-states, most of them in poetry, see n. 23.
25. Finley (1963) 45; Kolb (1984) 59; Runciman (1990) 348. *Contra* Hansen (1998) 15–16.
26. Xen. *Hell.* 5.2.4.

27. *IG* II² 43.70, 78.
28. Hansen (2000), the observation which we have called the *lex Hafniensis*; see Hansen (2004*b*) 150–2.
29. Hansen (2004*d*), the inverted *lex Hafniensis*.
30. Starr (1977) 98; Kolb (1984) 59, 66; Demand (1996*a*) 99.
31. Hampl (1937) 48–9; cf. Mertens (2002) 290; Zahrnt (1971) 10, 221; Lévy (1990) 54; Koerner (1985) 456–7; Knoepfler (1997) 401 n. 332.
32. In most historical studies of urbanism the terms 'city' and 'town' are used synonymously and indiscriminately (Hansen in *30 CSC*: 25) about nucleated settlements with a four-digit population; see *infra* ch. 9 n. 6.
33. *IG* XII.5 872.3 (*polis*) and 5 (*asty*); Hansen (1997*c*) 58–60.
34. Isoc. 15.299; Arist. *Pol.* 1252ᵇ16; Aristoxenos fr. 130, Wehrli. Hansen (1995*c*) 61–3.
35. Jones (1987) 4–10; *CPCInv.* 95–7. On these civic subdivisions, see *infra* 114–15.
36. Knoepfler (1997) 355–8, 389–92; *CPCInv.* 652.
37. *SEG* 22 370; Dem. 23.41. Dittenberger (1907); *CPCInv.* 58–69.
38. *CPCInv.* 454.
39. *Hell. Oxy.* 19.3; *IG* II² 43.79. There are, however, quite a few attestations of the toponym used about the *polis* as a state. In Aristotle's *Politics* Book 5, e.g., *poleis* in the political sense are referred to by toponym more frequently than by *ethnikon*, e.g. *Pol.* 1301ᵇ19, 21, 1303ᵃ3 ff., etc. *CPCInv.* 55–7. Cf. Hansen (1996*c*) 28 and 38; Whitehead (1996).
40. Gschnitzer (1955) 121–5; Hansen (1996*b*) 191–5.
41. Hansen (2004*a*) 11–16; see *infra* 76, 80, 82–3.
42. *IvO* 165; Paus. 6.13.6. Fraser (1995); Hansen (1996*b*) 176–81.
43. Dittenberger (1907) 15; Hansen (1996*b*) 191; *CPCInv.* 63–6.
44. Hansen (1996*b*) 190; *CPCInv.* 66–7.

Chapter 9: The Polis as City and State

1. I except historians who hold that every *polis* was a stateless society; see ch. 8 n. 5.
2. Thuc. 5.84–116.
3. *CPCInv.* no. 493, see *infra* 69–70.
4. Friedrichs (2000) 13.
5. Ammann (1978) 408; Johanek (2000) 296.
6. For the synonymous use of 'city' and 'town', and 1,000 inhabitants as the appropriate line of separation between city and village in ancient societies, see Bairoch (1988) 136; Horden and Purcell (2000) 93; Kolb (1984) 15. Smith (2005) 412 even includes two borderline cases of centres with 800 inhabitants. I endorse the view that to speak of a city or a town, a four-digit population is a requirement, but I also endorse

the view that 1,000 inhabitants are enough to make an 'early city'; see Hansen in *30 CSC*: 620 n. 108 and (2004*a*) 26. The size of population entails a number of important aspects of city life, some of which I have briefly described in Hansen (2004*a*) 30–1, viz. an urban demography, an urban economy, an urban administration and an urban mentality.

7. *Infra* 81.
8. Bintliff (1997) 236.
9. *CPCInv.* 626. See also Lauter (1993).
10. Hoepfner (1999) 352–67; *CPCInv.* no. 369.
11. See Hansen (1998) 114–23, in which points of difference and of resemblance are listed and discussed.
12. *Infra* 77–8.
13. *Infra* 89–90.
14. *CPCInv.* 128–9.
15. Hansen (1998) 75–6.
16. Hansen (1998) 36–40 (state), 53–67 (*polis*).
17. *Supra* 71.
18. Hansen (2002) 32–7.
19. Hansen (1998) 40–2 (state), 67–73 (*polis*).
20. Oppenheim (1992) 249: 'Since a federal state is itself a state, side by side with its member states, sovereignty is divided between the federal state on the one hand, and, on the other, the member states.' Hansen (1998) 46–7.

Chapter 10: Polis *as City*

1. Arist. *Pol.* 1275ᵃ7. Hom. *Od.* 7.131 and Pl. *Resp.* 370c are the only two passages in which *polites* seems to mean 'city-dweller'.
2. Hdt. 5.101.2; Dem. 18.215–16; Eur. *El.* 298–9.
3. Liddell–Scott–Jones, *A Greek English Lexicon*, s.v. *astos* has: '*townsman, citizen, Il.* 11.242; *Od.* 13.192 etc.', but in both these lines the sense is 'compatriot' rather than 'townsman', and I know of no other attestation of *astos* in the sense of 'townsman'.
4. See 111–12.
5. Men. *Georgos* fr. 5, Sandbach; Theophr. *Char.* 4.
6. Pl. *Phd.* 116d.

Chapter 11: The Settlement Pattern of the Ancient Greek City-States

1. Pečirka (1973) 115; Jameson, Runnels and van Andel (1994) 249, 375, 383; Shipley (1994) 218–19.
2. Finley (1981*a*) 3–5; Osborne (1985) 15–36.
3. Large surveys focusing *inter alia* on settlement pattern and population have been conducted on the island of Melos (Renfrew and Wagstaff

(1982)); in the territory of Metapontion in southern Italy (Carter (1990)); in central Boiotia (Bintliff and Snodgrass (1985); Snodgrass (1990)); on Northern Keos (Cherry, Davis and Mantzourani (1991)); in the southern Argolid (Jameson, Runnels and van Andel (1994)); on the peninsula of Methana (Mee and Forbes (1997)); in the Asea valley in Arkadia (Forsén and Forsén (1997, 2003)); and in central Lakonia (Cavanagh *et al.* (1996, 2002)). For a comparative study of landscape surveys, see Alcock and Cherry (2004).

4. Pečirka (1973); Snodgrass (1987–9); Roy *et al.* (1988); Carter (1990) 410; Catling (2002) 187–93.
5. Hansen (1997*c*) 22–5; *CPCInv.* 74–9.
6. *Polis* (Hansen (2000) 174–5); *polisma* (Flensted-Jensen (1995) 129–31); *asty* (Hansen (1997*c*) 58–60). *CPCInv.* 39–48.
7. Hansen (1995*c*) 61–71; see 69.
8. *IG* II² 1183.15; 1187.3.
9. Arist. *Poet.* 1448ᵃ35–7; Dem 57.10.
10. *Oikia kai chorion* (Finley (1952) 124, no. 14); *agros* (Men. *Dysc.* 5–7); *aule* (*Syll.*³ 169.40 ff.); *epaulion* (*Syll.*³ 344.98); see Pritchett (1956) 261–9. The only source in which the three types of settlement are juxtaposed is an inscription of *c.*304: *Syll.*³ 344.98: *kome—epaulion—polis.*
11. *SEG* 37 340.3–9; Arist. *Pol.* 1326ᵇ26, 27ᵃ3–5; Aen. Tact. 15.9–10. Hansen (1997*c*) 24–5.
12. Thuc. 3.94.4; Xen. *Hell.* 5.2.7; Palaiphatos 38; Arist. *Pol.* 1252ᵇ10–30; Ps.-Skylax 28, 30–2.
13. For these regions the ratio between *poleis* and smaller non-*polis* settlements is 39 : 31 (Arkadia), 8 : 6 (Triphylia), 12 : 7 (west Lokris) 29 : *c.*10 (Phokis), 11 : 7 (east Lokris), 83 : 26 (Chalkidike with Mygdonia and Bisaltia), 6 : 2? (Lesbos). See *CPCInv.* 78; Rousset (1999).
14. *CPCInv.* 78.
15. Stone (1997) 22, 26; Maisels (1990) 12–13, 253–61, 266–70.
16. 447 *poleis*: Hansen (2000) 179; *c.*30 *komai*: Hansen (1995*c*) 65–7.
17. Hansen (1995*c*) 51–2.
18. Finley (1987–9) 304–5; Brun (1999) 19; Horden and Purcell (2000) 105; Cartledge (2002) 20.
19. Davies (1998) 237.
20. Cherry, Davis and Mantzourani (1991) 235–7, 278–81, 337; *IG* XII.5 609; cf. Ruschenbusch (1982). Cherry, Davis and Mantzourani find that *c.*90 per cent of the population lived in the city (337–8). In an alternative interpretation of the evidence Whitelaw (1998) n. 35 finds that it was only *c.*60 per cent who lived in the city. Cf. Hansen (2004*a*) 11–12 and *infra* 80.

21. Jameson, Runnels and van Andel (1994) 18, 224, 545, 549–51, 562. Hansen (2004a) 12.
22. *CPCInv.* 437–59.
23. Bintliff (1997); Hansen (1997c) 62–3; (2004a) 13; (2006b) 84–7.
24. Surveys on the island of Melos, the peninsula of Methana, and in the territories of Metapontion and Asea; see *supra* ch. 10 n. 3. Preliminary investigations on the islands of Nisyros and Telos (Hoepfner (1999) 134–5, 170–89).
25. See also Osborne (1987) 95.
26. Thuc. 2.16.1, but see also Arist *Pol.* 1319ᵃ35–7.
27. *CPCInv.* 636.
28. Cavanagh *et al.* (2002) 205–11.
29. Hansen (2004a) 32.
30. Schuler (1998), with a survey of the epigraphical evidence 291–7. A large number of *komai* is attested in Strabo (first century BC) and Pausanias (second century AD) (Hansen 1995c) 48–52.

Chapter 12: The Size and Population of the Cities

1. Hansen (2004a) 33–40; *CPCInv.* 135–7.
2. Thuc. 2.17.1; Aen. Tact. 1.9, 2.2, 2.7; Xen. *Vect.* 2.6.
3. The *akropolis* of Phleious was uninhabited and often cultivated (Xen. *Hell.* 7.2.8).
4. Often called *proasteion*: Thuc. 5.2.4 (Torone). Part of the *proasteion* of Olynthos has been excavated (Hoepfner and Schwandner (1994) 92). This part of the city, called the Villa Section, covered at least 16 ha and may have been much larger (Cahill (2002) 29–32). For the meaning and reference of *proasteion*, see Audring (1989) 15–32. For the interpretation of the 'Villa Section' as a *proasteion*, see Hansen (2006b) 43.
5. Of the 1,035 *poleis*, 69 had a fortified *akropolis* but no (attested) city wall. *CPCInv.* 137.
6. Thuc. 2.2–6; Hdt. 7.233.2. Hansen (1997c) 27–8.
7. Hansen (2006b) 43.
8. Hoepfner and Schwandner (1994) 190.
9. The household varies in size in the course of a generation; see Gallant (1991) 11–33. In order to keep the population stationary, each woman had to give birth to five or six children, of whom two or three would survive to adulthood. In about a third of all families the father would die before his children came of age, and the orphans (and the widow) would often become members of a household of a male relative. The obligation to take care of one's parents also meant that most households during the first part of a generation included one grandmother and/or grandfather. If we assume, on average, half a slave per household, the

result over a generation of 30 years is *c*.5.5 persons per year. For a full treatment of the problems involved, see Hansen (2006b) 52–60.

10. Hoepfner and Schwandner (1994) 72–6; Cahill (2002) 30–2: the settlement on the South Hill covered 7 ha, that on the North and East Spur Hills *c*.28 ha.

11. According to Cahill (2002), the Villa Section, i.e. the *proasteion*, covered at least 16 ha, perhaps more, corresponding to a population of 2,400 persons min.

12. For a survey, see Hansen (2006b) 42.

13. In Kyrene, e.g., the walls enclosed 750 ha, but the archaeologists' estimate is that only some 250 ha seem to have been used for habitation (Laronde (1999) 82).

14. Hansen (2006b) 60–1, where I reckon 30–3 houses per ha habitation space, and an average household of five or six persons. Combining the minima, we get 150 persons per ha; combining the maxima, the result is 200 persons.

15. *Supra* ch. 11 n. 18.

Chapter 13: The Demography of the Greek City-State Culture

1. This chapter is a summary of the results reported in Hansen (2006b).

2. See *CPCInv*. 71 and the index, 1319–27. I have kept the most important of the double categories, viz. *poleis* with a territory size 1 or 2 (under 100 km²). The thirty-eight *poleis* with a territory size 2 or 3 (25–200 km²) have been divided equally between 2 and 3. Of the eleven *poleis* with a territory size 3 or 4 (100–500 km²), ten seem to belong in 3 (100–200 km²) rather than in 4 (200–500 km²), viz. Elateia, Ilion, Klazomenai, Kyparissos, Pellene, Priene, Pydna, Sestos, Teos and Thourioi. The hinterland of Pantikapaion was probably size 3, but including all the dependent *poleis* it was, of course, size 5. Of six *poleis* with territory size 4 or 5 (over 200 km²), I have little doubt that four belong in category 5 (Ainos, Gela, Megalopolis and Messene), whereas two were probably category 4 (Knidos and Barke).

3. There are, of course, regional differences. Phokis had many small *poleis*. Italia had few but mostly very large *poleis*. A large number of circuits are found in Epeiros, whereas no circuits of the Archaic and Classical periods are attested in Elis and Achaia.

4. *CPCInv*. 53–4 with the index, 1328–37.

5. To be on the safe side, I shall in the following assume that only *c*.50 per cent of the intramural space was used for habitation even in the very small *poleis* with an intramural area of under 10 ha.

6. Hansen (2004a) 11–16; see *supra* 71. The surveys in question are those of Melos, northern Keos, central Boiotia, southern Argolid, Asea in Arkadia, and Metapontion in southern Italy.

7. Hansen (2004*a*) 16, see *infra* 70–2.
8. Corvisier (1991) 159–227.
9. Fischer-Hansen (2002); Fischer-Hansen, Nielsen and Ampolo in *CPC Inv.* 172–6.
10. Hansen in *CPCInv.* 150–3.
11. Corvisier and Suder (2000) 32–5. For a ground-breaking account of the possible growth of the population in the Greek world between *c.*1,000 and 400, see Scheidel (2003).
12. In my calculation the population of every *polis* with a territory of more than 500 km² (size 5) is estimated at 27,300 persons. That may fit *poleis* such as Tanagra, Kleitor, Messene, Chalkis, Eretria and Histiaia/Oreos, but it is much too small a figure for Korkyra, Thebes, Corinth, Megalopolis, Argos and Athens. There is no attestation of a *polis* size 5 for which the population can be assumed to have been smaller than 27,300. Again, whenever we have specific information about the population of a *polis*, the total we reach is smaller, often much smaller, than the average suggested by the use of the shotgun method, see Hansen (2006*b*) 93–6.
13. If, e.g., we reckon with 200 persons per ha inhabited space instead of 150, the total goes up from 7 to 9.3 million people. If, furthermore, we follow Bintliff (1997) in assuming that the habitation area on average constituted *c.*55 per cent of the intramural area, the population goes up to over 10 million people.
14. Corvisier and Suder (2000) 32–5.
15. See *supra* ch. 11 n. 18.
16. Hansen (2004*a*) 11–16.
17. Horden and Purcell (2000) 92.
18. See Hansen (2004*a*) 16–18.
19. *CPCInv.*71 with the index, 1319–27.
20. See Table 9 on p. 81: 135,000 + 401,625 + 941,625 + 882,000 = 2,360,250.
21. Adults between 18 and 80+ constituted *c.*57.4 per cent of the total population; see Hansen (1985) 12.
22. Arist. *Pol.* 1267^{b}30–1 (utopian *polis*); *SEG* 9 1.6 (Kyrene); Diod. 11.49.1–2 (Aitna); Diod. 12.59.5 (Herakleia in Oiteia); see Schaefer (1961).
23. e.g. by Schaefer (1961).
24. Hansen in *CPCInv.* 7, 151 and the index, 1390–6.
25. See *supra*, 31.
26. Hansen (2006*b*) 30–3, 97–9.
27. For the regions from Spain to Adria we have some information about the size of the territory for thirty-five out of eighty-five *poleis* = 45 per cent. For the other regions outside the Greek homeland the figures are

107 out of 220 = 49 per cent (Thrace to the Hellespont) and 42 out of 103 = 41 per cent (Karia to Libya). For the Greek homeland the figures are 333 out of 442 = 75 per cent (Epeiros to Thessaly), 62 out of 105 = 59 per cent (Troas to Ionia), and 52 out of 57 = 91 per cent (Crete and Rhodes). For Macedonia the figure is two out of seventeen, and six *poleis* are unlocated.

28. Forty-three out of 408 colonies (= 11 per cent) had a territory size 5, while no more than twenty-four *poleis* in the Greek homeland out of 604 (= 4 per cent) had a territory size 5.

29. Hansen (2006*b*) 32.

Chapter 14: The Economy of the Cities: Max Weber's 'Ideal Type'

1. Weber (1921) republished with introduction and commentary by W. Nippel in *Max Weber Gesamtausgabe* I/22. 5 (1999). Max Weber focused on a sociological view of urbanisation. A more archaeological approach was suggested by V. Gordon Childe (1950), an incisive article in which he presents an extended list of altogether ten criteria for what constitutes a city. All the criteria emphasised by Max Weber are included, but Childe adds several others: e.g. monumental public architecture, naturalistic art and the use of writing.

2. Weber (1999) 59–63.

3. Weber (1999): *Konsumentenstadt* (63–5), *Produzentenstadt* (65); *Stadtgemeinde* (84); *Ackerbürgerstädte* (67).

4. On the Weberian ideal type, see Weber (1973) 190–205 and, in particular, 191: 'wie man z. B. die Idee der "Stadtwirtschaft" des Mittelalters als "genetischen" Begriff konstruirt hat. Tut man dies, so bildet man den Begriff "Stadtwirtschaft" *nicht* etwa als einen *Durchschnitt* der in sämtlichen beobachteten Städten tatsächlich bestehenden Wirtschaftsprinzipien, sondern ebenfalls als einen *Idealtypus*. Er wird gewonnen durch einseitige *Steigerung eines* oder *einiger* Gesichtspunkte und durch Zusammenschluß einer Fülle von diffus und diskret, hier mehr, dort weniger, stellenweise gar nicht, vorhandenen *Einzel*erscheinungen, die sich jenen einseitig herausgehobenen Gesichtspunkten fügen, zu einem in sich einheitlichen *Gedanken* bilde. In seiner begrifflichen Reinheit ist dieses Gedankenbild nirgends in der Wirklichkeit empirisch vorfindbar, es ist eine Utopie, und für die historische Arbeit erwächst die Aufgabe, in jedem *einzelnen Falle* festzustellen, wie nahe oder wie fern die Wirklichkeit jenem Idealbilde steht, inwieweit also der ökonomische Charakter der Verhältnisse einer bestimmten Stadt als "stadtwirtschaftlich" im begrifflichen Sinn anzusprechen ist.'

5. The dissociation of the urban from the political aspect of the *polis* has been carried to its extreme by, e.g., Morris (1997). In this general account of the Greek *polis* as a city-state, he treats the *polis* as a type of

state ranging between a citizen state and what Ernst Gellner (1983) 9 has called the agro-literate state (98b and *passim*). He discusses elites and characteristics of citizenship, and emphasises (95a, 102b) that 'in many areas there was a shift in the sixth century B.C. away from residence in nucleated villages towards dispersed settlement in rural farmsteads' (95a, 102b). Apart from a casual reference to emigrants settling in 'new cities around the western Mediterranean and Black Sea' (94b), there is nothing in this chapter to show that the *polis* had anything to do with urbanisation and urban form, and the only explicit mention of towns is on p. 103b where we are told that 'By 200 B.C., people were drifting back to the towns, breaking up the dispersed classical settlement pattern.' An equally negative view of the importance of cities and towns is expressed in Horden and Purcell (2000) 89–122. As set out in my text, I take the opposite line, and prefer to argue that the urban aspect of the *polis* was as important as the political and that the two aspects were inextricably intertwined.

6. Laslett (1956) 162; Finley (1983) 28–9. It is commonly emphasised, however, that Athens was too big to be a face-to-face society, and was, in this respect, different from the 'standard' *polis*; see most recently E. Cohen (1997).
7. Mattingly and Salmon (2001) 3–15.
8. Finley (1963) 45; Osborne (1987) 194.
9. Hopkins (1983) p. xi; Davies (1998) 237.
10. Starr (1957) 98; Wycherley (1967) 10; Finley (1987–9) 309; Nippel (1989) 1032; Snodgrass (1991) 9.
11. Finley criticised Weber's model of the Greek *polis* for being based on Athens, 'whereas everything we know about Greek history indicates that Athens was an exceptional *polis*' (Finley (1985*b*) 94); but, as Philippe Gauthier has pointed out: 'M. I. Finley lui même n'a-t-il pas le plus souvent extrapolé à partir de l'exemple athénien?' (Gauthier (1987–9) 188).
12. Later discussions of urbanism in a historical context are based on the views of Weber and Childe, e.g. Sjöberg (1960); Bairoch (1988) 8; cf. Hansen in *30 CSC*: 27 n. 20. A recent trend in anthropology is to skip population size and density altogether and define a town or a city as 'an urban centre that performs specialised functions in relation to a broader hinterland' (Trigger (2003) 120; Smith (2005) 431 n. 14).
13. Starr (1977) 98; Kolb (1984) 59, 66; Runciman (1990) 348; Demand (1996*a*) 99; Whitley (2001) 166.
14. Finley (1963) 45.
15. Snodgrass (1980) 157–8; Kolb (1984) 72; Morris (1991) 26, 40, 50; Hodkinson and Hodkinson (1981) 287; Schuler (1998) 18.

16. Thucydides called it a *polis kata komas oikoumene* (1.2.10). Hansen (1997c) 34–5.
17. Spartans of military age were required to live in the city (Xen. *Lac.* 5; Plut. *Lyc.* 15.3–4); 8,000 Spartans with their families (Hdt. 8.134.1) plus foreigners and some slaves. Hansen (1995c) 54–5; Cartledge (1998); Cavanagh *et al.* (2002) 207–8.
18. *Polis*: Hdt. 6.58.1; Thuc. 1.134.1; Xen. *Hell.* 3.3.10–11; 6.5.28. *Asty*: the oracular response quoted at Hdt. 7.220.4. *Polisma*: Aen. Tact. 2.2*bis*.
19. Xen. *Vect.* 4.50–1. Hansen (2000) 179, 182–202.
20. Hansen (2004*d*) 132–3.
21. Finley (1963) 45, repeated (1981*a*) 21.
22. Horden and Purcell (2000) 105–6.
23. The fourth-century city walls enclosed an area of 124 ha (Hodkinson and Hodkinson (1981) 257–8). On the assumption that only 50 per cent of this area was used for habitation and that the population density was no more than 150 persons per ha, the result is 9,300 inhabitants. If the population density was the same as in Plataiai, i.e. a minimum of 200 per ha, the urban population of Mantinea must have been *c.*12,400. Hodkinson and Hodkinson (1981) 279–86 assume *c.*7,000 inhabitants of whom *c.*10 per cent only were landowners. Hansen (2004*a*) 19–20.
24. One possible example is Tiryns in the Archaic period. It was probably a *polis* in the political sense; see Gehrke (1993) 54–6. No remains of an urban centre have been found, and it has been argued that it did not have one, see Koerner (1985). But the argument from silence is rejected as inadmissible by Morgan and Coulton (1997) 93.
25. Of the *c.*800–1,000 sites included in the Polis Centre's Inventory of Archaic and Classical *poleis*, 'barely 10% have been investigated to any significant extent (and even this varies greatly)'; Morgan and Coulton (1997) 87. Actually, the Inventory came to include no fewer than 1,035 sites.
26. Arist. *Pol.* 1326ᵇ16; Pl. *Leg.* 738e.
27. Laslett (1956) 158 and 163; Finley (1983) 28–9.
28. Hansen (1997c) 42–3.
29. Sombart (1902) ii. 198–205, 223; (1916) i. 142–54.
30. Weber (1999) 66–7.
31. Finley (1981*a*) 11 (Sombart), 13–18 (Weber); (1985*b*) 191–6.
32. Hopkins (1983) pp. xii–xiii; Horden and Purcell (2000) 105–8; but the model is criticised, e.g. in Mattingly and Salmon (2001).
33. *Supra* 35; Hansen (2004*a*) 11–21.
34. Hansen (2004*a*) 22.
35. Hdt. 8.134.1; see *supra* 87.
36. See the articles in Whitby (2002).

37. e.g. Euphiletos, the speaker of Lys. 1, described as a city-farmer at 11 and 22.
38. Hansen (1988) 7–13; Whitby (1998) 109–14.
39. Isager and Hansen (1975) 19–29; Whitby (1998) 114–27.
40. Garnsey (1998) 183–200.
41. Isager and Hansen (1975) 35–52; Hansen (2004a) 23–5.
42. Andoc. 1.133–4; Hansen (2004a) 23–5, 40–1.
43. Weber (1999) 65–6.
44. Weber (1999) 67.
45. Thuc. 2.38.2; Ps.-Xen. *Ath. Pol.* 2.7; Hermippos fr. 63, *PCG*; Isoc. 4.42, 45.
46. Cf. Bruhns (1985); Andreau (2002) 42.
47. The small Boiotian *polis* of Anthedon lay on the coast, and according to Heraklides Creticus all the inhabitants were fishermen (*Geographi Graeci Minores* I: 104, §23; cf. Archestratos fr. 15; Palaiphatos 27). The fourth-century author Archestratos of Gela wrote a gastronomical poem, known from numerous quotes in Athenaios. Most of the fragments (forty-seven out of sixty-one) concern fish courses, and indicate that fishermen constituted a significant part of the population of all coastal *poleis*; see Olson and Sens (1998). During the excavation of Olynthos fishing hooks were found in many houses, although the city was situated some 5 km from the coast (Cahill (2002) 250, 335 n. 68).
48. Isager and Skydsgaard (1992) 149–55; Hanson (1995).
49. Wagstaff and Augustson (1982) 108–10; Hansen (1987) 140 n. 68.
50. Xen. *Hell.* 5.4.3. For other sources, see Hansen (2004a) 17–18.
51. Weber (1999) 67–8.
52. Bairoch (1988) 15–16; Hertz (1989); Sandström (1996).
53. Sombart (1902) ii. 191–2, (1916) i. 136.
54. Weber (1999) 67.
55. Weber (1999) 68.
56. Finley (1981a) 15 and 20 connects the concept of *Ackerbürgerstadt* with the concept of *Konsumentenstadt*. That this is a misinterpretation of Weber has been argued persuasively by Bruhns (1985) 256–9, (1996) 1277–8; see also Bruhns and Nippel (1987–9).
57. Finley (1973) 138; Hopkins (1983) p. xi; Kolb (1984) 74–5; Davies (1992) 19–20, (1998) 237–8.
58. 'Magistrates' is the conventional but not quite satisfactory translation of *hai archai*, a term which refers to officials appointed by election or sortition for a shorter period, mostly a year, and entrusted with the day-to-day administration of the *polis* and the carrying into effect of the decisions made by the Assembly, the Council and the courts (Aischin. 3.13 ff.). The word *arche* actually means a magistracy, but it was used with just about equal frequency of the person holding the

magistracy (Andok. 1.84); hence *hai archai*, 'the magistrates', was the collective term for a group of people who constituted a branch of the government on a par with the *ekklesia* and the *dikasteria* (Arist. *Pol.* 1317^{b}35–6; Dem. 25.20; Hansen (1991) 225). For an account of the *archai* covering all *poleis*, see Fröhlich (2004).

59. Pl. *Resp.* 369b–74a; *Soph.* 223d; Xen. *Cyrop.* 8.2.5; Arist. *Pol.* 1321^b 12–18. Hansen (1997c) 47–51.

60. Ar. *Eccl.* 817 ff.

61. Meiggs–Lewis, *GHI* 30.A.6–12 (Teos); *Syll.*^{3} 354 (Ephesos); *IG* XII.6 46 (Samos); *IG* XII.2 3 (Mytilene); Heracl. Cret. 23 (Anthedon).

62. RO 96; cf. *SEG* 42 1663.

63. Thuc. 1.2.2, 5.1, 6.1, 7.1, 8.2; Eur. *Cycl.* 115–18.

64. Pl. *Leg.* 778d; Arist. *Pol.* 1330^{b}32–31^a 20.

65. Hom. *Il.* 3.153 ff. (Troy); 19.99 (Thebes); 2.559 (Tiryns); 18.514 (the shield of Achilleus); *Od.* 6.10, 266 (the city of the Phaiacians); cf. Scully (1990) 41–53; Alc. fr. 426; Anac. fr. 391 (the walls are the crown of the *polis*); Hes. *Scut.* 270. Hansen (1997c) 52–3.

66. *CPCInv.* 71, with the index, 1319–27.

67. *CPCInv.* 136–7, with the index, 1368–75. Hansen (2006b) 16–20.

68. e.g. *CPCInv.* 445 (Koroneia); 458 (three displaced blocks supposed to be remains of the city wall of Thespiai).

69. Hansen (2004a); *CPCInv.* 135.

Chapter 15: Polis *as City in the Archaic Period*

1. In the *Iliad* more than 100 lines mention high, long, steep and beautiful walls 'a wonder to see' (Prendergast (1875) s.v. *teichos*, p. 364). They have 'well-built towers' (s.v. *pyrgoi*, p. 347) and gates (s.v. *pylai*, p. 346), and the city has broad streets (s.v. *euryaguia*, p. 166). See *supra* 41–3.

2. Alc. fr. 426; Archil. fr. 49.7; *P.Oxy.* 4708 fr. 1.17, 20; Anac. fr. 391; Tyrt. fr. 10.3. Hansen (1997c) 52.

3. Morris (1991) 40; Kolb (1984) 72; Schuler (1998) 18.

4. Hansen (1997c) 40–1.

5. *Supra* 41.

6. V. von Graeve's report in *American Journal of Archaeology*, 99 (1995) 237–8: 'the early Archaic settlement is estimated at 4,000 houses together with an industrial area represented this season by further excavation of a large and well preserved potter's kiln.' Assuming that the early Archaic town was as large as the later town, the total area amounts to *c.*110 ha. Even assuming that almost all of the 110 ha were used for habitation, it is, I think, without parallel in the Greek world to have 4,000 houses squeezed into 110 ha. I do not doubt, however, that early Miletos was an impressive city, and many times larger than was supposed before the startling results of the new excavations. Even

if we halve the number of houses, Miletos must have had a population of, perhaps, 10,000. Greaves (2002) 99, 103; Hansen in *30 CSC*: 179 n. 208. If only part of the area was inhabited in the early phase, the population drops to less than 10,000.

7. Nicholls (1958–9). The defence wall enclosed an area of *c*.18 ha. But there are traces of extensive extramural habitation of the seventh century.

8. Lang (1996) 260–1.

9. The later walls enclose an area of *c*.80 ha. The excavations suggest that perhaps as much as half of that was inhabited in the late eighth and early seventh centuries. Remains of a defence wall of *c*.700 BC have been found. Whether they enclosed the entire city is still a moot point. See Altherr-Charon and Bérard (1980); Ainian (1987).

10. Lang (1996) 152–63 no. 1 (Athens); 165–73 no. 4 (Corinth); 174–7 no. 6 (Argos).

11. Di Vita (1981). Syracuse: *CPCInv*. no. 47, p. 228; Naxos: *CPCInv*. no. 41, p. 219; Megara Hyblaia: *CPCInv*. no. 36, p. 114, see 44–5. Cf. Fischer-Hansen (1996) 334–5 (Syracuse), 337–9 (Naxos), 345 (Megara Hyblaia). As the evidence stands, the largest of the early western colonies was Pithekoussai with a minimum population of 4,000–5,000 and perhaps as many as 5,000–10,000 (*CPCInv*. no. 65, p. 286).

12. Roebuck (1972) 106–7, 114–16, 125–7.

13. Thuc. 1.5.1, 1.10.2. Hansen (1997*c*) 35.

14. *Supra* 87.

15. Morgan and Coulton (1997) 87.

16. See Lang (1996), esp. 56–7 about sizes of settlements.

Chapter 16: The Greek Conception of Polis *as a City with a Hinterland*

1. *Chora*: Aen. Tact. *Prooem*. 1, 7.1, 15.9. *Ge*: Thuc. 2.71.1; *Syll*.³ 37–8.B.15 (Teos). In this chapter two important sources often cited are the fourth-century treatise on the siege of *poleis* by Aeneas the Tactician and the early third-century account of cities by Heraclides of Crete. See also the excellent description of the 'Durchschnittspolis' in Winterling (1991).

2. *Limen*: Aen. Tact. 8.2; Arist. *Pol*. 1327ᵃ32 ff.; Ps.-Skylax 13, 34. *Epineion*: Hellan. fr. 75; Thuc. 1.30.2.

3. Athens: *IG* I³ 1101A and B. Pantikapaion: Dem. 34.34. Rhodos: Dem. 56.47. Phasis: Hippoc. *De Aere Acquis et Locis* 15. Hansen (1997*a*) 85, (2006*b*).

4. Skandeia, the port of Kythera, called *polis* in the urban sense at Thuc. 4.54.1. Hansen (1995*b*) 43–4.

5. Peiraieus connected with Athens (Thuc. 1.107–8; Xen. *Hell*. 2.2.20, 4.8.9–10). Lecheion connected with Corinth (Xen. *Hell*. 4.4.13).

6. Naulochon, the port of Priene, is called a *polis* in the urban sense at *I.Priene* 1.6, but seems to have been a *polis* in the political sense too (Hansen (1995b) 44); *CPCInv.* no. 857.

7. *Supra* 95–6.

8. Hansen (1995c) 61–71; Gschnitzer (1991) 429, 434 ff.

9. In *c.*385 Helisson, a dependency of Mantinea, is called a *polis* in the urban sense at *SEG* 37 340.6–7 = RO 14. Nielsen (2002) 359–63. In the fifth century Mykalessos, a dependency of Tanagra (or, in that period, perhaps Thebes), is called a *polis* both in the urban and in the political sense, at Thuc. 7.29–30.

10. This typology is invented and developed by Snodgrass (1987–9) 56–64 and (1990) 130–1. Examples of type (A) are Haliartos in Boiotia, Eretria on Euboia, Aigeira and Aigion in Achaia. Examples of type (B) are Thespiai in Boiotia, Sparta, Athens and Argos; see also Morgan and Coulton (1997) 124.

11. e.g. in Thebes, see Symeonoglou (1985) 117–22. Amphipolis: Hornblower (1995) 321.

12. e.g. Kadmeia in Thebes: Symeonoglou (1985) 118; Fossey (1988) 204.

13. Orchomenos in Arkadia, see Osborne (1987) 118–19. Cf., however, Jost (1999) 240 n. 51.

14. Two separate walls, one around the *akropolis* and one around the city, are attested for 101 of the 1,035 *poleis* in *CPCInv.* index, 1368–75.

15. Crouch (1993); Wycherley (1967) 198–209. Famous fountain-houses are known from Athens, Corinth, Megara, Olynthos and Phigalea.

16. Public space: *IG* XII.3 86 (Nisyros). Private space: *IG* XII.7 67.43–4 (Arkesine). Jameson (1990); Hoepfner (1999).

17. *Supra* 42.

18. Arist. *Pol.* 1330^{b}24; Martin (1974) 221–52; Shipley (2005).

19. Fischer-Hansen (1996) 317–52.

20. Hoepfner and Schwandner (1994). The principal written sources are Aesch. *Supp.* 954–8; Pl. *Leg.* 779b and Arist. *Pol.* 1330^{b}21–31; see also Heracl. Cret. 1. On the passage from Aristotle see Gehrke (1989); on the Aischylos passage see Rösler (1989), and on the passage from Plato's *Laws* see Hansen (1989a).

21. Hansen (1991) 314, 319–20; Murray (1997).

22. For short surveys of public buildings in a Greek *polis*, see Wycherley (1967); Müller-Wiener (1988) 157–75; Martin (1974) 253–86.

23. Hdt. 3.57.3–4; Thuc. 2.15.2; Aen. Tact. 10.4; Arist. *Mund.* 400^{b}19. See S. G. Miller (1978); Hansen and Fischer-Hansen (1994) 30–7.

24. Hdt. 1.170.3; Thuc. 2.15.2; Aen. Tact. 10.4; Dem. 10.53. Gneisz (1990); Hansen and Fischer-Hansen (1994) 37–44.

25. Aen. Tact. 22.4; Arist. *Mund.* 400^{b}16; Xen. *Hell.* 5.4.58; Lys. 9.9;

Dem. 10.53. Hansen and Fischer-Hansen (1994) 79–80; Haensch (2003).

26. Arist. *Mund.* 400b16; Plut. *Tim.* 22.2; see Hansen and Fischer-Hansen (1994) 76–9.

27. *Syll.*³ 218.6–10 (Olbia, fourth century); see Hansen and Fischer-Hansen (1994) 53–75.

28. Hom. *Il.* 18.497; *Od.* 2.7, 6.266–7, 8.5. Raaflaub (1993) 54–5; Martin (1951); Hansen (1997*c*) 60–1; Kenzler (1999) 31–46.

29. e.g. Plut. *Mor.* 799E–F (Thebes before 362 BC); see Hansen and Fischer-Hansen (1994) 48–53.

30. Hansen and Fischer-Hansen (1994) 81, 85. Exceptions are the Archaic *prytaneion* on Siphnos (Hdt. 3.57.3–4), and *stoa basileios* and the old *bouleuterion* in Athens (Ober and Hedrick (1993) 73, 121).

31. The only attestations in the Classical period of the *agora* used as assembly place are in fifth-century laws from Gortyn (*I.Cret.* IV 72.X.34–5; XI.12–14). In Athens in 404 under the Thirty Tyrants an extraordinary meeting of the Assembly was held in the *agora* (Arist. *Ath. Pol.* 38).

32. Meiggs–Lewis, *GHI* 93.3 (Lykia); Thuc. 2.71.2 (Plataiai); Migeotte (1992) 69.9–21 (Kolophon). Schachter (1992); Marinatos and Hägg (1993).

33. Thuc. 1.10.1–2; Heracl. Cret. 28; Aen. Tact. 10.15; 31.15; Gruben (1986).

34. Heracl. Cret. 1, 28; Aen. Tact. 1.9, 3.5, 22.4. Rossetto and Sartorio (1994–6); Frederiksen (2002*a*) 85–7, 97–120.

35. Ehrenberg (1969) 28; Welwei (1998) 14.

36. The sanctuary of Poseidon Hippios in Mantinea (*CPCInv.* 518); of Hera on Samos (*CPCInv.* 1097).

37. The sanctuaries of Hera at Argos (*CPCInv.* 605), of Asklepios at Epidauros (*CPCInv.* 607). The major sanctuaries of Elis and Miletos were those at Olympia (*CPCInv.* 498) and Didyma (*CPCInv.* 1087).

38. De Polignac (1995) 21–5, 33–41.

39. Martin (1974) 253–5.

40. Schachter (1992) 36.

41. Festivals in the *polis*: Aen. Tact. 10.4; in the *chora*: Aen. Tact. 17.1.

42. Muggia (1997); Hansen (2006*b*) 37–47.

43. Lawrence (1979); Ducrey (1995) 253–5; *supra* 73.

44. Bertelli (1978) 41–4.

45. Hansen (1997*c*) 52–3.

46. Aen. Tact. 28.1–4.

47. Thuc. 7.29.3; Xen. *Hell.* 5.4.20.

48. Andoc. 1.38.

49. Arist. *Pol.* 1331ᵃ12.

50. Hdt. 1.153; cf. Hansen (1997c) 61; Heracl. Cret. 28; Arist. *Pol.* 1321ᵇ12. Kenzler (1999); cf. Hansen in *30 CSC*: 180 n. 255.
51. Aen. Tact. 8.2; Arist. *Pol.* 1327ᵃ32ff.; Ps.-Skylax 13, 34; *IG* IX² 717.4 (Chaleion).
52. Xen. *Hiero* 11.2; Thuc. 3.72.3 (Korkyra); Theopomp. fr. 62; Arist. *Oec.* 1346ᵇ19 (Byzantion).
53. Arist. *Pol.* 1321ᵇ13; Meiggs–Lewis, *GHI* 45 (10). Kenzler (1999).
54. Ar. *Ach.* 719; *IG* I³ 1087–90.
55. Arist. *Pol.* 1327ᵃ31; Theopomp. fr. 62; Hdt. 2. 178–9.
56. Hom. *Il.* 18.497; *Od.* 2.7, 6.266–7, 8.5; *I.Cret.* IV 43.Bb.5–6 (Gortyn); *SEG* 32 908.1 (Phaistos).
57. Hansen (1997c) 60–1. *Supra* ch. 16 n. 31.
58. Dem. 18.169.
59. One *stoa*: Xen. *Hell.* 5.2.29 (Thebes); two *stoai*: Heracl. Cret. 23 (Anthedon); three *stoai*: Heracl. Cret. 28 (Chalkis). Coulton (1976).
60. *IG* XII.2 14; cf. *SEG* 26 878; 34 850. Coulton (1976) 10–11.
61. Thuc. 7.29.5 (Mykalessos); Hdt. 6.27.2 (Chios); Paus. 6.9.6 (Astypalaia).
62. Anac. fr. 106.D.4, Campbell; Antiph. 3.β.3; Pl. *Euthyd.* 271c; Theophr. *Char.* 5.7.
63. Aen. Tact. 23.6; *I.Cret.* IV 64 (Gortyn); Heracl. Cret. 1 (Athens); Xen. *Hell.* 3.2.27 (Elis); Xen. *Hell.* 5.2.25 (Thebes).
64. Heracl. Cret. 28 (Chalkis); Arist. *Oec.* 1346ᵇ18 (Byzantion).
65. *SEG* 27 261 (law about the *gymnasion* of Beroia in Macedonia, second century). In the second century AD a *gymnasion* was seen as an institution that a city had to have in order to be a *polis*: Paus. 10.4.1; Delorme (1960) 93–230.
66. *SB* i. 30 no. 355 (Naukratis).
67. Alexis fr. 272.
68. A hippodrome is attested already in Homer *Il.* 23.330, but not again until the fourth century: Aeschin. 3.88 (Tamynai); Dem. 47.53, 76; Xen. *Hipp.* 3.1.5 (Athens); Xen. *Hell.* 3.4.16 (Ephesos); Xen. *Hell.* 6.5.30 (Sparta); Pl. *Criti.* 117c (Atlantis).
69. The oldest attestations of theatres in Greek literature are Hdt. 6.67.3 (Sparta) and Thuc. 8.93.1 (Mounichia in Peiraieus).
70. Müller-Wiener (1988) 166–8.
71. The only known Archaic theatre is that in Thorikos (phase 1: 525–480). In Metapontion there is a circular auditorium which may have been used as a theatre (phase I: late seventh century; phase II: mid-sixth century; phase III: 500–475). Theatres of the fifth century have been found in Argos, Athens, Chaironeia, Ikarion, Isthmia, Corinth and Syracuse. See Frederiksen (2002a, b).
72. Bieber (1961); Isler (1994).

Chapter 17: Polis *as State*

1. *Supra* 77.
2. Argos, Athens, Byzantion, Elis, Eretria, Kyrene, Megalopolis, Miletos, Pantikapaion, Rhegion, Rhodos, Sparta/Lakedaimon, Syracuse. *CPCInv.* 72.
3. *CPCInv.* 70–3.
4. Hansen in *30 CSC*: 613–14.
5. Athens: *IG* II² 1835–1923; Kroll (1972); Hansen (1991) 181–2. Kamarina: *SEG* 42 846; Cordano (1992); Murray (1997). Styra: *IG* XII.9 56.
6. Keos: *IG* XII.5 609; *supra* 70.
7. *IG* XII.9 240–9.
8. The size of the contingent of hoplites provided by each city-state is reported for the Battle of Plataiai in 479 by Hdt. 9.28 and for the Battle of Nemea in 394 by Xen. *Hell.* 4.2.16.
9. Hansen (1985) 11–13, 36–43.
10. Hdt. 6.92.1; Thuc. 1.105.2. Figueira (1981) 29–43 presumes that Aigina in the fifth century had a total population of *c.*35,000–45,000 (citizens, foreigners and slaves).
11. The walls of the city of Aigina enclosed an area of *c.*50 ha, and on the island there are no traces of other settlements of the Archaic or Classical periods.
12. Hansen (1985) 65, 69; (1988) 14–28.
13. Cawkwell (2002) 237–50.
14. Pl. *Resp.* 423a; *Pol.* 292e (full citizens); cf. Arist. *Pol.* 1262ª4; 1265ª 9–10.
15. Pl. *Leg.* 737e–38a, 745c; Arist. *Pol.* 1265ª10–17.
16. Hippodamos: Arist. *Pol.* 1267ᵇ30–1 (utopian *polis*). Aitna: Diod. 11. 49.1–2. Herakleia in Oiteia: Diod. 12.59.5. Kyrene: *SEG* 9 1.6. Schaefer (1961).
17. *Supra* 80 Table 7 and 81 Tables 8 and 9.
18. Arist. *Pol.* 1326ª18–20.
19. Hansen (1988) 10–11; Athens: Whitehead (1977); other *poleis*: Whitehead (1984).
20. Thuc. 1.55.1 (Korkyra); *IG* II² 1951; Thuc. 7.13.2; Isoc. 8.48; Dem. 4.36 (all Athens). Welwei (1974–7); Garlan (1988) 165–9; Graham (1998); Hunt (1998) 81–101.
21. Hdt. 7.229.1; Thuc. 7.75.5. Pritchett (1971) 49–51.
22. Ath. 272D. Hansen (1988) 11–12.
23. Hansen (2006*b*) 77–91.
24. 10 per cent: Ruschenbusch (1982) 180. 20 per cent: Cherry *et al.* (1991) 237; Bintliff (1991) 151. 50 per cent: Greaves (2002) 103.
25. Hansen (1996*a*).

26. Arist. *Pol.* 1252ª24–53a39.
27. Arist. *Pol.* 1253ᵇ2–7.
28. Arist. *Pol.* 1274ᵇ32–76ᵇ 15.
29. Arist. *Pol.* 1276ᵇ1. Hansen (1998) 133–4.
30. Arist. *Pol.* 1257ª7–8; 1326ª18–20.
31. Busolt (1920) 224–30.
32. Lycurg. 1.79; Arist. *Pol.* 1297ᵇ12–13. Hansen (1994*b*) 95–6.
33. Thuc. 2.37.1; Arist. *Pol.* 1274ᵇ38; cf. the 158 Aristotelian *politeiai*, i.e. descriptions of the constitutions of 158 different polities of which the majority were *poleis* (Diog. Laert. 5.27). Hansen (1994*b*).
34. The *politai* are the matter of the *polis* (Arist. *Pol.* 1325ᵇ39–26ª 5), the *politeia* is its form (Arist. *Pol.* 1276ᵇ2–11).
35. Aeschin. 3.8. Hansen (1998) 133 with n. 631.
36. Arist. *Pol.* 1278ᵇ8–10. Hansen (1994*b*).
37. Arist. *Pol.* 1279ª22–80ª 6. Each of the three basic forms is subdivided into a positive and a negative subspecies, so that Aristotle operates with altogether six forms: kingship and tyranny, aristocracy and oligarchy, citizen constitution and democracy. For *politeia* in the sense of 'citizen constitution' as the positive form of popular government, see Hansen (1994*b*) 95–7.
38. Pind. *Pyth.* 2.86–8; Hdt. 3.80–2; Xen. *Mem.* 4.6.12; *Cyrop.* 1.1.1; Pl. *Resp.* 338e, *Pol.* 291c–92a, *Leg.* 712c; Lys. 6.30; Aeschin. 1.4; Isoc. 12.132. De Romilly (1959); Bleicken (1979).
39. *I.Ilion* 25.19–22; *I.Erythrai* 503.2–6; *Tit. Cal.* XII 21–2.
40. Pierson (1996) 27–30.
41. Riesenberg (1992) 106–17, 140–86.
42. *IG* IV 841.12. Lévy (1985).
43. Solon fr. 4.6; Anac. *Anth. Gr.* 6.143.3–4 =fr. 106D, Campbell; Dem. 57.46. *Polites* and *astos* are juxtaposed at Arist. *Ath. Pol.* 26.4.
44. *Syll.*³ 1015.6–7 (Halikarnassos); *Egypt. I. Metr.* 33.1 (Naukratis). The feminine form *politis* is sometimes used about women who are citizens by birth: Arist. *Pol.* 1275ᵇ33; 1278ª28; *IG* XII.7 386.21 (Aigiale); *IG* V.2 268B.31 (Mantinea); *I.Kos* 178.6 (Kos). On Athens, see Mossé (1985). There is no attestation of *politis* applied to a female citizen who participates in the running of the political institutions.
45. By participating in the foundation of a new colony a colonist lost the status of citizen in the *metropolis*: Graham (1964) 111, 117. Double citizenship did occur, e.g. by naturalisation: Busolt (1920) 229–30; Hansen (1998) 115 n. 586.
46. Arist. *Pol.* 1275ᵇ22–4.
47. Arist. *Pol.* 1275ª22–3.
48. Arist. *Pol.* 1275ᵇ5–6.
49. Arist. *Pol.* 1292ª39–41, 1293ª12–17, 1320ᵇ25–6, 1308ª2 ff.

50. Arist. *Pol.* 1284ª3, 1287ª8–12, 1295ª17–21.

51. Aesch. *Supp.* 370–5. Hansen (1998) 75–6.

52. Arist. *Pol.* 1293ᵇ27–30; Soph. *Ant.* 737; Eur. *Supp.* 429–32; Aen. Tact. 10.11. Berve (1967) p. x.

53. *IG* XII.9 192.4–5 (Eretria); *Syll.*³ 222 (Miletos). Quass (1979); Gauthier (1993) 217–25; Ma (1999) 161.

54. Arist. *Pol.* 1286ᵇ20–2, 1291ᵇ7–13, 1296ª22–3, 1301ᵇ39–40. Demosthenes, on the other hand, claims that oligarchy is the most common form of constitution and that Athens is the only democracy left in Hellas (15.19).

55. *CPCInv.* 80–6 with the index, 1338–40.

56. Some oligarchies had no popular assembly (Arist. *Pol.* 1275ᵇ7) but many had (Arist. *Pol.* 1298ᵇ26–38). Among oligarchies with an Assembly are Sparta (Plut. *Lyc.* 6; cf. Andrewes (1966)) and Thebes (Hdt. 5.79.1). The typical Cretan *polis* seems to have had an Assembly of the People with limited powers (Arist. *Pol.* 1272ª10–12).

57. Syracuse under Dionysios I: Diod. 14.64.5; Arist. *Oec.* 1349ª34. Athens under the Peisistratids: Arist. *Ath. Pol.* 16.8. Rhodes (1981) 218–19.

58. Xen. *Hiero*; Arist. *Pol.* 1313ª34–15ᵇ 10. Mossé (1969).

59. *SEG* 9 1, trans. in Austin (1981) no. 264.

60. For a full list with references—all to *poleis* other than Athens—see Hansen (2002) 24–5.

61. Hansen (1987) 108–18 treating the Athenian material. For a survey of decrees and laws from all *poleis*, see Rhodes and Lewis (1997).

62. N. Jones (1987) 4–10.

63. Thus in Attika: Osborne (1985); Whitehead (1986); Eretria: Knoepfler (1997) 355–71; Rhodos: Gabrielsen (1997) 29–31, 116–20.

64. Mantinea: *SEG* 37 340; Xen. *Hell.* 5.2.7; T. H. Nielsen (2002) 358–9. Megara: Plut. *Mor.* 295B–C; *IG* VII 1; Legon (1981) 47–55. Naxos: Arist. fr. 566.

65. Many Dorian *poleis* were organised into three *phylai*: Hylleis, Dymanes and Pamphyloi: Tyrt. fr. 19.8 (Sparta); sometimes a fourth *phyle* was added for which each *polis* has a different name: *IG* IV 517 (Argos); *SEG* 39 411 (Megara); Hdt. 5.68 (Sikyon). Similarly, there were six old Ionian *phylai*: Aigikoreis, Argadeis, Boreis, Geleontes, Hopletes and Oinopes: *CIG* 3664. Roussel (1976) 161–310; N. Jones (1987) 11–12.

66. C.40 *phratriai* in Epidauros: *IG* IV².1 pp. 166–7. Roussel (1976) 93–157; on the *phratriai* in Athens, see Lambert (1993).

67. *Gene* in Kolophon: *American Journal of Philology* (1935) 377–9 no. 3; cf. Hansen (2004c) 126. Bourriot (1976); Parker (1996) 56–66, 284–327 about the *gene* in Athens.

68. On Samos the *gene* became identical with the *hekatostyes*: Shipley

(1987) 184–5. In Kamarina numbered *phratriai* were introduced *c.*460: Cordano (1992); cf. Lambert (1993) 9–10. Kamiros created a system of *patrai*: Andrewes (1957).

69. For all the activities within the powers of civic subdivisions, see Analytical Index III in N. Jones (1987) 396–404. For the Attic demes, see Whitehead (1986). Two of the best sources for civic subdivisions outside Athens are the regulations for the *phratria* of the Labyadai at Delphi (*CID* I 9, fourth century) and the decrees passed by the *phratria* of the Klytidai at Chios (Michel, *Recueil* 997, fourth century).

70. For all the activities not performed by civic subdivisions the evidence is negative, i.e. an argument from silence based on the very rich sources we have for what civic subdivisions actually did.

71. Arist. *Pol.* 1253ᵃ1–4.

72. Arist. *Pol.* 1283ᵇ42–84ᵃ 3; 1324ᵃ15, 27; 1326ᵇ5–9.

73. Hansen (1989*b*); Murray (1990) 19–22, (1996).

Chapter 18: Army

1. Stesimbrotos (*FGrHist* 107) fr. 9; Isae. 5.42. T. H. Nielsen (2004) 56–8; *CPCInv.* 49–50.

2. *Hell. Oxy.* 19.4; Thuc. 4.93.4.

3. Cf. Herodotos' description of the Greek army at Plataiai in 479 (Hdt. 9.28; cf. Meiggs–Lewis, *GHI* 27) and Thucydides' description of the Boiotian army at Delion in 424 (Thuc. 4.93.3–4).

4. Hanson (1989); Pritchett (1985) 1–93; Schwartz (2004).

5. *IG* I³ 1.8–10.

6. Arist. *Pol.* 1321ᵃ5–14.

7. Raaflaub (1997*b*) 53.

8. Arist. *Pol.* 1265ᵇ26–9, 1279ᵇ2–4, 1297ᵇ1–16; Thuc. 8.97.1.

9. Arist. *Pol.* 1297ᵇ24–5. Called *politeia* in the specific sense.

10. Murray (1993) 159–80.

11. Plut. *Lyc.* 6.2; Hornblower (1992) 1–2; Hansen (1999*b*).

12. e.g. by Raaflaub (1997*b*) 53–7, emphasising the gradual development and the constant interaction of the military and political aspects. The emergence of the hoplite *phalanx* is now dated to the eighth century (Hanson (1991) 64–5, 74–8).

13. Thuc. 2.13.7, 2.31.1–2. Whitehead (1977) 82–6.

14. Aen. Tact. 13.1–4; Dem. 1.19–22. Parke (1933); Griffith (1934); Bettalli (1995); McKechnie (1989) 79–100.

Chapter 19: Religion

1. Fustel de Coulanges (1864) 5, 194–219 *et passim*. For a perspicacious critique of Fustel de Coulanges' basic idea and method, see Glotz (1928) 2–6.

2. Sourvinou-Inwood (1990) 295, 322; Kearns (1996*a*) 1300.

3. Zaidman and Schmitt Pantel (1992) 8.

4. Sourvinou-Inwood (1990) 322; Kearns (1996*a*) 1300; Bowden (2005) 7–11.

5. In my endeavour to see religion as one important aspect of the *polis* but not necessarily the predominant one, I follow Walter Burkert (1985), (1992) and (1995). With Moses Finley (1981*b*) 23 I share the 'insistence on the secular quality of public life', and with Oswyn Murray I share the view of the *polis* as an essentially rational community centred on its political institutions; see Murray (1990) 19–22, (2000) 241–2, and Hansen (1989*b*), (1991) 63–4, (1997*c*), 57.

6. Snodgrass (1980) 33, 58; Sourvinou-Inwood (1993) 11; de Polignac (1994) 15; Voyatzis (1999) 150–3.

7. The temple for Apollo in Syracuse built by Kleomenes (*IG* XIV 1. Hellmann (1999) 100); the temple for Apollo in Delphi re-erected by the Alkmaionidai (Hdt. 5.62.2–63.1; Arist. *Ath. Pol.* 19.4); a temple for Artemis in Skillous built by Xenophon (Xen. *An.* 5.3.7–9).

8. Thus the priestess of Athena Nike *c*.450 (Meiggs–Lewis, *GHI* 44).

9. *SEG* 43 630. Jameson *et al.* (1993) 114–16.

10. Arist. *Ath. Pol.* 60.2.

11. Parker (1983) 160–3.

12. Mikalson (1975).

13. *IG* XII *Suppl.* 236 (Koresia); Costabile (1992) nos. 1–39 (Epizephyrian Lokris). Migeotte (1998).

14. See also N. Jones (1999) 132–3.

15. Sacrifice before a battle: Thuc. 6.69; Pritchett (1971) 109–15. Sacrifice before a meeting of the Assembly: Aeschin. 1.23; Hansen (1987) 90.

16. Vidal-Naquet (1983) 26; Bruhns (1994) 79–83. In almost all sources the exclusion of women from politics and armed forces is taken for granted, and therefore not explicitly prohibited. For Athens, see the shocking idea 'to hand over the *polis* to the women' and give them political rights (Ar. *Eccl.* 210) or to allow them to join in the defence of the *polis* (Pl. *Resp.* 451c–57c). The explicit exclusion of women from the *prytaneion* of the *polis* is attested, e.g., for Naukratis (Ath. 150A). Again, although in the Hellenistic period there are numerous honorific decrees for women (e.g. *IG* XII.7 36, Amorgos, second century BC), it is extremely rare to find citizenship among the privileges bestowed on a female honourand. One example is the poet Aristodama of Smyrna (third century BC). In Chalaia she is honoured with *proxenia*, and her brother with *politeia* (*F. Delphes* III.3 145), but in Lamia she herself obtains both *proxenia* and *politeia* (*Syll.*³ 532). Another example is the Molossians' grant of citizenship to Philista, the wife of Antimachos, during the reign of Neoptolemos (fourth century BC) (*AE* (1956/9) 3).

In the Hellenistic period women are sometimes honoured as *euergetai* and entrusted with liturgies; see van Bremen (1996) 13–19, 25–30.

17. *Supra* 111–12.
18. Just (1989) 23; Parker (1996) 80; N. Jones (1999) 123–8.
19. 'Women were sometimes excluded from the cults of Poseidon, Zeus, and Ares, all emphatically masculine gods' (Parker (1983) 85). For the exclusion of women from the cult of Poseidon, see, e.g., *Syll.*³ 1024.9 = *LSCG* 96, Mykonos, *c*.200 BC.
20. A cult for Demeter celebrated by married women of citizen status. The *thesmophoria* are the most widespread Greek festival and attested in a large number of *poleis*. Burkert (1985) 242–6.
21. Holdermann (1985); van Bremen (1996) 28–30.
22. Kearns (1996*b*); N. Jones (1999) 122–33.
23. Arist. *Pol.* 1322ᵇ18–22.
24. Hansen (1991) 63. In Aristotle's ideal *polis* too the priests are separated from the magistrates (Arist. *Pol.* 1331ᵇ4–5).
25. Arist. *Pol.* 1322ᵇ22–5.
26. Burkert (1992) 534.
27. Sinn (1993).
28. In *c*.632 BC Kylon attempted to set himself up as the tyrant of Athens. He escaped, and his followers took refuge at an altar on the *akropolis*. Although they were manifestly guilty of treason, it was considered a sacrilege and a pollution of the whole city when the Athenian archons had them dragged away from the altar and executed (Thuc. 1.126.10–11). The Spartan officials did not dare to have Pausanias killed in the temple of the goddess of the brazen House (Thuc. 1.134.1–2).
29. Zaidman and Schmitt-Pantel (1992) 102–11.
30. Pl. *Resp.* 419a. Aleshire (1994) discusses the difference in Athens between private cults and state cults.
31. *Syll.*³ 1015 (Halikarnassos). It must of course be remembered that even private sacrifices were made at public shrines with the services of the public priest(ess).
32. Jost (1992) 262–80.
33. Burkert (1995) 202.
34. *Supra* ch. 19 n. 15.
35. e.g. *IG* XII.8 356 (sixth century BC), where Dionysos and Herakles are commemorated as the protectors of the *polis* Thasos. See Cole (1995) 297–301, noting that some *poleis* had no identifiable patron divinity, whereas others had several.
36. Both Dionysos and Herakles are shown on the coins of Thasos (Head (1911) 264–6.
37. McDonald (1943) 115, 132, 135–7, 167, 179, 200, 279–83.
38. *IG* II² 1496.131–2, 140–1. Raubitschek (1962).

39. Head (1911) 616; *SNG Cop. Caria* 305.
40. Balty (1981).
41. S. G. Miller (1978).

Chapter 20: State and Society

1. Claimed already by Benjamin Constant in 1819 ((1980) 495), followed by Fustel de Coulanges (1864) 280–6 and still maintained by, e.g., Finley (1963) 49–50; Ostwald (1986) p. xix. *Contra* Hansen (1998) 84–97.
2. Popper (1962) 102–3 quotes and discusses Pl. *Leg.* 739c ff., 942a ff.
3. Pl. *Resp.* 544a; *Ep.* 326a; Arist. *Pol.* 1260^{b}34–5.
4. Xen. *Lac. Pol. passim*. A. Powell (1988) 214–62.
5. Pl. *Leg.* 666d ff.; Plut. *Lyc.* 24.1.
6. Xen. *Lac. Pol.* 8.1, 10.4. Both passages emphasise the difference between Sparta and other *poleis*.
7. e.g. Pl. *Cri.* 52e, *Resp.* 544c; Arist. *Pol.* 1269^{a}29–71^b 19, see also 1288^{b}41–89^a 1, 1293^{b}16–18, 1296^{a}18–21. We must not forget, however, that both Plato and Aristotle took a very critical view of many Spartan institutions; Aristotle's account in Book 2 of this allegedly well-ordered *polis* amounts to one long series of points of criticism. The philosophers' principal reservation is that Spartan society is one-eyed and focused on the military aspects of human life (Pl. *Lach.* 182e; Arist. *Pol.* 1271^{b}2–3, 1324^{b}7–9, 1333^{b}12–35, 1334^{a}40–^{b} 4, 1338^{b}9–14). But in spite of the frequent strictures passed on Sparta by Plato and Aristotle, their basic view seems to be that it is better to be one-eyed than blind. For an illuminating account of Plato's and Aristotle's views of Sparta see Rawson (1969) 61–80.
8. Thuc. 2.39.2; Dem. 20.105–8.
9. Dem. 24.192–3; 18.210 (Athens); *IG* V.2 6.A.II.39 (Tegea); *IG* XII.9 189.36–7 (Eretria); Hornblower (1982) M7.2 (Labraunda). Musti (1985); Hansen (1998) 86–91.
10. One example is the laws about schools. All schools were private, but in the speech *Against Timarchos* Aischines quotes some laws about the age of children sent to school, the number of children in a class, opening hours of schools and sports centres, etc. (Aeschin. 1.9–11); for laws about schools see also Pl. *Cri.* 50c–e.
11. To live as one likes (*zen hos bouletai tis*) is cherished by the Athenian democrats as a fundamental ideal (Thuc. 2.37.2, 7.69.2; Lys. 26.5; Dem. 10.4, 25.25; cf. Hdt. 3.83.2), but it is dismissed as a democratic vice by the critics of popular rule (Pl. *Resp.* 557b–58c, *Leg.* 701b–c. *Def.* 412d; Isoc. 7.20, 37; 12.131; Theopomp. fr. 62. Cf. also Arist. *Pol.* 1317^{b}11–17, 1310^{a}32, 1316^{b}24, 1318^{b}39–40, 1319^{b}30).
12. Hdt. 5.78.1; Eur. *Supp.* 438–41; Aeschin. 1.173; Dem. 9.3, 20.105–8.

Dover (1988) ii. 135–8; Hansen (1995*d*) 19–21. The limits of freedom of speech are stressed by Mulgan (1984) 15.

13. Hansen (1998) 105–6.

14. Rousseau (1782) 957: 'Sparte n'etoit qu'une ville, il est vrais; mais par la seule force de son institution cette ville donna des loix à toute la Grece, en devint la capitale, et fit trembler l'Empire persan. Sparte étoit le foyer d'ou sa législation étendoit ses effets tout autour d'elle.' Swoboda (1913) 11–13; Rawson (1969); Hansen (1992) 18.

15. A typical example is Benjamin Constant's famous and influential essay *De la liberté des anciens comparée à celle des modernes* (1819) in which Sparta is repeatedly singled out as the typical *polis* ((1980) 494–5, 500, 509), whereas Athens is taken to be the exception (496, 500 with n. 14).

16. Roberts (1994) 238–55.

17. Gehrke (1986).

18. Hansen (1998) 98–106. But against the view of, *inter alios* me, Hodkinson (2005) argues that Sparta in many respects was a typical *polis*.

19. Cartledge (2000) 16.

Chapter 21: Civil War (Stasis)

1. *Supra* ch. 18 n. 1. T. H. Nielsen (2004).

2. Pl. *Resp.* 422e; 551d; *Leg.* 945e; Arist. *Pol.* 1310ª4 ff.; Eur. fr. 173, Nauck; cf. Thuc. 3.82–83.4; Bederman (2001) 130–4.

3. Pl. *Resp.* 555b, 557a; Arist. *Pol.* 1266ª37–8, 1289ᵇ27–40, 1290ᵇ18–20, 1302ª10–13, 1303ª1–2.

4. Arist. *Pol.* 1303ª25–ᵇ 7 with eight examples: Sybaris, Thourioi, Byzantion, Antissa, Zankle, Apollonia Pontika, Syracuse and Amphipolis.

5. Arist. *Pol.* 1305ᵇ2–6ᵇ 2 with twenty-two examples.

6. Thuc. 3.82.8; Arist. *Pol.* 1301ª20–5 and the rest of Book 5. Gehrke (2001).

7. Thuc. 3.82.1; Arist. *Pol.* 1307ᵇ19–25; Ps.-Xen. *Ath. Pol.* 1.14, 3.10; Isoc. 16.17.

8. *Stasis* in the Archaic period: Lintott (1982) 13–81; in the Classical period: Gehrke (1985); southern Italy and Sicily are covered by Berger (1992).

9. (1) Hdt. 9.21.2; (2) Hermagoras fr. 10, Matthes; (3) Thuc. 7.50.1; (4) Thuc. 4.71.1; Arist. *Ath. Pol.* 13.4; (5) Arist. *Pol.* 1302ª9–13; (6) Solon fr. 4.19; Hdt. 8.3.1.

10. Hdt. 1.59–60 (Athens); Thuc. 4.71.1 (Megara); Thuc. 7.50.1 (Akragas); Arist. *Oec.* 1348ᵇ1 (Phokaia).

11. Or, rather, hardly ever. For an exceptional use of *stasis* to denote a constitutional faction, see Thuc. 2.22.3.

12. Hansen (1987) 74.

13. *CPCInv.* 124–9 with the index, 1361–2. Earlier surveys in Gehrke (1985); Berger (1992).
14. Thuc. 5.33.1 (Parrhasian *poleis* in Arkadia); Xen. *Hell.* 7.1.41–3 (Achaian *poleis* in 366).
15. Berger (1992) 34–53.
16. *IG* I³ 14.32 ff. (Erythrai); Meiggs–Lewis, *GHI* 83 (Thasos); *IG* XII.9 190 (Eretria); Tod, *GHI* 191 (Eresos); *Syll.*³ 360 (Chersonesos); *I.Ilion* 25 (Ilion).
17. Seibert (1979) 353–407; McKechnie (1989) 16–33.
18. *IvO* 22 (Selinus); *IG* XII.2 6 (Mytilene); Tod, *GHI* 192 (Chios); *SEG* 30 1119 (Nakona); Arist. *Ath. Pol.* 39 (Athens). Seibert (1979) 401–2.
19. Gehrke (1985) 359; cf. Thuc. 4.86.4–5.
20. Ste Croix (1954–5) 29, countering Ehrenberg's claim ((1947) 48) that liberty (*eleutheria*) and independence (*autonomia*) were the fundamental values of the *polis*.
21. Xen. *Mem.* 4.4.16. Thériault (1996).

Chapter 22: Relationships between Poleis

1. Kienast (1973); Adcock and Mosley (1975); Bederman (2001) 88–120.
2. *Presbeis*: Thuc. 1.24.6 (Epidamnos). *Presbeutai*: *IG* XII.5 1004.3 (Ios). Kienast (1973) 507–10.
3. Meiggs–Lewis, *GHI* 65.16–17; Plut. *Per.* 17.2.
4. Meiggs–Lewis, *GHI* 45.(9); *CID* II 31.49; Adcock and Mosley (1975) 152–4.
5. Perlman (2000) 14–16, 45–60.
6. Hom. *Il.* 6.224–31. Herman (1987).
7. Gschnitzer (1973); Marek (1984); Bederman (2001) 130–4.
8. Wallace (1970) 190; Gschnitzer (1973) 632. *Proxenos* can also mean 'one who assists a foreigner': Marek (1984) 387.
9. Meiggs–Lewis, *GHI* 82.
10. De Romilly (1968) 207–11.
11. A. H. M. Jones (1940) 236, 256; Camp (2000) 50.
12. Kelly (1976) 49–50, 64–5, 73–7, 86–9, 95, 99, 127–8, 138.
13. Meritt, Wade-Gery and McGregor (1939) 461–566; *CPCInv.* 111–14 with the index, 1356–60.
14. Wickert (1961).
15. *Supra* 53.
16. *CPCInv.* 120–3 with the index, 1363–4.
17. Paus. 8.28.1. Demand (1990) 59–61; Piérart (1997) 333–7; J. M. Hall (1995).
18. Shipley (1997); J. M. Hall (2000). *Contra* Mertens (2002), countered by Hansen (2004*b*).

19. Huxley (1966) 120–2. On the conditions after the King's Peace of 386, see Debord (1999) 279–82.
20. Diod. 14.82.1 = *Staatsverträge* no. 225.
21. Meiggs (1972); Schuller (1974).
22. Wickert (1961); Ste Croix (1972) 96–124; Lendon (1994).
23. Helisson was dependent on Mantinea (*SEG* 37 340 = RO 14); Mykalessos was dependent on Tanagra (Thuc. 7.29–30; Strabo 9.2.11, 14) or Thebes (*CPCInv.* 88 n. 4); Notion was dependent on Kolophon (Arist. *Pol.* 1303^{b}10). Hansen (1997*d*) 31, 35.
24. The Corinthian colonies in western Greece were to some extent governed from their *metropolis*, i.e. Corinth: Graham (1964) 118–53; one of them was Ambrakia (Thuc. 2.80.3; Arist. *Pol.* 1304^{a}1–3, 1311^{a}40): Hansen (1997*d*) 33.
25. Xen. *Hell.* 5.1.31 (the King's Peace of 386), thus e.g. Mylasa (Tod, *GHI* 138; Hansen (1997*d*) 36).
26. The Boiotian Federation was dominated by Thebes, and the Thebans deprived all the smaller Boiotian *poleis* of their *autonomia* and reduced them to dependencies: Xen. *Hell.* 3.5.18, 4.8.15, 5.1.32–6, 6.4.3; Andoc. 3.13, 20; Isoc. 4.175–6, 15.10, 17. Hansen (1995*a*) 35, (1996*d*), (2004*b*) 157–60; *CPCInv.* 92–3. *Contra* Keen (1996); Rhodes (1998).
27. Thuc. 1.67.2; 1.139.1, 3; 1.140.3–4; 1.144.2; 3.10.5; 4.87.5; 7.57.3; 3.46.5. Schuller (1974) 109–24; Ste Croix (1972) 96–101.
28. Gauthier (1993); Millar (1993).
29. *Contra* the peer polity interaction model, described in Renfrew and Cherry (1986).
30. *Contra* all historians who claim that *eleutheria* and/or *autonomia* (understood as independence) were the essential characteristics of the *polis*: Will (1972) 416; Thomas and Griffeth (1981) pp. xiii, xv; Thomas (1981) 40; Duthoy (1986) 7; Osborne (1987) 11; Murray (1993) 62; Snodgrass (1986) 47; Zeidman and Schmitt-Pantel (1992) 7; Cawkwell (1996) 98–115.
31. Hansen (1995*a*); (1996*d*); (1997*d*); Hansein in *30 CSC*: 172–3; Hansen (2004*b*) 157–60.
32. Orth (1977) 179–80; Gauthier (1993) 212; Ma (1999) 163–5.
33. J. A. O. Larsen (1968); Beck (1997). Both called leagues, but in fact federations.
34. *Hell. Oxy.* 19. Salmon (1978).
35. Thuc. 4.91.1; *Hell. Oxy.* 19.3.
36. *Staatsverträge* nos. 273, 277, 283, 345.
37. *Hell. Oxy.* 19.3–4.
38. Hansen (1995*b*) 54 n. 21.
39. Chorsiai: *SEG* 24 361; Siphai: Thuc. 4.76.1; Schwandner (1977); Eutresis and Thisbai: *Hell. Oxy.* 19.3.

40. Hes. *Op.* 639–40 & 222; Arist. fr. 580.
41. Hansen (1995*b*) 20–1.
42. J. A. O. Larsen (1966) 33, 38; Beck (1997) 94.
43. Xen. *Hell.* 5.2.19.
44. Roesch (1982) 441–500; Beck (1997) 174–9.

Chapter 23: The Hellenistic Polis

1. Carlsson (2005) 147–66.
2. Carlsson (2005); O'Neill (1995) 103–20.
3. A. H. M. Jones (1940) 113–15, 120–1.
4. Gauthier (1993) 217–25.
5. Davies (1984) 313.
6. Van Bremen (1996); Carlsson (2005) 92–109.
7. A. H. M. Jones (1940) 220–6.
8. Chankowski (forthcoming); Chaniotis (2005) 46–56.
9. Green (1990) 319, 506.
10. Dunand (1973).
11. Thériault (1996).
12. Best attested in Athens; see Whitehead (1986) 360–3.
13. Wilson (1996).
14. Gabrielsen (1997) 123–9.
15. Camp (2000) 50–1.
16. I. Nielsen (1999) 112–28.
17. Kockel (1995).
18. Frederiksen (2002*a*) 111–20.
19. Coulton (1976) 55–74.
20. Von Hesberg (1995).
21. Gauthier (1995). The importance of the *gymnasion* is attested in a second-century law from Beroia in Macedonia about the institution and its personnel (*SEG* 27 261); cf. Gauthier and Hatzopoulos (1993).
22. Martin (1974) 353–5.
23. Martin (1974) 113–18, 163–76; Shipley (2000) 89–96.
24. Nevett (1999) 114–23.
25. Hansen and Fischer-Hansen (1994) 81–5.
26. Hansen (1995*c*) 48–52.
27. J. A. O. Larsen (1968) 173–504.
28. Carlsson (2005) 167–77.
29. Davies (1984) 309; Gawantka (1975).
30. Schmitt (1969).
31. Ager (1996).
32. Tscherikower (1927) and G. M. Cohen (1995).
33. Ma (1999) 153–74.
34. Binder (1999).

35. G. M. Cohen (1995) 63–71.
36. Green (1990) 155–70.

Chapter 24: The *Polis Compared with Other City-State Cultures*

1. *6 CSC*: 12–13 with n. 55. City-state cultures arising by devolution are: (1) possibly the Sumerian city-states *c*.3000; (2) the Sumerian city-states after the collapse of the Assyrian empire (*c*.2250–2200) and in the Isin–Larsa period, (*c*.2000–1800); (3) the Neo-Hittite city-states after *c*.1200; (4) the Syrian city-states after *c*.1000; (5) the Neo-Babylonian city-states after *c*.900; (6) the Chinese city-states in the Spring-and-Autumn period (771–481); (7) the Bènizàa city-states after *c.* AD 800; (8) the Italian city-states after AD 875; (9) the Swiss city-states after AD 1218; (10) the Maya city-states in the post-Mayapan period after *c.* AD 1450; (11) the city-states in Nepal after AD 1482.
2. *30 CSC*: 16–17 with n. 65. Parallels are in the Near East: the first phase of the Syrian and Palestinian city-state cultures, Assur, the Phoenician city-states in the homeland; in the Far East: Sriwijaya, the Taklamakan and Tai city-states; in Europe the Etruscan and Latin city-states; and probably all the African city-state cultures.
3. Thomas and Conant (1999) xxvi–xxviii; Schnapp-Gourbeillon (2002).
4. *Supra* 41.
5. Bintliff (2002) 156, 162.
6. Bintliff (2002) 162, 173.
7. Cycles of city-state cultures are attested, e.g., in Mesopotamia (at least three periods of Sumerian city-states later followed by a fourth period of Babylonian city-states), in Syria (at least three periods of city-states), in Tuscany (Etruscan city-states in antiquity, Italian city-states in the Middle Ages), in East Asia (Sriwijaya in the Middle Ages, the Malay city-states in the Early Modern period), in Mesoamerica (two periods of city-states among the Maya). See *6 CSC*: 7–8, 13–14 with n. 59.
8. *Supra* 44–5.
9. *30 CSC*: 17, 602, 610 (general), 133, 136 (Philistine), 252–4 (Viking), 447 (Mzâb), 584 (Aztec).
10. *30 CSC*: 17 with n. 74; *6 CSC*: 13.
11. *Supra* 25 and 45.
12. Hatzopoulos (1996) 167–260; *CPCInv*. 794.
13. *Supra* 50.
14. *30 CSC*: 593 (Aztec), 531 (Kotoko).
15. *Supra* 11 and 89–90; *30 CSC*: 17, 601.
16. *30 CSC*: 17.
17. *Supra* 55; *30 CSC*: 18, 602.
18. Arist. *Eth. Nic.* 1170^{b}31–2.
19. *30 CSC*: 512–13 (Old Oyo), 586 (Tenochtitlan).

20. *30 CSC*: 215, 602.
21. *30 CSC*: 602, 612; *6 CSC*: 18.
22. *30 CSC*: 18.
23. *30 CSC*: 16.
24. *30 CSC*: 614 with n. 107.
25. *Supra* 58–9.
26. *Supra* 68–9.
27. *30 CSC*: 620 n. 107 (Sumer, quote from Kuhrt (1995) 31); 570 (Mixtec); 587 (Aztecs); 286 (fourteenth century Italy).
28. *Supra* 57–8. *30 CSC*: 16 with n. 57.
29. *Qrt* (Phoenician); *civitas* (Latin); *città* (medieval and Renaissance Italian); *ilu* (Yoruba); *birni* (Hausa); *oman* (Akan); *mji* (Swahili); *guo* (Chinese in the Spring-and-Autumn period); *negeri* (Malay, from Sanskrit); *müang* (Tai); *ahawlel* (Maya); *yuhuitaya* (Mixtec); *Altepetl* (Aztec).
30. *30 CSC*: 31 n. 80.
31. *Supra* 59–61.
32. *30 CSC*: 614–15.
33. *30 CSC*: 79–82, 85–6.
34. *30 CSC*: 90, 96, 98–9, 103.
35. *30 CSC*: 457–8.
36. *30 CSC*: 241–3, 246–8.
37. *30 CSC*: 540–1, 544.
38. *30 CSC*: 468–75.
39. *30 CSC*: 420, cf. 417–21, 423–7.
40. Quoted from Smith (1996) 114.
41. Thuc. 2.38.2; see *supra* 92–3.
42. Not all city-state cultures were trading communities. The Chinese and Philistine city-state cultures, e.g., were basically agrarian; see *30 CSC*: (Philistine) and 371–2 (Chinese).
43. Hansen (1995a) 21–5.
44. Hansen (1995a) 43; *supra* 48–50 and 64–5.
45. Hansen (1998) 46–7; *30 CSC*: 606–8.
46. *30 CSC*: 606; *6 CSC*: 14.
47. *30 CSC*: 277–8, 288–9. For the view, however, that many subject cities were still—to some extent—polities, see Chittolini (1991) 598–9.
48. Thuc. 5.33.1 and 3, 6.84.2–3, 7.57.3; *Hell. Oxy.* 24.1. *CPCInv.* 87–94.
49. *Supra* 49, 55, 130–1.
50. *30 CSC*: 17–19, 606–7, 613–14.
51. Hansen (1993) 18–20; (1995a); *CPCInv.* 87–94.
52. *30 CSC*: 611–12; *6 CSC*: 17.
53. *30 CSC*: 279, 283–5, 288–90.
54. *30 CSC*: 448.

55. *30 CSC*: 470–1, 480.
56. *30 CSC*: 513–14.
57. Hallpike (1972) 66–71.
58. *30 CSC*: 422.
59. *Supra* 112.
60. Jacobsen (1943) even assumed that the early Sumerian city-states were democracies.
61. *6 CSC*: 31, 36; Barjamovic (2004) 49–53.
62. Hansen (2005*b*) 10–11; Millar (2002).
63. Waley (1978) 28–9.
64. P. Jones (1997) 505–19.
65. *Encyclopaedia Britannica*, 1st edn. (1771), ii. 415, s.v. *democracy*; but see Müller (1954).
66. *Supra* 112–14.
67. *30 CSC*: 203–4 (Etruscan); 214 (Latin); 286, 290 (Italian); 307–8 (German; cf. *6 CSC*: 91–106); 329 (Swiss); 348, 350 (Dutch).
68. *30 CSC*: 489–93 (Hausa); 508, 515 (Yoruba).
69. Barjamovic (2004) 55–77.
70. *30 CSC*: 369–72.
71. *30 CSC*: 424–6.
72. *30 CSC*: 589.
73. *30 CSC*: 17 no. 12.
74. *30 CSC*: 32, additional note.
75. *30 CSC*: 491 (Hausa), 589 (Aztec). *6 CSC*: 121–2 (Nepal).
76. *30 CSC*: 361 (Chinese), 520 (Fante).
77. *Supra* 83, 86, 93–4, 141.

References

Works Published by the Polis Centre

1. *Acts*

CPCActs 1   M. H. Hansen (ed.), *The Ancient Greek City-State*, Acts of the Copenhagen Polis Centre 1, Det Kongelige Danske Videnskabernes Selskab, Historisk-filosofiske Meddelelser 67 (Copenhagen, 1993).

CPCActs 2   M. H. Hansen (ed.), *Sources for the Ancient Greek City-State*, Acts of the Copenhagen Polis Centre 2, Det Kongelige Danske Videnskabernes Selskab, Historisk-filosofiske Meddelelser 72 (Copenhagen, 1995).

CPCActs 3   M. H. Hansen (ed.), *Introduction to an Inventory of Poleis*, Acts of the Copenhagen Polis Centre 3, Det Kongelige Danske Videnskabernes Selskab, Historisk-filosofiske Meddelelser 74 (Copenhagen, 1996).

CPCActs 4   M. H. Hansen (ed.), *The Polis as an Urban Centre and as a Political Community*, Acts of the Copenhagen Polis Centre 4, Det Kongelige Danske Videnskabernes Selskab, Historisk-filosofiske Meddelelser 75 (Copenhagen, 1997).

CPCActs 5   M. H. Hansen. *Polis and City-State: An Ancient Concept and its Modern Equivalent*, Acts of the Copenhagen Polis Centre 5, Det Kongelige Danske Videnskabernes Selskab, Historisk-filosofiske Meddelelser 76 (Copenhagen, 1998).

CPCActs 6   T. Heine Nielsen (ed.), *Defining Ancient Arkadia*, Acts of the Copenhagen Polis Centre 6, Det Kongelige Danske Videnskabernes Selskab, Historisk-filosofiske Meddelelser 78 (Copenhagen, 1999).

CPCActs 7   M. H. Hansen (ed.), *The Imaginary Polis*, Acts of the Copenhagen Polis Centre 7, Det Kongelige Danske Videnskabernes Selskab, Historisk-filosofiske Meddelelser 91 (Copenhagen, 2005).

2. *Papers*

CPCPapers 1   D. Whitehead (ed.), *From Political Architecture to Ste-*

phanus Byzantius, Papers from the Copenhagen Polis Centre 1, *Historia* Einzelschriften 87 (Stuttgart, 1994).

CPCPapers 2   M. H. Hansen and K. Raaflaub (eds.), *Studies in the Ancient Greek* Polis, Papers from the Copenhagen Polis Centre 2, *Historia* Einzelschriften 95 (Stuttgart, 1995).

CPCPapers 3   M. H. Hansen and K. Raaflaub (eds.), *More Studies in the Ancient Greek* Polis, Papers from the Copenhagen Polis Centre 3, *Historia* Einzelschriften 108 (Stuttgart, 1996).

CPCPapers 4   T. Heine Nielsen (ed.), *Yet More Studies in the Ancient Greek* Polis, Papers from the Copenhagen Polis Centre 4, *Historia* Einzelschriften 117 (Stuttgart, 1997).

CPCPapers 5   P. Flensted Jensen (ed.), *Further Studies in the Ancient Greek* Polis, Papers from the Copenhagen Polis Centre 5, *Historia* Einzelschriften 138 (Stuttgart, 2000).

CPCPapers 6   T. Heine Nielsen (ed.), *Even More Studies in the Ancient Greek* Polis, Papers from the Copenhagen Polis Centre 6, *Historia* Einzelschriften 162 (Stuttgart, 2002).

CPCPapers 7   T. Heine Nielsen (ed.), *Once Again: Studies in the Ancient Greek* Polis, Papers from the Copenhagen Polis Centre 7, *Historia* Einzelschriften 180 (Stuttgart, 2004).

3. *City-State Cultures*

30 CSC   M. H. Hansen (ed.), *A Comparative Study of Thirty City-State Cultures*, Det Kongelige Danske Videnskabernes Selskab, Historisk-filosofiske Skrifter 21 (Copenhagen, 2000).

6 CSC   M. H. Hansen (ed.), *A Comparative Study of Six City-State Cultures*, Det Kongelige Danske Videnskabernes Selskab, Historisk-filosofiske Skrifter 27 (Copenhagen, 2002).

4. *The Inventory*

CPCInv.   M. H. Hansen and T. Heine Nielsen (eds.), *An Inventory of Archaic and Classical* Poleis (Oxford, 2004).

5. *Alia*

Polis and Politics   P. Flensted-Jensen, T. Heine Nielsen and L. Rubinstein (eds.), *Polis and Politics: Studies in Ancient Greek History Presented to Mogens Herman Hansen on his Sixtieth Birthday, August 20, 2000* (Copenhagen, 2000).

Nielsen (2002)	T. H. Nielsen, *Arkadia and its* Poleis *in the Archaic and Classical Periods*, Hypomnemata 140 (Göttingen).
Hansen (2003)	M. H. Hansen, '95 Theses about the Ancient Greek *Polis* in the Archaic and Classical Periods: A Report on the Results Obtained by the Copenhagen Polis Centre in the Period 1993–2003', *Historia*, 52: 257–82.

Other Works

Adcock, F. and Mosley, D. J. 1975. *Diplomacy in Ancient Greece* (London).

Ager, S. L. 1996. *Interstate Arbitrations in the Greek World 337–90 B.C.* (Berkeley and Los Angeles).

Ainian, A. M. 1987. 'Geometric Eretria', *Antike Kunst*, 30: 1–24.

—— 1997. *From Rulers' Dwellings to Temples: Architecture, Religion and Society in Early Iron Age Greece (1100–700 B.C.)* (Jonsered).

Alcock, S. E. and Cherry, J. F. (eds.) 2004. *Side-by-Side Survey: Comparative Regional Studies in the Mediterranean World* (Oxford).

Aleshire, S. B. 1994. 'Towards a Definition of "State Cult" for Ancient Athens', in R. Hägg (ed.), *Ancient Greek Cult Practice from the Epigraphical Evidence* (Stockholm), 9–16.

Altherr-Charon, A. and Bérard, C. 1980. 'Erétrie: l'organisation de l'espace et la formation d'une cité grecque', in A. Schnapp (ed.), *L'Archéologie aujourd'hui* (Paris), 229–49.

Ammann, H. 1978. 'Wie gross war die mittelalterliche Stadt?', in C. Haase (ed.), *Die Stadt des Mittelalters*, 3 vols. (Darmstadt), i: 415–22.

Andreau, J. 2002. 'Twenty Years after Moses I. Finley's *The Ancient Economy*', in Scheidel and von Reden (2002) 33–49.

Andrewes, A. 1957. 'The *Patrai* of Kamiros', *Annual of the British School at Athens*, 52: 30–7.

—— 1966. 'The Government of Classical Sparta', in *Ancient Society and Institutions* (Oxford), 8–17.

Arnold, C. J. 1997. *An Archaeology of the Early Anglo-Saxon Kingdoms*, 2nd edn. (London).

Audring, G. 1989. *Zur Struktur des Territoriums griechischer Poleis in archaischer Zeit (nach den schriftlichen Quellen)* (Berlin).

Austin, M. M. 1981. *The Hellenistic World from Alexander to the Roman Conquest* (Cambridge).

—— and Vidal-Naquet, P. 1977. *Economic and Social History of Ancient Greece* (London).

Bairoch, P. 1988. *Cities and Economic Development from the Dawn of History to the Present* (Chicago).

Balty, J. Ch. 1981. 'Antiocheia', in *Lexicon Iconographicum Mythologiae Classicae* (Zurich and Munich), i. 840–51.

Barjamovic, G. 2004. 'Civic Institutions and Self-Government in Southern Mesopotamia in the Mid-First Millennium BC', in J. G. Dercksen (ed.), *Assyria and Beyond: Studies Presented to Mogens Trolle Larsen* (Leuven), 47–98.

—— 2005. 'A Historical Geography of Ancient Anatolia in the Assyrian Colony Period' (unpublished thesis, Copenhagen University).

Baurain, C. 1997. *Les Grecs et la Méditerranée orientale* (Paris).

Beck, H. 1997. *Polis und Koinon* (Stuttgart).

Bederman, D. J. 2001. *International Law in Antiquity* (Cambridge).

Bengtson, H. 1977. *Griechische Geschichte*, 5th edn. (Munich).

Bennet, J. 1997. 'Homer and the Bronze Age', in Morris and Powell (1997), 511–34.

Benveniste, E. 1973. *Indo-European Language and Society* (London).

Berent, M. 1996. 'Hobbes and the "Greek Tongues"', *History of Political Thought*, 17: 36–59.

—— 2000. 'Anthropology and the Classics: War, Violence and the Stateless *Polis*', *Classical Quarterly*, NS 50: 257–89.

—— 2004. 'In Search of the Greek State: A Rejoinder to M. H. Hansen', *Polis*, 21: 107–46.

Berger, S. 1992. *Revolution and Society in Greek Sicily and Southern Italy* (Stuttgart).

Bertelli, S. 1978. *Il potere oligarchico nello stato-città medievale* (Florence).

Bertrand, J. M. 1992. *Cités et royaumes du monde grec: espace et politique* (Paris).

Berve, H. 1967. *Die Tyrannis bei den Griechen*, 2 vols. (Munich).

Bettalli, M. 1995. *I mercenari nel mondo greco*, i (Pisa).

Bieber, M. 1961. *History of the Greek and Roman Theatre*, 2nd edn. (Princeton).

Binder, V. 1999. '*Koine*', in *Der Neue Pauly* (Stuttgart), vi. 631–3.

Bintliff, J. 1991. 'Die Polis-Landschaften Griechenlands: Probleme und Aussichten der Bevölkerungsgeschichte', in Olshausen and Sonnabend (1991) 149–202.

—— 1997. 'Further Considerations on the Population of Ancient Boeotia', in J. Bintliff (ed.), *Recent Developments in the History and Archaeology of Central Greece* (London), 231–52.

—— 2002. 'Rethinking Early Mediterranean Urbanism', *Mauerschau*, 1: 153–77.

—— and Snodgrass, A. 1985. 'The Boiotia Survey, a Preliminary Report: The First Four Years', *Journal of Field Archaeology*, 12: 123–61.

Bleicken, J. 1979. 'Zur Entstehung der Verfassungstypologie im 5. Jahrhundert v. Chr. (Monarchie, Aristokratie, Demokratie)', *Historia*, 28: 148–72.

Bluntschli, J. 1885/6. *Allgemeine Staatslehre*, 6th edn. (Stuttgart, 1886), English edn. (London, 1885).

Bourriot, F. 1976. *Recherches sur la nature du genos* (Lille).

Bowden, H. 2005. *Classical Athens and the Delphic Oracle* (Cambridge).

Bremen, R. van 1996. *The Limits of Participation* (Amsterdam).

Brock, R. and Hodkinson, S. (eds.) 2000. *Alternatives to Athens* (Oxford).

Bruhns, H. 1985. 'De Werner Sombart à Max Weber et Moses I. Finley: la typologie de la ville antique et la question de la ville de consommation', in Ph. Leveau (ed.), *L'Origine des richesses dépensées dans la ville antique* (Aix-en-Provence), 255–73.

——— 1994. 'Verwandschaftstrukturen, Geschlechterverhältnisse und Max Weber's Theorie der antiken Stadt', in C. Meier (ed.), *Die Okzidentale Stadt nach Max Weber* (Munich), 59–94.

——— 1996. 'Max Weber, l'économie et l'histoire', *Annales*, 51: 1259–87.

——— and Nippel, W. 1987–9. 'Max Weber, M. I. Finley et le concept de cité antique', *Opus*, 6–8: 29–50.

Brun, P. 1999. 'Les nouvelles perspectives de l'étude démographique des cités grecques', in M. Bellancourt-Valdher and J.-N. Corvisier (eds.), *La Démographie historique antique* (Artois), 13–25.

Bryce, T. 1986. *The Lycians* (Copenhagen).

Burke, P. 1986. 'City-States', in J. A. Hall (ed.), *States in History* (Oxford), 137–53.

——— 1992. *History and Social Theory* (Cambridge).

Burkert, W. 1985. *Greek Religion* (Oxford).

——— 1992. 'The Formation of Greek Religion at the Close of the Dark Ages', *Studi italiani di filologia classica*, III vol. 10, fasc. 1–2: 533–51.

——— 1995. 'Greek *Poleis* and Civic Cults', *CPCPapers* 2: 201–10.

Busolt, G. 1920. *Griechische Staatskunde*, i (Munich).

Cahill, N. 2002. *Household and City Organization at Olynthos* (New Haven).

Cambitoglou, A. 1981. *Archaeological Museum of Andros: Guide to the Finds from the Excavations of the Geometric Town of Zagora* (Athens).

Camp, J. 2000. 'Walls and the *Polis*', in *Polis and Politics*, 41–57.

Carlsson, S. 2005. *Hellenistic Democracies: Freedom, Independence and Political Procedure in Some East Greek City-States* (Uppsala).

Carter, J. C. 1990. 'Metapontum—Land, Wealth, and Population', in J. P. Descœudres (ed.), *Greek Colonists and Native Populations* (Oxford), 405–51.

Cartledge, P. 1993. *The Greeks* (Oxford).

——— 1996. 'Trade, Greek', in *Oxford Classical Dictionary*, 3rd edn., 1535–7.

——— 1998. 'City and Chora in Sparta: Archaic to Hellenistic', in W. G. Cavanagh and S. E. C. Walker (eds.), *Sparta in Laconia* (Athens), 39–47.

——— 2000. 'Greek Political Thought: The Historical Context', in C. Rowe and M. Schofield (eds.), *Greek and Roman Political Thought* (Cambridge), 11–22.

—— 2002. 'The Economy (Economies) of Ancient Greece', in Scheidel and von Reden (2002) 11–32.

Catling, R. 2002. 'The Survey Area from the Early Iron Age to the Classical Period', in W. Cavanagh *et al.* (2002), ii. 151–255.

Cauer, P. 1923. *Grundfragen der Homerkritik*, 3rd edn. (Leipzig).

Cavanagh, W. *et al.* (eds.) 1996. *Continuity and Change in a Greek Rural Landscape: The Laconia Survey*, ii (London).

—— 2002. *Continuity and Change in a Greek Rural Landscape: The Laconia Survey*, i (London).

Cawkwell, G. 1996. 'The End of Greek Liberty', in Wallace and Harris (1996) 98–121.

—— 2002. 'The Decline of Sparta', in M. Whitby (ed.), *Sparta* (Edinburgh), 236–57.

Chamoux, F. 1953. *Cyrène sous la monarchie des Battiades* (Paris).

Chaniotis, A. 2005. *War in the Hellenistic World* (Oxford).

Chankowski, A. S. Forthcoming. *L'Éphébie hellénistique: étude d'une institution civique dans les cités grecques des îles de la mer Égée et de l'Asie Mineure (IVe–I^e siècles avant J.C.)* (Paris).

Cherry, J. F. 1986. 'Polities and Palaces: Some Problems in Minoan State Formation' in Renfrew and Cherry (1986) 19–45.

—— Davis, J. L. and Mantzourani, E. 1991. *Landscape Archaeology as Long-Term History* (Los Angeles).

Childe, G. V. 1950. 'The Urban Revolution', *Town Planning Review*, 21: 3–17.

Chittolini, G. 1991. 'The Italian City-State and its Territory', in A. Molho *et al.* (eds.), *City-States in Classical Antiquity and Medieval Italy* (Stuttgart), 589–602.

Cohen, E. 1997. 'A Modern Myth: Classical Athens as a Face-to-Face Society', *Common Knowledge*, 6: 97–124.

Cohen, G. M. 1995. *The Hellenistic Settlements in Europe, the Islands and Asia Minor* (Berkeley and Los Angeles).

Coldstream, J. N. 1993. 'Mixed Marriages at the Frontiers of the Early Greek World', *Oxford Journal of Archaeology*, 12: 89–107.

Cole, S. G. 1995. 'Civic Cult and Civic Identity', *CPCActs* 2: 292–325.

Compernolle, R. van 1992. 'Lo stanziamento di *apoikoi* greci presso capo Zefirio (Capo Bruzzano) nell'ultimo terzo del'VIII secolo A.C.', *Ann Pisa*, 22: 774–80.

Constant, B. 1819. *De la liberté des anciens comparée de celle des modernes*, repr. in M. Gauchet (ed.), *De la liberté chez des modernes: écrits politiques* (Paris, 1980), 491–515.

Cordano, F. 1992. *Le tessere pubbliche dal tempio di Atene a Camarina* (Rome).

Corvisier, J.-N. 1991. *Aux origines du miracle grec* (Paris).

—— 1999. 'Continuité et discontinuité dans les tissus urbains grecs', in M. Bellancourt-Valdher and J.-N. Corvisier (eds.), *La Démographique historique antique* (Artois), 141–52.

—— and Suder, W. 2000. *La Population de l'Antiquité classique* (Paris).

Costabile, F. (ed.) 1992. *Polis ed Olympieion a Locri Epizefiri* (Catanzaro).

Coulton, J. J. 1976. *The Architectural Development of the Greek Stoa* (Oxford).

Crouch, D. 1993. *Water Management in Ancient Greek Cities* (Oxford).

Dakaris, S. I. 1972. Θεσπρωτία: Ἀρχαῖες Ἑλληνικές πόλεις (Athens).

Davies, J. K. 1984. 'Cultural, Social and Economic Features of the Hellenistic World', in *Cambridge Ancient History*, 2nd edn. (Cambridge), vii.1: 304–20.

—— 1992. 'Greece after the Persian Wars', in *Cambridge Ancient History*, 2nd edn. (Cambridge), v. 15–33.

—— 1998. 'Ancient Economies: Models and Muddles', in H. Parkins and C. Smith (eds.), *Trade, Traders and the Ancient City* (London), 225–56.

De Angelis, F. 2003. *Megara Hyblaia and Selinous: The Development of Two Greek City-States in Archaic Sicily* (Oxford).

Debord, P. 1999. *L'Asie Mineure au IVe siècle (412–323 a.C)* (Bordeaux).

Delorme, J. 1960. *Gymnasion: étude sur les monuments consacrés à l'éducation en Grèce* (Paris).

Demand, N. H. 1990. *Urban Relocation in Archaic and Classical Greece* (Bristol).

—— 1996a. *A History of Ancient Greece* (New York).

—— 1996b. '*Poleis* on Cyprus and Oriental Despotism', *CPCPapers* 3: 7–15.

Dittenberger, W. 1907. 'Ethnika und Verwandtes III', *Hermes*, 42: 1–34, 161–234.

Di Vita, A. 1956. 'La penetrazione siracusana nella Sicilia sud-orientale alla luce delle più recenti scoperti archeologiche', *Kokalos*, 2: 177–205.

—— 1981. 'L'urbanistica più antica delle colonie di Magna Graecia e di Sicilia', *Annuario della Scuola archeologica di Atene*, 59: 63–79.

Dover, K. J. 1988. 'The Freedom of the Intellectual in Greek Society', in K. J. Dover, *The Greeks and Their Legacy* (Oxford), ii. 135–58.

Drögemüller, H.-P. 1970. 'Städtischer Raum und politischer Machtbereich in der Entwicklung der griechischen Polis', *Gymnasium*, 77: 484–507.

Ducrey, P. 1986. *Warfare in Ancient Greece* (New York).

—— 1995. 'La muraille est-elle un élément constitutif d'une cité?', *CPC Acts* 2: 245–56.

198   *References*

Dunand, F. 1973. *Le Culte d'Isis dans le Bassin orientale de la méditerranée* (Leiden).

Duthoy, R. 1986. 'Qu'est-ce qu'une *Polis?*', *Les Études classiques*, 54: 3–20.

Effenterre, H. van 1985. *La Cité grecque des origines à la défaite de Marathon* (Paris).

Ehrenberg, V. 1947. 'Polypragmosyne: A Study in Greek Politics', *Journal of Hellenic Studies*, 67: 46–67.

—— 1969: *The Greek State* (London).

—— 1973. 'The Greek Country and the Greek State', in *Aspects of the Ancient World* (New York), 29–52.

Elazar, D. J. 1994. *Federal Systems of the World* (Jerusalem).

Figueira, T. 1981. *Aegina: Society and Politics* (Salem).

Finer, S. E. 1997. *The History of Government*, 3 vols. (Oxford).

Finley, M. I. 1952. *Land and Credit in Ancient Athens 500–200 B.C.* (New Brunswick).

—— 1956. *The World of Odysseus* (London).

—— 1963. *The Ancient Greeks* (London).

—— 1973. *The Ancient Economy* (London).

 —— 1981a. 'The Ancient City: From Fustel de Coulanges to Max Weber and Beyond', in B. D. Shaw and R. P. Saller (eds.), *Economy and Society in Ancient Greece* (London), 3–23.

—— 1981b. 'Politics and Political Theory', in M. Finley (ed.), *The Legacy of Greece* (Oxford), 22–64.

—— 1983. *Politics in the Ancient World* (London).

—— 1985a. 'Further Thoughts', in 2nd edn. of Finley (1973) 177–207.

—— 1985b. 'Max Weber and the Greek City-State', in *Ancient History. Evidence and Models* (London), 88–103.

—— 1987–9. 'The City', *Opus*, 6–8: 303–13.

Fischer-Hansen, T. 1996. 'The Earliest Town-Planning of the Western Greek Colonies, with Special Regard to Sicily', *CPCActs* 3: 317–73.

—— 2002. 'Reflections on Native Settlements in the Dominions of Gela and Akragas—as Seen from the Perspective of the Copenhagen Polis Centre', *CPCPapers* 6: 125–86.

Flensted-Jensen, P. 1995. 'The Bottiaians and their *Poleis*', *CPCPapers* 2: 103–32.

—— and Hansen, M. H. 1996. 'Pseudo-Skylax' Use of the Term *Polis*', *CPCPapers* 3: 137–67.

Forde, D. 1964. *Yakö Studies* (Oxford).

Forsén, J. and Forsén, B. 1997. 'The *Polis* of Asea: A Case Study of How Archaeology Can Expand Our Knowledge of the History of a *Polis*', *CPCPapers* 4: 163–76.

—— —— 2003. *The Asea Valley Survey* (Stockholm).

Fossey, J. M. 1988. *Topography and Population of Ancient Boiotia* (Chicago).

Fowler, R. L. 1998. 'Genealogical Thinking, Hesiod's *Catalogue*, and the Creation of the Hellenes', *Proceedings of the Cambridge Philological Society*, 44: 1–19.

Fraser, P. 1995. 'Citizens, Demesmen and Metics in Athens and Elsewhere', *CPCActs* 2: 64–90.

Frederiksen, R. 2002*a*. 'The Greek Theatre', *CPCPapers* 6: 65–124.

—— 2002*b*. 'Typology of the Greek Theatre. Building in Late Classical and Hellenistic Times', *Proceedings of the Danish Institute at Athens*, 3: 135–75.

Friedrichs, C. R. 2000. *Urban Politics in Early Modern Europe* (London).

Frisk, H. 1970. *Griechisches etymologisches Wörterbuch*, ii (Heidelberg).

Fröhlich, P. 2004. *Les Cités grecques et le contrôle des magistrats (IVe–Ier siècle avant J.-C.)* (Geneva).

Funke, P. 1997. 'Polisgenese und Urbanisierung in Aitolien im 5. und 4. Jh. v. Chr.', *CPCActs* 4: 145–88.

Fustel de Coulanges, N. D. 1864. *La Cité antique* (Paris).

Gabrielsen, V. 1997. *The Naval Aristocracy of Hellenistic Rhodes* (Aarhus).

Gallant, T. W. 1991. *Risk and Survival in Ancient Greece* (Cambridge).

Gantz, T. 1993. *Early Greek Myth* (Baltimore).

Garlan, Y. 1988. *Slavery in the Ancient World* (Ithaca, NY).

Garnsey, P. 1998. *Cities, Peasants and Food in Classical Antiquity* (Cambridge).

—— 1999. *Food and Society in Classical Antiquity* (Cambridge).

Gat, A. 2002. 'Why City-States Existed. Riddles and Clues of Urbanisation and Fortifications', *6 CSC*: 125–39.

Gauthier, Ph. 1987–9. 'Grandes et petits cités: hégémonie et autarcie', *Opus*, 6–8: 187–202.

—— 1988. 'Métèques, perièques et *paroikoi*: Bilan et points d'interrogation', in R. Lonis (ed.), *L'Étranger dans le monde grec* (Nancy), 23–46.

—— 1993. 'Les cités hellénistiques', *CPCActs* 1: 211–31.

—— 1995. 'Notes sur le rôle du gymnase dans les cités hellénistiques', in Wörrle and Zanker (1995) 1–11.

—— and Hatzopoulos, M. 1993. *La Loi gymnasiarchique de Beroia* (Athens).

Gawantka, W. 1975. *Isopolitie: ein Beitrag zur Geschichte der zwischenstaatlichen Beziehungen in der griechischen Antike* (Munich).

Gehrke, H.-J. 1985. *Stasis: Untersuchungen zur den inneren Kriegen in der griechischen Staaten des 5. und 4. Jahrhunderts v. Chr.* (Munich).

—— 1986. *Jenseits von Athen und Sparta: das dritte Griechenland und seine Staatenwelt* (Munich).

—— 'Bemerkungen zu Hippodamos von Milet', in Schuller *et al.* (1989) 58–68.

—— 1993. 'Gesetz und Konflikt: Überlegungen zur frühen Polis', in J. Bleicken (ed.), *Colloqium aus Anlass des 80. Geburtstages von Alfred Heuss* (Kallmünz), 49–67.

—— 1994/5. 'Die kulturelle und politische Entwicklung Akarnaniens vom 6. bis zum 4. Jh v. Chr.', *Geographica Antiqua*, 3/4: 41–8.

—— 2001. 'Verfassungswandel', in O. Höffe (ed.), *Aristoteles, Politik* (Berlin), 137–50.

Gellner, E. 1983. *Nations and Nationalism* (Cambridge).

Giovannini, A. 1971. *Untersuchungen über die Natur und die Anfänge der bundesstaatlichen Sympolitie in Griechenland* (Göttingen).

Glotz, G. 1928. *La Cité grecque* (Paris).

Gneisz, D. 1990. *Das antike Rathaus* (Vienna).

Graham, A. J. 1964. *Colony and Mother City in Ancient Greece* (Manchester).

—— 1980–1. 'Religion, Women and Greek Colonization', in *Atti: Centro ricerche e documentazione sull' antichità classica* (Rome), 11: 293–314.

—— 1982. 'The Colonial Expansion of Greece', in *Cambridge Ancient History*, 2nd edn. (Cambridge), iii.3: 83–162.

—— 1998. 'Thucydides 7.13.2 and the Crews of Athenian Triremes. An Addendum', *Transactions of the American Philological Association* 128: 89–114.

Greaves, A. M. 2002. *Miletos: A History* (London).

Green, P. 1990. *Alexander to Actium: The Historical Evolution of the Hellenistic Age* (Berkeley and Los Angeles).

Greenhalgh, P. A. L. 1973. *Early Greek Warfare* (Cambridge).

Griffith, G. T. 1934. *The Mercenaries of the Hellenistic World* (Cambridge).

Gruben, G. 1986. *Die Tempel der Griechen* (Darmstadt).

Gruen, E. S. 1993. 'The Polis in the Hellenistic World', in R. M. Rosen and J. Farrell (eds.), *Nomodeiktes: Greek Studies in Honor of Martin Ostwald* (Ann Arbor), 339–54.

Gschnitzer, F. 1955. 'Stammes- und Ortsgemeinden im alten Griechenland', *Wiener Studien*, 68: 120–44.

—— 1973. '*Proxenos*', in *Paulys Real-Encyclopädie der classischen Altertumswissenschaft*, suppl. xiii: 629–730.

—— 1988. 'Die Stellung der Polis in der politischen Entwicklung des Altertums', *Oriens Antiquus*, 27: 287–302.

—— 1991. 'Zum Verhältnis von Siedlung, Gemeinde und Staat in der griechischen Welt', in Olshausen and Sonnabend (1991) 429–42.

Haensch, R. 2003. 'Amtslokal und Staatlichkeit in den griechischen Poleis', *Hermes*, 131: 172–95.

Hainsworth, J. B. 1968. 'Greek Views of Greek Dialectology', in *Transactions of the Philological Society* (Oxford), 62–76.

—— 1982. 'The Greek Language and the Historical Dialects', in *Cambridge Ancient History*, 2nd edn. (Cambridge), iii.1: 850–65.

Haldon, J. 1999. 'The Idea of the Town in the Byzantine Empire', in C. P. Brogiolo and B. Ward-Perkins (eds.), *The Idea and Ideal of the Town between Late Antiquity and the Early Middle Ages* (Leiden), 1–23.

Hall, E. 1989. *Inventing the Barbarian: Greek Self-Definition through Tragedy* (Oxford).

Hall, J. M. 1995. 'How Argive Was the Argive Heraion? The Political and Cultic Geography of the Argive Plain, 900–400 B.C.', *American Journal of Archaeology*, 99: 577–613.

—— 1997. *Ethnic Identity in Greek Antiquity* (Cambridge).

—— 2000. 'Sparta, Lakedaimon and the Nature of Perioikic Dependency', *CPCPapers* 5: 73–89.

—— 2002. *Hellenicity* (Chicago).

Hallpike, C. R. 1972. *The Konso of Ethiopia* (Oxford).

Hampl, F. 1937. 'Die Lakedämonischen Periöken', *Hermes*, 72: 1–49.

—— 1939. 'Poleis ohne Territorium', *Klio*, 32: 1–60.

Hansen, M. H. 1985. *Demography and Democracy* (Herning).

—— 1987. *The Athenian Assembly* (Oxford).

—— 1988. *Three Studies in Athenian Demography* (Copenhagen).

—— 1989a. 'Note', in Schuller *et al.* (1989) 14, 113.

—— 1989b. 'On the Importance of Institutions in an Analysis of Athenian Democracy', in *The Athenian Ecclesia*, ii. *A Collection of Articles 1983–89* (Copenhagen), 263–9.

—— 1991. *The Athenian Democracy in the Age of Demosthenes* (Oxford; 2nd edn. Bristol, 1999).

—— 1992. 'The Tradition of the Athenian Democracy A.D. 1750–1990', *Greece and Rome*, 39: 14–30.

—— 1993. 'Introduction', *CPCActs* 1: 7–29.

—— 1994a. 'Polis and City-State, 600–323 B.C.: A Comprehensive Research Programme', *CPCPapers* 1: 9–17.

—— 1994b. 'Polis, Politeuma and Politeia: A Note on Arist. *Pol.* 1278b6–14', *CPCPapers* 1: 91–8.

—— 1995a. 'The "Autonomous City-State": Ancient Fact or Modern Fiction?', *CPCPapers* 2: 21–43.

—— 1995b. 'Boiotian *Poleis*: A Test Case', *CPCActs* 2: 13–63.

—— 1995c. '*Kome*: A Study in How the Greeks Designated and Classified Settlements Which were not *Poleis*', *CPCPapers* 2: 45–81.

—— 1995d. *The Trial of Sokrates—From the Athenian Point of View* (Copenhagen).

—— 1996a. 'Aristotle's Two Complementary Views of the Greek *Polis*', in Wallace and Harris (1996) 196–210.

—— 1996b. 'City-Ethnics as Evidence for *Polis* Identity', *CPCPapers* 3: 169–96.

—— 1996c. '*Πολλαχῶς πόλις λέγεται* (Arist. *Pol.* 1276a23): The Copenhagen Inventory of *Poleis* and the *Lex Hafniensis de Civitate*', *CPCActs* 3: 7–72.

—— 1996d. 'Were the Boiotian *Poleis* Deprived of their *Autonomia*?', *CPC Papers* 3: 127–36.

—— 1997a. '*Emporion*: A Study of the Use and Meaning of the Term in the Archaic and Classical Periods', *CPCPapers* 4: 83–105.

—— 1997b. '*Πόλις* as the Generic Term for State', *CPCPapers* 4: 9–15.

—— 1997c. 'The *Polis* as an Urban Centre and as a *Political Community*', *CPCActs* 4: 9–86.

—— 1997d. 'A Typology of Dependent *Poleis*', *CPCPapers* 4: 29–37.

—— 1998. Polis *and City-State: An Ancient Concept and its Modern Equivalent*, *CPCActs* 5.

—— 1999a. 'Aristotle's Reference to the Arkadian Federation at *Pol.* 1261a 29', *CPCActs* 6: 80–8.

—— 1999b. 'Review of E. W. Robinson *The First Democracies*', *Bryn Mawr Classical Review*, 17 Sept. 1999.

—— 2000. 'A Survey of the Use of the Word *Polis* in Archaic and Classical Sources', *CPCPapers* 5: 173–215.

—— 2001. *Polis et cité-État: un concept antique et son équivalent moderne* (Paris). Revised French edn. of Hansen (1998).

—— 2002. 'Was the *Polis* a State or a Stateless Society?', *CPCPapers* 6: 17–47.

—— 2003. '95 Theses about the Ancient Greek *Polis* in the Archaic and Classical Periods: A Report on the Results Obtained by the Copenhagen Polis Centre in the Period 1993–2003', *Historia*, 52: 257–82.

—— 2004a. 'The Concept of the Consumption City Applied to the Greek *Polis*', *CPCPapers* 7: 9–47.

—— 2004b. 'The Perioikic *Poleis* of Lakedaimon', *CPCPapers* 7: 149–64.

—— 2004c. 'The Use of Sub-ethnics as Part of the Name of a Greek Citizen', *CPCPapers* 7: 117–29.

—— 2004d. 'Was Every *Polis* State centred on a *Polis* Town?', *CPCPapers* 7: 131–47.

—— 2006a. 'Emporion: A Study of the Use and Meaning of the Term in the Archaic and Classical Periods', in G. R. Tsetskhladze (ed.), *Greek Colonization: An Account of Greek Colonies and Other Settlements Overseas* (Leiden), 1–39.

—— 2006b. *The Shotgun Method: The Demography of the Ancient Greek*

City-State Culture, The Fordyce Mitchel Memorial Lectures 2004 (Columbia, Mo.).

—— and Fischer-Hansen, T. 1994. 'Monumental Political Architecture in Archaic and Classical Greek *Poleis*', *CPCPapers* 1: 23–90.

Hanson, V. D. 1989. *The Western Way of War* (New York).

—— 1991. 'Hoplite Technology in Phalanx Battle', in V. D. Hanson (ed.), *Hoplites: The Classical Greek Battle Experience* (London), 63–84.

—— 1995. *The Other Greeks* (New York).

Hatzopoulos, M. 1996. *Macedonian Institutions under the Kings*, 2 vols. (Athens).

Hayden, B. J. 1988. 'Fortifications of Postpalatial and Early Iron Age Crete', *Archäologischer Anzeiger*, 1–21.

Head, B. V. 1911. *Historia Numorum*, 2nd edn. (London).

Hellmann, M.-C. 1999. *Choix d'inscriptions architecturales grecques* (Lyon).

Herman, G. 1987. *Ritualised Friendship and the Greek City* (Cambridge).

Hertz, M. 1989. 'Avlsbrugere og avling på købstadsjorder', *Bol og By*, 72–92.

Hesberg, H. von 1995. 'Das griechische Gymnasion im 2. Jh. v. Chr.', in Wörrle and Zanker (1995) 13–27.

Hicks, J. 1969. *A Theory of Economic History* (Oxford).

Hodkinson, S. 2005. 'The Imaginary Spartan *Politeia*', *CPCActs* 7: 222–81.

—— and Hodkinson, H. 1981. 'Mantinea and the Mantinike: Settlement and Society in a Greek Polis', *Annual of the British School at Athens*, 76: 239–96.

Hoepfner, W. (ed.) 1999. *Geschichte des Wohnens*, i. *5000 v.Chr–500 n. Chr.* (Ludwigsburg).

—— and Schwandner, E.-L. 1994. *Haus und Stadt im klassischen Griechenland*, 2nd edn. (Berlin).

Holder, G. and Peatrik, A.-M. 2004. 'Cité, centre, capitale: pour une anthropologie du statut politique de la ville', *Journal des africanistes*, 74: 9–34.

Holderman, E. S. 1985. 'Le sacerdotesse: requisiti, funzioni, poteri', in G. Arrigone (ed.), *Le donne in Grecia* (Bari), 299–330.

Hope Simpson, R. and Lazenby, J. F. 1970. *The Catalogue of Ships in Homer's Iliad* (Oxford).

Hopkins, K. 1983. 'Introduction', in P. Garnsey, K. Hopkins and C. R. Whittaker (eds.), *Trade in the Ancient Economy* (London), pp. ix–xxv.

Horden, P. and Purcell, N. 2000. *The Corrupting Sea: A Study in Mediterranean History* (Oxford).

Hornblower, S. 1982. *Mausolus* (Oxford).

—— 1991. *A Commentary on Thucydides*, i (Oxford).

—— 1992. 'Creation and Development of Democratic Institutions in

Ancient Greece', in J. Dunn (ed.), *Democracy: The Unfinished Journey 508 BC to AD 1993* (Oxford), 1–16.

—— 1995. *A Commentary on Thucydides*, ii (Oxford).

Hunt, P. 1998. *Slaves, Warfare and Ideology in the Greek Historians* (Cambridge).

Huxley, A. L. 1966. *The Early Ionians* (London).

Isager, S. and Hansen, M. H. 1975. *Aspects of Athenian Society* (Odense).

—— and Skydsgaard, J. E. 1992. *Ancient Greek Agriculture* (London).

Isler, H. P. 1994. 'Die antike Theaterarchitektur', in Rossetti and Sartorio (1994–6) i. 86–124.

Jacobsen, T. 1943. 'Primitive Democracy in Ancient Mesopotamia', *Journal of Near Eastern Studies*, 2: 159–72.

Jameson, M. H. 1990. 'Private Space and the Greek City', in Murray and Price (1990) 171–95.

—— Runnels, C. N. and van Andel, T. H. 1994. *A Greek Countryside* (Stanford, Calif.).

—— *et al.* 1993. *A Lex sacra from Selinous* (Durham, NC).

Jehne, M. 1994. *Koine Eirene: Untersuchungen zu den Befriedungs- und Stabilisierungsbemühungen in der griechischen Poliswelt des 4. Jahrhunderts v. Chr.* (Stuttgart).

Jensen, M. Skafte 1980. *The Homeric Question and the Oral-Formulaic Theory* (Copenhagen).

Johanek, P. 2000. 'Imperial and Free Towns of the Holy Roman Empire: City-States in Pre-Modern Germany?', *30 CSC*: 295–319.

Jones, A. H. M. 1940. *The Greek City from Alexander to Justinian* (Oxford).

—— 1964. *The Later Roman Empire 284–602* (Oxford).

Jones, N. 1987. *Public Organization in Ancient Greece* (Philadelphia).

—— 1999. *The Associations of Classical Athens* (New York).

Jones, P. 1997. *The Italian City-State: From Commune to Signoria* (Oxford).

Jost, M. 1992. *Aspects de la vie religieuse en Grèce*, 2nd edn. (Paris).

—— 1999. 'Les schemas de peuplement de l'Arcadie aux époques archaïque et classique', *CPCActs* 6: 192–247.

Just, R. 1989. *Women in Athenian Law and Life* (London).

Kearns, E. 1996a. 'Religion, Greek', in *Oxford Classical Dictionary*, 3rd edn., 1300–1.

—— 1996b. 'Women in Cult', in *Oxford Classical Dictionary*, 3rd edn., 1624–5.

Keen, A. G. 1996. 'Were the Boiotian *Poleis Autonomoi*?', *CPCPapers* 3: 113–25.

Kelly, T. 1976. *A History of Argos to 500 B.C.* (Minneapolis).

Kenzler, U. 1999. *Studien zur Entwicklung und Struktur der griechischen Agora in archaischer und klassischer Zeit* (Frankfurt am Main).

Kienast, D. 1973. 'Presbeia', in *Paulys Real-Encyclopädie der classischen Altertumswissenschaft*, suppl. xiii. 499–628.

Knoepfler, D. 1997. 'Le territoire d'Erétrie et l'organisation politique de la cité (*dēmoi, chōroi, phylai*)', *CPCActs* 4: 352–449.

Kockel, V. 1995. '*Bouleuteria*: Architektonische Form und urbanistischer Kontext', in Wörrle and Zanker (1995) 29–40.

Koerner, R. 1985. 'Tiryns als Beispiel einer frühen dorischen Polis', *Klio*, 67: 452–7.

——— 1993. *Inschriftliche Gesetzestexte der frühen griechischen Polis* (Cologne).

Kolb, F. 1984. *Die Stadt im Altertum* (Munich).

Kroll, J. H. 1972. *Athenian Bronze Allotment Plates* (Cambridge, Mass.).

Kuhrt, A. 1995. *The Ancient Near East*, 2 vols. (London).

Lambert, S. D. 1993. *The Phratries of Attica* (Oxford).

Lang, F. 1996. *Archaische Siedlungen in Griechenland* (Berlin).

Laronde, A. 1999. 'A propos de la population et des familles cyrénéennes', in M. Bellancourt-Valdher and J.-N. Corvisier (eds.), *La Démographie historique antique* (Artois), 81–90.

Larsen, J.A.O. 1966. *Representative Government in Greek and Roman History* (Berkeley and Los Angeles).

——— 1968. *Greek Federal States* (Oxford).

Larsen, M. T. 1976. *The Old Assyrian City-State and its Colonies* (Copenhagen).

Laslett, P. 1956. 'The Face to Face Society', in P. Laslett (ed.), *Philosophy, Politics and Society*, i (Oxford), 157–84.

Lauter, H. 1993. *Attische Landgemeinden in klassischer Zeit* (Marburg).

Lawrence, A. W. 1979. *Greek Aims in Fortification* (Oxford).

——— 1996. *Greek Architecture*, 5th edn. revised by R. A. Tomlinson (New Haven).

Legon, R. 1981. *Megara: The Political History of a Greek City-State to 336 B.C.* (Ithaca, NY).

Lendon, J. L. 1994. 'Thucydides and the "Constitution" of the Peloponnesian League', *Greek Roman and Byzantine Studies*, 35: 159–77.

Leschhorn, W. 1984. *Gründer der Stadt* (Stuttgart).

Lévy, E. 1985. '*Astos* et *polites* d'Homère à Hérodote', *Ktema*, 10: 53–66.

——— 1990. 'La cité grecque: invention moderne ou réalité antique?' *Cahiers du Centre Glotz*, 1: 53–67.

Lintott, A. 1982. *Violence, Civil Strife and Revolution in the Classical City 750–330 BC* (London).

Lord, A. B. 1962. 'Homer and Other Epic Poetry', in Wace and Stubbings (1962) 179–214.

Lübtow, U. von 1972. 'Gab es in der Antike den Begriff des Stadtstaates?', in *Festschrift für Ernst Heinitz* (Berlin), 89–109.

Lyons, J. 1977. *Semantics*, i (Cambridge).

Ma, J. 1999. *Antiochos III and the Cities of Western Asia Minor* (Oxford).

Madvig, J. N. 1840. *Blik på Oldtidens Statsforfatninger med hensyn til Udviklingen af Monarchiet og en omfattende Statsorganisme*, Indbydelsesskrift til Universitetsfesten den 6te juli 1840 in Anledning af Deres Majestæters Kong Christian den Ottendes og Dronning Caroline Amalies Salving og Kroning (Copenhagen).

Maisels, C. K. 1990. *The Emergence of Civilization: From Hunting and Gathering to Agriculture, Cities and the State in the Near East* (London).

Malkin, I. 1987. *Religion and Colonization in Ancient Greece* (Leiden).

—— 1994. 'Inside and Outside: Colonisation and the Formation of the Mother City', in B. D'Agostino and D. Ridgway (eds.), *Apoikia* (Naples), 1–9.

Marek, C. 1984. *Die Proxenie* (Frankfurt am Main).

Marinatos, N. and Hägg, R. (eds.) 1993. *Greek Sanctuaries: New Approaches* (London).

Martin, R. 1951. *Recherches sur l'agora grecque* (Paris).

—— 1974. *L'Urbanisme dans la Grèce antique*, 2nd edn. (Paris).

Mattingly, D. J. and Salmon, J. (eds.) 2001. *Economies beyond Agriculture in the Classical World* (London).

McDonald, W. A. 1943. *The Political Meeting Places of the Greeks* (Baltimore).

McInerney, J. 1999. *The Folds of Parnassos* (Austin, Tex.).

McKechnie, P. 1989. *Outsiders in the Greek Cities in the Fourth Century BC* (London).

Mee, Chr. and Forbes, H. (eds.) 1997. *A Rough and Rocky Place* (Liverpool).

Meiggs, R. 1972. *The Athenian Empire* (Oxford).

Mellaart, J. 1967. *Qatal Hüyük: A Neolithic Town in Anatolia* (London).

—— 1975. 'The Origins and Development of Cities in the Near East', in L. L. Orlin (ed.), *Janus: Essays in Ancient and Modern Studies* (Ann Arbor), 5–22.

Meritt, B. D., Wade-Gery, H. T. and McGregor, M. F. 1939. *The Athenian Tribute Lists*, i (Princeton).

Mertens, N. 2002. 'οὐχ ὁμοῖοι, ἀγαθοὶ δέ: The *Perioikoi* in the Classical Lakedaimonian *Polis*', in A. Powell and S. Hodkinson (eds.), *Sparta: Beyond the Mirage* (London), 285–303.

Mieroop, M. van de 1997. *The Ancient Mesopotamian City* (Oxford).

Migeotte, L. 1992. *Les Souscriptions publiques dans les cités grecques* (Geneva).

—— 1998. 'Finances sacrées et finances publiques dans les cités grecques', in *Actas del IX Congreso Español de Estudios Clásicos* (Madrid), 179–85.

—— L. 2002. *L'Économie des cités grecques* (Paris).

Mikalson, J. D. 1975. *The Sacred and Civil Calendar of the Athenian Year* (Princeton).

Millar, F. 1993. 'The Greek City in the Roman Period', *CPCActs* 1: 232–60.

—— 2002. *The Roman Republic in Political Thought* (Hanover).

Miller, J. 1984. *Rousseau: Dreamer of Democracy* (New Haven).

Miller, S. G. 1978. *The Prytaneion* (Berkeley and Los Angeles).

Mithen, S. 2003. *After the Ice Age: A Global Human History 20,000–5,000 BC* (London).

Moggi, M. 1976. *I sinecismi interstatali greci*, i (Pisa).

Momigliano, A. 1977. 'The Fault of the Greeks', in *Essays in Ancient and Modern Historiography* (Oxford), 9–23.

Monier-Williams, M. 1899. *A Sanskrit–English Dictionary* (Oxford).

Montesquieu. 1951. *Œuvres complètes*, ii, ed. R. Caillois (Paris).

Moretti, L. 1959. 'Olympionikai, i vincitori negli antichi agoni olimpici', in *Atti della Accademia Nazionale dei Lincei*. Serie 8: Memorie, Classe di Scienze morali, storiche e filologiche, 8: 59–198.

Morgan, C. 1993. 'The Origins of Pan-Hellenism', in Marinatos and Hägg (1993) 18–44.

—— 2003. *Early Greek States beyond the Polis* (London).

—— and Coulton, J. J. 1997. 'The *Polis* as a Physical Entity', *CPCActs* 4: 87–144.

—— and Hall, J. M. 1996. 'Achaian *Poleis* and Achaian Colonisation', *CPC Acts* 3: 164–232.

Morpurgo Davies, A. 1963. *Mycenaeae Graecitatis Lexicon* (Rome).

—— 1987. 'The Greek Notion of Dialect', *Verbum*, 10: 7–28.

Morris, I. 1986. 'The Use and Abuse of Homer', *Classical Antiquity*, 5: 81–138.

—— 1991. 'The Early Polis as City and State', in Rich and Wallace-Hadrill (1991) 25–57.

—— 1996. 'The Absolute Chronology of the Greek Colonies in Sicily', *Acta Archaeologica*, 67: 51–9.

—— 1997. 'An Archaeology of Equalities? The Greek City-States', in Nichols and Charlton (1997) 91–105.

—— and Powell, B. (eds.) 1997. *A New Companion to Homer* (Leiden).

Mossé, C. 1969. *La Tyrannie dans la Grèce ancienne* (Paris).

—— 1985. 'ΑΣΤΗ ΚΑΙ ΠΟΛΙΤΙΣ: la dénomination de la femme athénienne dans les plaidoyers démosthéniens', *Ktema*, 10: 77–9.

—— and Schnapp-Gourbeillon, A. 1990. *Précis d'histoire grecque* (Paris).

Müller, A. 1954. 'Die Ratsverfassung der Stadt Basel von 1521 bis 1798', *Basler Zeitschrift für Geschichte und Altertumskunde*, 53: 5–98.

Müller-Wiener, W. 1988. *Griechisches Bauwesen in der Antike* (Munich).

Muggia, A. 1997. *L'area di rispetto nelle colonie magno-greche e siceliote* (Palermo).

Mulgan, R. G. 1984. 'Liberty in Ancient Greece', in Z. Pelczynski and J. Gray (eds.), *Conceptions of Liberty in Political Philosophy* (New York), 7–26.

Murray, O. 1990. 'Cities of Reason', in Murray and Price (1990), 1–25.

—— 1993. *Early Greece*, 2nd edn. (London).

—— 1996. 'Polis', in *Oxford Classical Dictionary*, 3rd edn., 1205–6.

—— 1997. 'Rationality and the Greek City: The Evidence from Kamarina', *CPCActs* 4: 493–504.

—— 2000. 'What is Greek about the *Polis?*', in *Polis and Politics*, 231–48.

—— and Price S. (eds.) 1990. *The Greek City from Homer to Alexander* (Oxford).

Musti, D. 1985. 'Pubblico e privato nella democrazia periclea', *Quaderni Urbinati di Cultura Classica*, 20: 7–17.

Nevett, L. C. 1999. *House and Society in the Ancient Greek World* (Cambridge).

Nicholls, R. V. 1958–9. 'Old Smyrna: the Iron Age Fortifications and Associated Remains on the City Perimeter', *Annual of the British School at Athens*, 53–4: 35–137.

Nichols, D. L. and Charlton, T. H. (eds.) 1997. *The Archaeology of City-States* (Washington).

Nielsen, I. 1999. *Hellenistic Palaces* (Aarhus).

Nielsen, T. Heine. 2002. *Arkadia and its Poleis in the Archaic and Classical Periods* (Göttingen).

—— 2004. 'The Concept of *Patris* in Archaic and Classical Sources', *CPC Papers* 7: 49–76.

Nippel, W. 1989. 'Polis', in *Historisches Wörterbuch der Philosophie* (Basel), vii. 1031–4.

Nowicki, K. 1992. 'Fortifications in Dark Age Krete', in S. van de Maele and J. M. Fossey (eds.), *Fortificationes Antiquae* (Amsterdam), 53–76.

Ober, J. and Hedrick, C. W. 1993. *The Birth of Democracy: An Exhibition Celebrating the 2500th Anniversary of Democracy* (Washington).

Olsen, O. 1989. 'Royal Power in Viking Age Denmark', in *Les Mondes normands (VIIIᵉ–XIIᵉ s.): Actes du IIe congrès international d'archéologie médiéval* (Caen), 27–32.

Olshausen, E. and Sonnabend, H. (eds.) 1991. *Geographica Historica*, v (Stuttgart).

Olson, S. D. and Sens, A. 2000. *Archestratos of Gela* (Oxford).

O'Neill, J. L. 1995. *The Origins and Development of Ancient Greek Democracy* (Lanham, Md.).

Oppenheim, L. F. L. 1992. In R. Jennings and A. Watts (eds.), *Oppenheim's International Law*, 9th edn. (Harlow).

Orth, W. 1977. *Königlicher Machtanspruch und städtische Freiheit* (Munich).

Osborne, R. 1985. *Demos: The Discovery of Classical Attika* (Cambridge).
—— 1987. *Classical Landscape with Figures* (London).
—— 1998. 'Early Greek Colonization? The Nature of Greek Settlement in the West', in N. Fischer and H. van Wees (eds.), *Archaic Greece: New Approaches and New Evidence* (London), 251–69.
Ostwald, M. 1982. *Autonomia: Its Genesis and Early History* (New York).
—— 1986. *From Popular Sovereignty to the Sovereignty of Law* (Berkeley and Los Angeles).
Palmer, L. R. 1980. *The Greek Language* (London).
Parke, H. W. 1933. *Greek Mercenary Soldiers* (Oxford).
Parker, R. 1983. *Miasma* (Oxford).
—— 1996. *Athenian Religion: A History* (Oxford).
Parkins, H. 1998. 'Time for Change? Shaping the Future of the Ancient Economy', in Parkins and Smith (1998) 1–15.
—— and Smith, C. (eds.) 1998. *Trade, Traders and the Ancient Economy* (London).
Pečírka, J. 1973. 'Homestead Farms in Classical and Hellenistic Hellas', in M. I. Finley (ed.), *Problèmes de la terre en Grèce ancienne* (Paris), 113–47.
Perlman, P. 2000. *City and Sanctuary in Ancient Greece: The Theorodokia in the Peloponnese* (Göttingen).
Piérart, M. 1997. 'L'attitude d'Argos à l'égard des autres cités d'Argolide', *CPCActs* 4: 321–51.
Pierson, C. 1996. *The Modern State* (London).
Pleket, H. 1996. 'L'agonismo sportivo', in S. Settis (ed.), *Noi e i Greci*. i (Turin), 507–37.
Pöhlmann, E. 1992. 'Homer Mykene und Troja: Probleme und Aspekte', *Studia Troica*, 2: 187–99.
Polignac, F. de 1994. 'Mediation, Competition and Sovereignty: The Evolution of Rural Sanctuaries in Geometric Greece', in S. E. Alcock and R. Osborne (eds.), *Placing the Gods* (Oxford), 3–18.
—— 1995. *Cults, Territory and the Origins of the Greek City-State* (Chicago).
Popper, K. R. 1962. *The Open Society and its Enemies*, i (London).
Postgate, N. 1992. *Ancient Mesopotamia* (London).
Poulsen, F. 1924. *Den Delfiske Gud og hans Helligdom* (Copenhagen).
Powell, A. 1988. *Athens and Sparta* (London).
Powell, B. 1991. *Homer and the Origin of the Greek Alphabet* (Cambridge).
—— 1997. 'Homer and Writing', in Morris and Powell (1997) 3–32.
Prendergast, G. L. 1875. *A Complete Concordance to the Iliad of Homer* (London).
Pritchett, W. K. 1956. 'The Attic Stelai II', *Hesperia*, 25: 178–328.
—— 1971. *The Greek State at War*, i (Berkeley and Los Angeles).
—— 1985. *The Greek State at War*, iv (Berkeley and Los Angeles).

Quass, F. 1979. 'Zur Verfassung der griechischen Städte im Hellenismus', *Chiron*, 9: 37–52.

Raaflaub, K. 1993. 'Homer to Solon: The Rise of the Polis. The Written Sources', *CPCActs* 1: 41–105.

—— 1997*a*. 'Homeric Society', in Morris and Powell (1997) 624–48.

—— 1997*b*. 'Soldiers, Citizens and the Evolution of the Early Greek *Polis*', in L. G. Mitchell and P. J. Rhodes (eds.), *The Development of the Polis in Archaic Greece* (London), 49–59.

Raubitschek, A. 1962. 'Demokratia', *Hesperia*, 31: 238–44.

Rawson, E. 1969. *The Spartan Tradition in European Thought* (Oxford).

Renfrew, C. and Cherry, J. F. (eds.) 1986. *Peer Polity Interaction and Socio-Political Change* (Cambridge).

—— and Wagstaff, M. 1982. *An Island Polity* (Cambridge).

Rhodes, P. J. 1981. *A Commentary on the Aristotelian* Athenaion Politeia (Oxford).

—— 1995. 'Epigraphical Evidence: Laws and Decrees', *CPCActs* 2: 91–112.

—— 1998. 'Sparta, Thebes and *Autonomia*', *Eirene*, 35: 33–40.

—— and Lewis, D. M. 1997. *The Decrees of the Greek States* (Oxford).

Rich, J. and Wallace-Hadrill A. (eds.) 1991. *City and Country in the Ancient World* (London).

Riesenberg, P. 1992. *Citizenship in the Western Tradition: Plato to Rousseau* (Chapel Hill, NC).

Robert, L. 1967. 'Sur des inscriptions d'Éphèse', *Revue de philologie*, 41: 7–84.

Roberts, J. T. 1994. *Athens on Trial: The Antidemocratic Tradition in Western Thought* (Princeton).

Roebuck, C. 1972. 'Some Aspects of Urbanization in Corinth', *Hesperia*, 41: 96–127.

Roesch, P. 1982. *Études béotiennes* (Paris).

Rösler, W. 1989. 'Typenhäuser bei Aischylos?', in Schuller *et al.* (1989) 109–14.

Romilly, J. de 1959. 'Le classement des constitutions d'Hérodote à Aristote', *Revue des études grecques*, 72: 81–9.

—— 1968. 'Guerre et paix entre cités', in J.-P. Vernant (ed.), *Problèmes de la guerre en Grèce ancienne* (Paris), 207–20.

Rossetti, P. C. and Sartorio, G. P. (eds.) 1994–6. *Teatri greci e romani*, 3 vols. (Rome).

Rostovtzeff, M. 1926. *The Social and Economic History of the Roman Empire* (Oxford).

Rousseau, J.-J. 1782. *Considérations sur le gouvernement de Pologne* (Geneva), cited from the Pléiade edn. (Paris, 1964) iii. 951–1041.

Roussel, D. 1976. *Tribu et cité* (Paris).

Rousset, D. 1999. 'Centre urbain, frontière et espace rural dans les cités de Grèce centrale', in M. Brunet (ed.), *Territoires des cités grecques* (Paris), 35–77.

Roy, J. *et al*. 1988. 'Tribe and Polis in the Chora of Megalopolis: Changes in Settlement Pattern in Relation to Synoikism', *Praktika*, 12: 179–82.

Runciman, W. G. 1990. 'Doomed to Extinction: The *Polis* as an Evolutionary Dead-End', in Murray and Price (1990) 347–67.

Ruschenbusch, E. 1982. '*IG* XII 5 609: eine Bürgerliste von Ioulis und Koresia auf Keos', *Zeitschrift für Papyrologie und Epigraphik*, 48: 175–88.

—— 1985. 'Die Zahl der griechischen Staaten und Arealgrösse und Bürgerzahl der Normalpolis', *Zeitschrift für Papyrologie und Epigraphik*, 59: 233–7.

Sakellariou, M. B. 1989. *The Polis State: Definition and Origin* (Athens).

Salmon, P. 1978. *Étude de la Confédération béotienne (447/6–386)* (Brussels).

Sandström, Å. 1996. *Plöjande borgare och handlande bönder* (Stockholm).

Sansone, D. 1988. *Greek Athletics and the Genesis of Sport* (Berkeley).

Saradi-Mendelovici, H. 1988. 'The Demise of the Ancient City and the Emergence of the Medieval City in the Eastern Roman Empire', *Échos du monde classique*, 7: 365–401.

Schachter, A. 1985. 'Kadmos and the Implications for the Tradition of Boiotian History', in *La Béotie antique* (1985) 145–53.

—— 1992. 'Policy, Cult and the Placing of Greek Sanctuaries', in Schachter (ed.), *Le Sanctuaire grec* (Geneva), 1–57.

—— 2000. 'Greek Deities: Local and Panhellenic Identities', *CPCPapers* 5: 9–17.

Schaefer, H. 1961. 'Polis Myriandros', *Historia*, 10: 292–317.

Scheer, T. S. 1993. *Mythische Vorväter: zur Bedeutung griechischer Heroenmythen im Selbstverständnis kleinasiatischer Städte* (Munich).

Scheidel, W. 2003. 'The Greek Demographic Expansion: Models and Comparisons', *Journal of Hellenic Studies*, 123: 120–40.

—— and von Reden, S. (eds.) 2002. *The Ancient Economy* (Edinburgh).

Schmidt, M. 2004. 'πόλις, πτόλις', in *Lexikon des frühgriechischen Epos* (Göttingen), xx. 1345–79.

Schmitt, H. H. 1969. *Die Staatsverträge des Altertums: die Verträge der griechisch-römischen Welt von 338 bis 200 v. Chr.*, iii (Munich).

Schnapp-Gourbeillon, A. 2002. *Aux origines de la Grèce* (Paris).

Schuler, Chr. 1998. *Ländliche Siedlungen und Gemeinden im hellenistischen und römischen Kleinasien* (Munich).

Schuller, W. 1974. *Die Herrschaft der Athener im Ersten Attischen Seebund* (Berlin).

—— Hoepfner, W. and Schwandner, E. L. (eds.) 1989. *Demokratie und Architektur: der hippodamische Städtebau und die Entstehung der Demokratie* (Berlin).

Schwandner, E. L. 1977. 'Die Böotische Hafenstadt Siphai', *Archäologischer Anzeiger*, 519–25.

Schwartz, A. 2004. *Hoplitkrigsførelse i Arkaisk og Klassisk Tid* (Copenhagen).

Scully, S. 1990. *Homer and the Sacred City* (Ithaca, NY).

Seibert, J. 1979. *Die politischen Flüchtlinge und Verbannten in der griechischen Geschichte*, 2 vols. (Darmstadt).

Shipley, G. 1987. *A History of Samos 800–188 B.C.* (Oxford).

—— 1994. '*Perioikos*: The Discovery of Classical Lakonia', in J. M. Sanders (ed.), *ΦΙΛΟΛΑΚΩΝ: Lakonian Studies in Honour of Hector Catling* (London), 211–26.

—— 1997. '"The Other Lakedaimonians": The Dependent Perioikic *Poleis* of Laconia and Messenia', *CPCActs* 4: 189–281.

—— 2000. *The Greek World after Alexander, 330–30 BC* (London).

—— 2005. 'Little Boxes on the Hillside: Greek Town Planning, Hippodamos and Polis Ideology', *CPCActs* 7: 335–403.

Sinn, U. 1993. 'Greek Sanctuaries as Places of Refuge', in Marinatos and Hägg (1993) 88–109.

Sjöberg, G. 1960. *The Preindustrial City* (Glencoe, Ill.).

Smith, M. E. 1996. *The Aztecs* (Oxford).

—— 2005. 'City Size in Late Postclassic Mesoamerica', *Journal of Urban History*, 31: 403–34.

Snodgrass, A. 1980. *Archaic Greece* (London).

—— 1986. Review of van Effenterre (1985), *Classical Review*, NS 36: 261–5.

—— 1987–9. 'The Rural Landscape and its Political Significance', *Opus*, 6–8: 53–70.

—— 1990. 'Survey Archaeology and the Rural Landscape of the Greek City', in Murray and Price (1990) 113–36.

—— 1991. 'Archaeology and the Study of the Greek City', in Rich and Wallace-Hadrill (1991) 1–23.

Sombart, W. 1902. *Der moderne Kapitalismus*, 2 vols. (Leipzig), 2nd edn., 3 vols. (1916).

Sourvinou-Inwood, C. 1990. 'What is *Polis* Religion?' in Murray and Price (1990) 295–322.

—— 1993. 'Early Sanctuaries, the Eighth Century and Ritual Space: Fragments of a Discourse', in Marinatos and Hägg (1993) 1–17.

Southall, A. 1998. *The City in Time and Space* (Cambridge).

Starr, C. G. 1957. 'The Early Greek City-State', *La parola del passato*, 12: 96–108.

—— 1977. *The Economic and Social Growth of Early Greece 800–500* (New York).

Ste. Croix, G. E. M. de 1954–5. 'The Character of the Athenian Empire', *Historia*, 3: 1–41.

—— 1972. *The Origins of the Peloponnesian War* (London).

—— 1981. *The Class Struggle in the Ancient Greek World* (London).

Stone, E. 1997. 'City-States and their Centers', in Nichols and Charlton (1997) 15–26.

Strunk, K. 1970. 'Verkannte Spuren eines weiteren Tiefstufentyps im Griechischen', *Glotta*, 47: 1–8.

Swoboda, H. 1913. *Lehrbuch der griechischen Staatsaltertümer*, 6th edn. (Tübingen).

Symeonoglou, S. 1985. *The Topography of Thebes* (Princeton).

Talbert, R. 1974. *Timoleon and the Revival of Greek Sicily 344–317 B.C.* (Cambridge).

Thériault, G. 1996. *Le Culte d'*Homonoia *dans les cités grecques* (Lyon).

Thomas, C. G. 1981. 'The Greek *Polis*', in Thomas and Griffeth (1981) 31–69.

—— and Conant, C. 1999. *Citadel to City-State* (Bloomington, Ind.).

—— and Griffeth R. (eds.) 1981. *The City-State in Five Cultures* (Santa Barbara, Calif.).

Thumb, A. and Scherer, A. 1959. *Handbuch der griechischen Dialekte*, ii (Heidelberg).

Toner, J. 2004. *Greek Key Words* (Cambridge).

Trigger, B. 1993. *Early Civilizations: Ancient Egypt in Context* (Cairo).

—— 2003. *Understanding Early Civilizations* (Cambridge).

Tscherikower, V. 1927. *Die hellenistischen Städtegründungen von Alexander dem grossen bis auf die Römerzeit, Philologus* suppl. 19: 1–111.

Vidal-Naquet, P. 1983. *Le Chasseur noir* (Paris).

Voyatzis, M. E. 1999. 'The Role of Temple Building in Consolidating Arkadian Communities', *CPCActs* 6: 130–68.

Wace, A. J. B. 1962. 'Houses and Palaces', in Wace and Stubbings (1962) 489–97.

—— and Stubbings, F. H. (eds.) 1962. *A Companion to Homer* (London).

Wagstaff, M. and Augustson, S. 1982. 'Traditional Land Use', in Renfrew and Wagstaff (1982) 106–33.

Waley, D. 1978. *The Italian City-Republics*, 2nd edn. (London).

Wallace, M. B. 1970. 'Early Greek *Proxenoi*', *Phoenix*, 24: 189–208.

Wallace, R. W. and Harris, E. H. (eds.) 1996. *Transitions to Empire: Essays in Graeco-Roman History 360–146 B.C. in Honor of E. Badian* (Norman, Okl.).

Wallace-Hadrill, A. 1991. 'Introduction', in Rich and Wallace-Hadrill (1991), pp. ix–xvii.

Ward-Perkins, B. 1998. 'The Cities', in *Cambridge Ancient History*, 2nd edn. (Cambridge), xiii. 371–410.

Weber, M. 1973. 'Die "Objektivität" sozialwissenschaftlicher und Sozialpolitischer Erkenntnis' (1904), repr. in *Gesammelte Aufsätze zur Wissenschaftslehre*, 4th edn. (Tübingen), 146–214.

—— 1999. 'Die Stadt: eine soziologische Untersuchung', *Archiv für Sozialwissenschaft und Sozialpolitik*, 47 (1920–1), 621–772; repr. in *Max Weber Gesamtausgabe*, ed. W. Nippel, I 22.5 (Tübingen).

Welwei, K.-W. 1974–7. *Unfreie im antiken Kriegsdienst*, 2 vols. (Wiesbaden).

—— 1998. *Die griechische Polis*, 2nd edn. (Stuttgart).

Whitby, M. 1998. 'The Grain Trade of Athens in the Fourth Century B.C.', in Parkins and Smith (1998) 102–28.

—— (ed.) 2002. *Sparta* (Edinburgh).

Whitehead, D. 1977. *The Ideology of the Athenian Metic* (Cambridge).

—— 1984. 'Immigrant Communities in the Classical Polis: Some Principles for a Synoptic Treatment', *L'Antiquité classique*, 53: 47–59.

—— 1986. *The Demes of Attica 508/7–ca. 250 B.C.* (Princeton).

—— 1996. '*Polis*-Toponyms as Personal Entities (in Thucydides and elsewhere)', *Museum Helveticum*, 53: 1–11.

Whitelaw, T. 1998. 'Colonisation and Competition in the Polis of Koressos: The Development of Settlement in North-West Keos from the Archaic to the Late Roman Periods', in L. G. Mendoni and A. J. Mazarakis Ainian (eds.), *Keos–Kythnos: History and Archaeology* (Athens), 227–57.

Whitley, J. 2001. *The Archaeology of Ancient Greece* (Cambridge).

Wickert, K. 1961. *Der peloponnesische Bund von seiner Entstehung bis zum Ende des archidamischen Krieges* (Königsberg).

Will, E. 1972. *Le Monde grec et l'Orient*, i. *Le Ve siècle (510–403)* (Paris).

Wilson, S. G. 1996. 'Voluntary Associations: An Overview', in J. S. Kloppenborg and S. G. Wilson (eds.), *Voluntary Associations in the Graeco-Roman World* (London), 1–15.

Winter, F. E. 1971. *Greek Fortifications* (Toronto).

Winterling, A. 1991. 'Polisbegriff und Stasistheorie des Aeneas Tacticus', *Historia*, 40: 193–229.

Wörrle, M. and Zanker, P. (eds.) 1995. *Stadtbild und Bürgerbild im Hellenismus* (Munich).

Wycherley, E. R. 1967. *How the Greeks Built Cities* (London).

Yalouris, A. and Yalouris, N. 1995. *Olympia* (Athens).

Yoffee, N. 1997. 'The Obvious and the Chimerical: City-States in Archaeological Perspective', in Nichols and Charlton (1997) 255–63.

—— 2005. *Myths of the Archaic State* (Cambridge).

Zahrnt, M. 1971. *Olynth und die Chalkidier* (Munich).

Zaidman, L. B. and Schmitt-Pantel, P. 1992. *Religion in the Ancient Greek City* (Cambridge).

Index of Sources

I. LITERARY TEXTS

Acts of the Apostles
14.11: 154

Aeneas Tacticus
Prooem. 1: 173
1.9: 165, 175
2.2: 165
2.2*bis*: 170
2.7: 165
3.5: 175
7.1: 173
8.2: 173, 176
10.4: 174*bis*, 175
10.11: 179
10.15: 175
13.1–4: 180
15.9: 173
15.9–10: 161, 164
17.1: 175
22.4: 174, 175
23.6: 176
28.1–4: 175
31.15: 175

Aeschines
1.4: 178
1.9–11: 183
1.23: 181
1.173: 183
3.8: 178
3.13 ff.: 171
3.88: 176

Aeschylus
Persae
213: 154
511–12: 154, 161
715: 154
781: 154
Supplices
370–5: 179
954–8: 174

Alcaeus
Fr. 426: 172*bis*

Alexis
Fr. 272: 176

Anacreon
Fr. 391, Page: 172*bis*
Anth. Gr. 6.143.3–4: 176, 178

Andocides
1.38: 175
1.84: 172
1.133–4: 171
3.13: 186
3.20: 186

Antiphon
3.b.3: 176

Archestratus (Olson and Sens)
Fr. 15: 171

Archilochus (West)
Fr. 13.2: 155
Fr. 49.7: 155, 172
Fr. 228: 155

Aristophanes
Acharnenses
719: 176

Ecclesiazusae
210: 181
817 ff.: 172

Aristotle
Athenaion Politeia
13.4: 184
16.8: 179
19.4: 181
26.4: 178
38: 175

39: 185
60.2: 181

De mundo
400ᵇ16: 174, 175
400ᵇ19: 174

Nicomachean Ethics
1170ᵇ31–2: 188

Oeconomica
1343ᵃ10: 160
1346ᵇ18: 176
1346ᵇ19: 176
1348ᵇ1: 184
1349ᵃ34: 179

Poetics
1448ᵃ35–7: 164

Politics
1252ᵃ1–7: 160
1252ᵃ24–53ᵃ39: 178
1252ᵇ8–9: 153
1252ᵇ10–30: 164
1252ᵇ16: 162
1253ᵃ1–4: 180
1253ᵇ2–7: 178
1257ᵃ7–8: 178
1260ᵇ34–5: 183
1261ᵃ29: 160
1262ᵃ4: 177
1265ᵃ9–10: 177
1265ᵃ10–17: 177
1265ᵇ26–9: 180
1266ᵃ37–8: 184
1267ᵇ30–1: 167, 177
1269ᵃ29–71ᵇ19: 183
1271ᵇ2–3: 183
1271ᵇ34–5: 152
1272ᵃ10–12: 179
1274ᵇ32–76ᵇ15: 178
1274ᵇ38: 178
1274ᵇ41: 160*bis*
1275ᵇ7: 163
1275ᵃ22–3: 178
1275ᵇ5–6: 178
1275ᵇ7: 179
1275ᵇ22–4: 178
1275ᵇ33: 178
1276ᵃ8–16: 161
1276ᵃ17–27: 160
1276ᵇ1: 178

1276ᵇ1–3: 160
1276ᵇ2–11: 178
1278ᵃ28: 178
1278ᵇ8–10: 178
1279ᵃ22–80ᵃ6: 178
1279ᵇ2–4: 180
1283ᵇ42–84ᵃ3: 180
1284ᵃ3: 179
1286ᵇ20–2: 179
1287ᵃ8–12: 179
1288ᵇ41–89ᵃ1: 183
1289ᵇ27–40: 184
1290ᵇ18–20: 184
1291ᵇ7–13: 179
1292ᵃ39–41: 178
1293ᵃ12–17: 178
1293ᵇ16–18: 183
1293ᵇ27–30: 179
1295ᵃ17–21: 179
1296ᵃ18–21: 183
1296ᵃ22–3: 179
1297ᵇ1–16: 180
1297ᵇ12–13: 178
1297ᵇ24–5: 180
1298ᵇ26–38: 179
1301ᵃ20–5: 184
1301ᵇ19: 162
1301ᵇ21: 162
1301ᵇ39–40: 179
1302ᵃ9–13: 184
1302ᵃ10–13: 184
1303ᵃ1–2: 184
1303ᵃ3 ff.: 162
1303ᵃ25–ᵇ7: 184
1303ᵇ10: 186
1304ᵃ1–3: 186
1305ᵇ–6ᵇ2: 184
1307ᵇ7–10: 161
1307ᵇ19–25: 184
1308ᵃ2 ff.: 178
1310ᵃ4 ff.: 184
1310ᵃ32: 183
1311ᵃ40: 186
1313ᵃ34–15ᵇ10: 179
1316ᵇ24: 183
1317ᵇ11–17: 183
1317ᵇ35–6: 172
1318ᵇ39–40: 183
1319ᵃ35–7: 165
1319ᵇ30: 183
1320ᵇ25–6: 178
1321ᵃ5–14: 180
1321ᵇ12: 176

1321^{b}12–18: 172
1321^{b}13: 176
1322^{b}18–22: 182
1322^{b}22–5: 182
1324^{a}15: 180
1324^{a}27: 180
1324^{b}7–9: 183
1325^{b}39–26^{a}5: 178
1326^{a}18–20: 152, 177, 178
1326^{b}5–9: 180
1326^{b}16: 170
1326^{b}26: 164
1327^{a}3–5: 164
1327^{a}31: 176
1327^{a}32: 161
1327^{a}32 ff.: 173, 176
1327^{b}17–32: 153
1327^{b}20–33: 154
1327^{b}32: 160
1330^{b}21–31: 174
1330^{b}24: 174
1330^{b}32–31^{a}20: 172
1331^{a}12: 175
1331^{b}4–5: 182
1333^{b}12–35: 183
1334^{a}40–^{b}4: 183
1338^{b}9–14: 183

Fragments (Gigon)
476: 160
477: 160
487–8: 160
489: 160
502–5: 160
566: 179
580: 187
601: 159

Fragments (Rose)
498: 161

Aristoxenus (Wehrli)
Fr. 124: 153
Fr. 130: 162

Arrian
Anabasis
1.9.9: 159
1.26.4: 153
6.30.3: 153

Athenaeus
150A: 181

272D: 177

Callisthenes (*FGrHist* 124)
Fr. 25: 159

Craterus (*FGrHist* 342)
Fr. 18: 161

Demosthenes
1.19–22: 180
4.36: 177
9.3: 183
10.4: 183
10.53: 174, 175
15.19: 179
18.169: 176
18.210: 183
18.215–16: 160, 163
20.105–8: 183*bis*
21.31–5: 161
23.41: 162
24.192–3: 183
25.20: 172
25.25: 183
34.34: 173
47.53: 176
47.76: 176
56.47: 173
57.10: 164
57.46: 178
59.103: 159

Dinarchus
1.24: 159
1.77: 160

Diodorus
7.16: 161
11.49.1–2: 167, 177
12.9–10: 159
12.59.5: 167, 177
14.64.5: 179
14.82.1 = *Staatsverträge* no. 225: 186
15.48.1–49.4: 159
15.94.1–3: 159
16.53.3: 159
16.60.2: 159
16.82.5: 152
17.14.3: 159
17.109.1: 152
18.8: 152

Diogenes Laertius
5.27: 178

Etymologicum Magnum
680.1–4: 160

Euripides
Cyclops
115–18: 172

Electra
298–9: 163

Ion
294: 161

Iphigenia in Aulis
1400: 153

Supplices
429–32: 179
438–41: 183

Fragments (Nauck)
173: 184

Harpocration
s.v. *Keioi*: 161

Hellanicus
Fr. 75: 173

Hellenica Oxyrhynchia (Chambers)
19: 186
19.3: 162, 186*bis*
19.3–4: 186
19.4: 180
20.3: 159*bis*
24.1: 189

Heraclides Creticus (GGM)
1: 174, 175, 176
23: 172, 176
28: 175*bis*, 176*ter*
104.23: 171

Hermagoras (Matthes)
Fr. 10: 184

Hermippus (*PCG*)
Fr. 63: 171

Herodotus
1.14.4: 159
1.58.1: 154
1.59–60: 184
1.76.2: 154
1.146.2–3: 153
1.153: 176
1.170.3: 160, 174
2.154.2: 153
2.178–9: 176
3.57.3–4: 174, 175
3.80–2: 178
3.83.2: 183
3.139.1: 152
4.59: 154
4.108.2: 153
5.3.1: 159
5.62.2–63.1: 181
5.68: 179
5.78.1: 183
5.79.1: 179
5.101.2: 163
6.21: 159
6.27.2: 176
6.59.1: 170
6.67.3: 176
6.92.1: 177
7.58.2: 160
7.156.2: 159*bis*
7.220.4: 170
7.229.1: 177
7.233.2: 165
8.3.1: 184
8.26.2–3: 154
8.134.1: 170*bis*
8.144.2: 152
8.144.3: 36
9.21.2: 184
9.28: 177, 180

Hesiod
Opera et dies
222: 187
639–40: 187

Scutum
270: 172

Hippocrates
De aëre aquis et locis
12–24: 153
15: 173

Homer
Iliad
1.39: 156
2.484–759: 43
2.559: 172
2.591–602: 156
2.645–52: 43
2.867: 153
3.153 ff.: 172
5.446: 156
6.224–31: 185
6.242 ff.: 155
6.297–300: 156
7.83: 156
11.242: 163
18.490–540: 42
18.497: 175, 176
18.514: 172
19.99: 172
23.330: 176

Odyssey
1.365: 155
2.7: 175, 176
3.387 ff.: 155
4.20 ff.: 155
6.7–10: 42
6.10: 156, 172
6.262–72: 42
6.266: 172
6.266–7: 175, 176
7.81 ff.: 155
7.131: 163
8.5: 175, 176
13.192: 163

Isaeus
5.42: 180

Isocrates
4.42: 171
4.45: 171
4.175–6: 186
5.124: 153
7.20: 183
7.37: 183
8.48: 177
12.100: 159
12.131: 183
12.132: 178
15.10: 186
15.17: 186
15.299: 162

16.17: 184

Libanius
Orationes
11.266: 158
16.14: 158

Lycurgus
1.79: 178

Lysias
1.11: 171
1.22: 171
6.30: 178
9.9: 174
24.22–3: 160
26.5: 183

Menander
Dyscolus
5–7: 164

Georgus
Fr. 5 Sandbach: 163

Palaephatus
27: 171
38: 164

Pausanias
1.26.6: 160
6.9.6: 176
6.13.6: 162
8.27.1–8: 159
8.28.1: 185
8.43.1: 158, 159
9.5.2: 158
10.4.1: 176

Pherecydes (*FGrHist* 3)
Fr. 41d: 158

Phocylides
Fr. 4 Diehl: 155, 160

Pindar
Pythian Odes
2.86–8: 178

Plato
Apology
50c: 160
17d: 154

Critias
117c: 176

Crito
50c–e: 183
52e: 183
53a: 152

Definitions
412d: 183
415c: 160

Euthydemus
271c: 176

Laches
182e: 183

Laws
666d ff: 183
701b–c: 183
712c: 178
737e–38a: 177
738e: 170
739c ff: 183
745b: 161
745c: 177
778d: 172
779b: 174
942a ff: 183
945e: 184

Letters
326a: 183

Menexenus
245d–e: 152

Phaedo
109b: 152*bis*
116d: 163

Politicus
262d: 153
291c–92a: 178
292e: 177

Republic
338e: 178
369b–74a: 172
370c: 163
371b: 160
419a: 182

422e: 184
423a: 177
435e: 153
451c–57c: 181
544a: 183
544c: 183
551d: 184
555b: 184
557a: 184
557b–58c: 183

Sophist
223d: 172

Symposium
182b: 154

Plutarch
Demetrius
53.7: 160

Lycurgus
6: 179
6.2: 180
15.3–4: 170
24.1: 183

Moralia
295B–C: 179
799E–F: 175

Pelopidas
18.1: 160

Pericles
17.2: 185

Timoleon
22.2: 175
23.4–6: 159

Polybius
2.41.7: 159

Posidippus (*PCG*)
Fr. 30: 37
Fr. 30.3: 154

Pseudo-Scylax
5: 154
13: 173, 176
21: 154
28: 164

30–2: 164
33: 152, 160
34: 152, 173, 176
35: 152
36: 152
46: 152
61: 152
63: 152
64: 152
65: 152

Pseudo-Scymnus
551: 159

Pseudo-Xenophon
Ath. Pol.
1.14: 184
2.7: 171
3.10: 184

Solon
Fr. 4.6: 178
Fr. 4.19: 184

Sophocles
Antigone
737: 179

Stesimbrotus (*FGrHist* 107)
Fr. 9: 180

Stobaeus
Florilegium
2.7: 160

Strabo
7 fr. 24: 160
9.2.11: 186
9.2.14: 186
9.5.15: 160

Theophrastus
Characters
4: 163
5.7: 176

Theopompus
Fr. 62: 176*bis*, 183

Thucydides
1.2.2: 172
1.2.10: 170
1.3.4: 154

1.5.1: 172, 173
1.6.1: 172
1.6.6: 153
1.7.1: 172
1.8.2: 172
1.10.1–2: 175
1.10.2: 173
1.24.6: 185
1.30.2: 173
1.55.1: 177
1.67.2: 186
1.105.2: 177
1.107–8: 173
1.108.5: 159
1.126.10–11: 182
1.134.1: 170
1.134.1–2: 182
1.139.1: 186
1.139.3: 186
1.140.3–4: 186
1.144.2: 186
2.2–6: 165
2.9.1–2: 161
2.13.7: 180
2.15.1–2: 158
2.15.2: 174*bis*
2.15.6: 155, 160
2.16.1: 165
2.17.1: 165
2.22.3: 184
2.31.1–2: 180
2.37.1: 178
2.37.2: 183
2.38.2: 171, 189
2.39.2: 183
2.71.1: 173
2.71.2: 161, 175
2.72.3: 161
2.80.3: 186
2.80.8: 158
2.97.6: 160
3.10.5: 186
3.46.5: 186
3.68.2: 159
3.72.3: 176
3.82–83.4: 184
3.82.1: 184
3.82.8: 184
3.92–3: 159
3.94.4: 164
3.94.5: 36
3.102.2: 159
4.3.2–3: 155

4.26.2: 155
4.54.1: 173
4.71.1: 184*bis*
4.76.1: 186
4.86.4–5: 185
4.87.5: 186
4.91.1: 186
4.93.3–4: 180
4.93.4: 180
5.2.4: 165
5.18.6: 158
5.33.1: 185, 189
5.33.3: 189
5.84–116: 162
5.116.4: 159
6.2–6: 157
6.5.2–3: 152
6.5.3: 159
6.49.4: 159
6.69: 181
6.84.2–3: 189
6.88.6: 154
7.13.2: 177
7.29–30: 174, 186
7.29.3: 175
7.29.5: 176
7.50.1: 184*bis*
7.57.3: 186, 189
7.57.4: 159
7.69.2: 183
7.75.5: 177
7.77.7: 160
7.80.2: 152
8.72.1: 161
8.93.1: 176
8.97.1: 180

Timaeus (*FGrHist* 556)
Fr. 56: 159

Tyrtaeus (West)
Fr. 4.4: 155
Fr. 4.5: 155
Fr. 4.8: 155
Fr. 4.9: 155
Fr. 10.3: 155, 172
Fr. 12.28: 155
Fr. 19.8: 179

Xanthus (*FGrHist* 765)
Fr. 16: 154

Xenophon
Anabasis
1.2.17: 154
3.1.26: 154
3.2.1: 154
5.3.7–9: 181
5.4.2–4: 153
5.4.4–5: 154
6.1.30: 154
7.1.29: 152

Cyropaedia
1.1.1: 178
8.2.5: 172

De republica Lacedaemoniorum: 183
5: 170
8.1: 183
10.4: 183

Hellenica
2.2.20: 173
2.3.35: 160
3.2.27: 176
3.3.10–11: 170
3.4.16: 176
3.5.18: 186
4.1.1: 154
4.2.16: 177
4.4.13: 173
4.8.9–10: 173
4.8.15: 186
5.1.31: 157, 186
5.1.32–6: 186
5.2.4: 161
5.2.7: 159, 164, 179
5.2.19: 187
5.2.25: 176
5.2.29: 176
5.4.3: 171
5.4.20: 175
5.4.49: 161
5.4.58: 174
6.4.3: 186
6.5.28: 170
6.5.30: 176
7.1.41–3: 185
7.2.8: 165
7.5.5: 159

Hiero: 179
11.2: 176

Hipparchicus
3.1.5: 176

Memorabilia
4.4.16: 185
4.6.12: 178

Vectigalia
2.6: 165
4.50–1: 170

II. INSCRIPTIONS AND PAPYRI

CID I
9: 180

CID II
4: 160
4.I.14–15: 161
31.49: 185

CIG
3664: 179

Egypt. I. Metr.
33.1: 178

F. Delphes II
84: 153

F. Delphes III.3
145: 181

I.Cret. IV
4.13: 155
43.Bb.5–6: 176
64: 176
72.X.34–5: 175
72.XI.12–14: 175
144.9: 161

I.Erythrai
503.2–6: 178

IG I³
1.8–10: 180
14.32 ff.: 185
270.V.22: 159
1087–90: 176
1101A and B: 173

IG II²
43: 161
43.70: 162
43.78: 161, 162
43.79: 162

1183.15: 164
1187.3: 164
1496.131–2: 182
1496.140–1: 182
1835–1923: 177
1951: 177

IG IV
517: 179
841.12: 178

IG IV².1
95.8: 159
p. 166–7: 179

IG V.2
6.A.II.39: 183
268B.31: 178

IG VII
1: 179

IG IX²
717.4: 176

IG XII.1
677.13–19: 160

IG XII.2
3: 172
4.7: 160
6: 185
14: 176
17: 160

IG XII.3
86: 174

IG XII.5
609: 164, 177
872.3: 162
872.5: 162
1004.3: 185

IG XII.6
46: 172

IG XII.7
36: 181
67.43–4: 174
386.21: 178

IG XII.8
356: 182

IG XII.9
56: 177
189.36–7: 183
190: 185
192.4–5: 179
240–9: 177
245A.36: 159
249B.361: 159

IG XII *Suppl.*
236: 181

IG XIV
1: 181

I.Ilion
25: 185
25.19–22: 178

I.Kos
178.6: 178

I.Priene
1.6: 174

IvO
22: 185
165: 162

Kn As
1517.12: 154

Koerner (1993)
No. 90: 155

LSCG
96 = *Syll.*³ 1024.9: 182

Meiggs–Lewis, *GHI*
2.1–2: 155
5: 159
20: 159

27: 180
30.A.6–12: 172
44: 181
45: 176
45.(9): 185
65.16–17: 185
82: 185
83: 185
86.28–9: 155
93.3: 175

Michel, *Recueil*
997: 180

Nomima
1.1: 155
1.81: 155

OGIS
229.9–16: 158

P.Oxy.
4708 fr. 1.17: 172
4708 fr. 1.20: 172

RO
14 = *SEG* 37 340: 174, 186
96: 172
101: 152

SB
i.30 no. 355: 176

SEG
9 1: 179
9 1.6: 167, 177
22 370: 162
24 361: 186
26 878: 176
27 261: 176, 187
30 1119: 185
32 908.1: 176
34 850: 176
36 331.A.31–3: 159
37 340 = RO 14: 179, 186
37 340.3–9: 164
37 340.6–7: 174
39 411: 179
42 846: 177
42 1663: 172
43 310.1–4: 160
43 630: 181
47 1745.1–29: 158

*Syll.*³
37–8.B.15: 173
147.3–7: 161
169.40 ff.: 164
218.6–10: 175
222: 179
344: 159
344.98: 164*bis*
354: 172
357.2: 159
359.3–5: 160
360: 185
532: 181
1015: 182
1015.6–7: 178
1024.9 = *LSCG* 96: 182

Staatsverträge
No. 225 = Diodorus 14.82.1: 186
No. 273: 186
No. 277: 186
No. 283: 186
No. 345: 186

Tit. Cal.
XII 21–2: 178

Tod, *GHI*
138: 186
191: 185
192: 185
201–2: 152

Index of Names

Abai 37
Abdera 99
Abyssinians 22
Aceh 20, 143
Achaia 45, 47, 49, 54, 80, 166, 174
Achaian cities, *poleis* 128, 185
Achaian League 15, 130
Acheron 33, 151, 152
Achilleus 42, 172
Aden 25, 141
Adria 167
Aegean (islands) 44, 46, 78, 81, 84,
    137, 151
Aegean (sea) 54
Aeneas Tacticus, Aeneas the Tactician
    160, 173
Afghanistan 31
Africa, African 21, 25, 50, 141, 144,
    145, 148, 188
Ai Khanoum 31
Aigeira 174
Aigiale 178
Aigikoreis 179
Aigina 95, 106, 108, 109, 177
Aigion 174
Ainos 166
Aiolis 81, 151
Aischines 183
Aischylos 174
Aitna 88, 108, 167, 177
Aitolia, Aitolians 36, 47, 49, 52, 54,
    80, 158, 159, 160
Aitolian League 15, 130
Akan 189
Akarnania, Akarnanians 47, 49, 52,
    54, 80, 158, 160
Akkadian 17
Akragas 87, 184
Akrai 152
Ålborg 9
Alexander the Great 18, 37, 53, 77,
    109, 134, 152, 157
Alexandria 134
Alkaios 98
Alkinoos 155

Alkmaionidai 181
Alps 93
Ambrakia 186
American War of Independence 15
America, Americans 15, 23
Amorgos 181
Amphipolis 174, 184
Anakreon 98
Anatolia, Anatolian 10, 13, 17, 138,
    141, 142
Anavlochos 40
Andokides 92
Andorra 9, 11, 60
Andros 44
Anglo-Saxon 8, 26, 45, 157
Ankara 7
Ano Englianos 156
Anthedon 95, 171, 172, 176
Antigonos Monophthalmos 159
Antimachos 181
Antioch at the Orontes 121, 134
Antissa 184
Antoninus Pius 158
Aphrodite 103
Apollo 38, 103, 156, 181
Apollonia Pontika 184
Arab, Arabian 18, 19, 25
Aramaic 18
Archestratos of Gela 171
Archilochos 41, 98
Ares 182
Argadeis 179
Argolis, Argolid 46, 70, 71, 129, 164,
    166
Argos 46, 87, 99, 128, 129, 167, 173,
    174, 175, 176, 177, 179
Århus 9
Aristion 60
Aristodama of Smyrna 181
Aristophanes 95
Aristotle, Aristotelian 37, 90, 94, 95,
    108, 109, 110, 112, 115, 116, 119,
    123, 139, 144, 160, 174, 178, 182,
    183
Aristotle's *Politics* 109, 110, 122, 162

Arkadia, Arkadian, Arkadians 49, 52,
54, 68, 80, 154, 160, 164, 166,
174, 185
Arkesine 174
Artemis 181
Arwad 18
Asante 21
Asea 164, 165
Asia, Asian 11, 20, 25, 134, 144, 148
Asia Minor 7, 12, 13, 16, 17, 18, 33,
45, 46, 47, 48, 49, 54, 74, 78, 81,
82, 84, 99, 129, 130, 134, 151,
158
Asklepios 175
Askra 63, 131
Assur 16, 17, 141, 188
Assyria, Assyrian 10, 13, 17, 18, 27,
138, 142, 186
Astypalaia 159, 176
Athena 103, 156
    Boulaia 121
    Nike 181
Athenaios 171
Athens, Athenian, Athenians 1, 9, 11,
12, 36, 41, 43, 46, 48, 49, 51, 53,
62, 63, 71, 87, 91, 92, 93, 94, 95,
99, 106, 108, 109, 110, 119, 121,
123, 124, 128, 129, 139, 140, 141,
152, 153, 156, 157, 167, 169, 173,
174, 175, 176, 177, 178, 179, 180,
181, 182, 183, 184, 185, 187
Atlantic 22, 25
Atlantis 176
Attic, Attika 37, 46, 51, 63, 68, 69, 88,
91, 106, 109, 179, 180
Attic orators 123
Austrian 85
Aztec, Aztecs 10, 12, 13, 22, 26, 31,
138, 141, 143, 146, 188, 189, 190

Babylon, Babylonian 10, 13, 18, 31,
43, 188
Baltic 40
Barke 166
Basle 144
Belbina 106
Bènizàa 22, 188
Berber 13, 21
Beroia 176, 187
Bisaltia 164
Black Sea 18, 31, 33, 34, 46, 54, 91,
169
Boiotia, Boiotian, Boiotians 49, 52, 54,

59, 63, 68, 69, 71, 95, 154, 160,
164, 166, 171, 174, 180, 186
Boiotian Federation 60, 71, 130, 186
Boreis 179
Bornu Empire 11, 21, 138, 143
Bremen 9
British 16
Brunei 20
Bug 31
Burkert, Walter 120
Byblos 18
Byzantion 176, 177, 184

Caere 19
Caliphate 21
Cameroon 10
Carolingian 19
Carthage 18
Çatal Höyük 7, 8, 149
Catalogue of the Ships 43
Caucasus 36
Central America 22, 23, 26, 31
Central Asia 13
Central Europe 19
Chad, Lake 10, 13
Chaironeia 48, 69, 176
Chalaia 181
Chaldean 18
Chaleion 176
Chalestre 152
Chalkidian Federation 131
Chalkidike 68, 75, 164
Chalkis 46, 159, 167, 176
Chersonesos 185
Childe, V. Gordon 168, 169
China, Chinese 10, 13, 20, 27, 143,
145, 146, 161, 188, 189, 190
Chios 176, 180, 185
Chorsiai 131, 186
Constant, Benjamin 184
Copenhagen 1
Corinth, Corinthian 45, 46, 47, 48, 62,
87, 99, 106, 107, 129, 152, 159,
167, 173, 174, 176, 186
Corinthian Gulf 54
Corinthian War 129
Council 50, 103, 112, 113, 114, 132,
133, 134, 145, 171
Council-house 121
Crete, Cretan 40, 41, 43, 46, 84, 137,
151, 168, 179
Crook, John v
Cyprus 18, 45, 138, 151

Damokles, sword of 126
Danish 58, 148
Danish National Research Foundation
    1
Danmark 59
Danzig 9
Delian Naval League 49, 54, 128, 129,
    130
Delion 69, 180
Delos 96
Delphi 35, 37, 52, 88, 96, 180, 181
Demeter 104, 182
Demetrias 54
Demokratia 121
Denmark, Danes 8, 9, 12, 59, 60, 149,
    157
Deucalion 36
Diaz, Bernal 141
Didyma 37, 175
Diocletian 50
Dionysios I 42, 55, 179
Dionysos 103, 182
Dodone 37
Donoussa 44
Drakon 155
Dreros 40, 41
Dublin 19
Durhumit 18
Dutch 13, 15, 20, 141, 143, 145, 190
Dymanes 179
Dystos 63

East 19, 36
East Africa 13
East Asia 26, 144, 188
Ebla 17, 142
Egypt, Egyptian 8, 9, 26, 33, 82, 91,
    113, 133, 142, 151, 161
Ekron 18
Elateia 166
Elis 47, 88, 166, 175, 176, 177
Elymians 81
Emporion 31
Encyclopaedia Britannica 144
England, English 8, 14, 19, 26, 45, 58,
    60, 147, 157
Epeiros, Epeirotes 33, 47, 49, 52, 54,
    81, 82, 84, 151, 158, 166, 168
Ephesos 95, 172, 176
Epidamnos 185
Epidauros 60, 159, 175, 179
Epitalion 88
Eresos 185

Eretria 46, 54, 59, 63, 99, 107, 108,
    127, 140, 156, 167, 174, 177, 179,
    183, 185
Erythrai 54, 185
Estonia 12
Ethiopia 22
Etruscan, Etruscans 13, 18, 26, 27, 38,
    145, 154, 188, 190
EU, European Union 65, 142
Euboia 43, 45, 46, 54, 59, 63, 107,
    161, 174
Eumenes II of Pergamon 158
Euphiletos 171
Euphrates 18
Euripides 95
Europa 51
Europe, European 13, 17, 20, 21, 22,
    25, 26, 58, 60, 62, 64, 123, 142,
    144, 145, 149, 188
Eurytanes 36
Eutresis 131, 186

Fante 13, 21, 143, 146, 190
Far East 188
Fertile Crescent 13, 26, 138
Finley, Moses 41, 88, 89, 90, 94, 96,
    153, 169
Florence 19, 27, 144
Founding Fathers of the American
    Revolution 15
France, French 9, 12, 14, 21, 33, 58,
    78, 82, 147, 148
French Revolution 15, 111
Fulani 21
Funeral Oration 92
Fustel de Coulanges 118, 180

Gat, Azar 27
Gauthier, Philippe 169
Gaza 18
Geitosyros 38
Gela 166, 171
Geleontes 179
Gelon 53
Gelonoi 153
Geneva 15
Genoa 92
German empire 161
Germany, German 9, 13, 14, 19, 58,
    62, 63, 83, 111, 123, 141, 143,
    145, 147, 148, 157, 190
Ghana 21
Gibraltar 33

Gold Coast 13, 21
Gordian 40
Gortyn 96, 155, 175, 176
Gothic 156
Goulfeil 11
Graham 153
Greece, Greeks, Greek *passim*
Greenland ice 155
Grote, George, *History of Greece* 123
Grynchai 54, 159
Gurkhas 21

Haliartos 174
Halieis 70
Halikarnassos 53, 120, 178, 182
Hama 18
Hamburg 11
Hannover 9
Hansa cities 92
Harald Bluetooth 9
Hausa 13, 21, 145, 146, 161, 189, 190
Hazor 17
Hedeby 9
Hekataios of Miletos 34, 152
Helike 54
Helisson 174, 186
Hellas, Hellenes, Hellenic 33, 34, 36,
    37, 78, 80, 81, 82, 84, 151, 152,
    153, 159, 179
Hellen 36
Hellespont 82, 168
Hera 104, 175
Herakleia 52, 167, 177
Herakles 182
Hermione 70
Herodotos 37, 38, 108, 123, 160
Hesiodos, Hesiod 63, 131
Hestia 103, 121
Hicks, John 16
Hieron 108
Hippodamian plan 74, 102
Hippodamos 102, 108, 177
Histiaia/Oreos 167
Hittite, Hittites 18, 27, 142
Homer, Homeric 37, 41, 42, 43, 89,
    95, 98, 104, 155, 156
Homonoia 133
Hopletes 179
Hyksos 142
Hylleis 179
Hysiai 54, 129

Idomeneus 43

Ikarion 176
Iliad 42, 43, 172
Ilion 166, 185
Illyria 33, 82
Inca Empire 9
India 134, 141, 149
Indo-European 39, 40, 154
Indonesia, Indonesian 13, 161
Indus 31, 54
Ionia, Ionian 37, 45, 46, 54, 74, 81,
    84, 95, 151, 168
Ios 185
Ireland, Irish 13, 19, 45, 138, 142,
    143, 157
Isin–Larsa period 188
Isis 133
Islamic 20, 21
Israeli 27
Isthmia 176
Isthmos 37, 45, 46
Italia 166
Italy, Italian, Italic 2, 12, 13, 19, 26,
    27, 33, 44, 45, 54, 78, 82, 93, 111,
    137, 143, 144, 145, 146, 148, 153,
    164, 166, 184, 188, 189, 190

Javanese 20
Jelling 9
Jensen, Minna Skafte 43
Julianus 158
Justinian 50

Kadmeia 174
Kadmos 51
Kaisareia 158
Kamarina 53, 152, 159, 177, 180
Kamiros 180
Kanesh 16, 17, 18
Kappadokia 154, 158
Karia, Karians 47, 82, 121, 151, 153,
    157, 168
Karkamis 18, 142
Karyanda 33
Kasmenai 152
Kassite 18, 27
Kathmandu 13, 20, 21
Kenya 13, 21
Keos 62, 69, 107, 164, 166, 177
Keressos 69
King's Peace 49, 186
Kition 45
Klazomenai 166
Kleanthes 160

Kleitor 167
Kleomenes 181
Klytidai 180
Knidos 121, 166
Knossos 41, 42
Kolb 99
Kolophon 54, 175, 179, 186
Konso 22, 144
Koresia 62, 70, 107, 181
Korkyra 167, 176, 177
Koroneia 69, 172
Kos 178
Kotoko 10, 13, 21, 138, 143, 188
Koukounaris 44
Kyklades 44
Kyklopes 95
Kylon 182
Kyparissos 166
Kyrene 31, 52, 55, 87, 95, 107, 108, 113, 139, 166, 167, 177
Kyros, King 129
Kyros, Prince 36
Kythera 173

Labraunda 183
Labyadai 180
Lagash 17
Lakedaimon, Lakedaimonian 46, 48, 55, 71, 91, 106, 129, 154, 177
Lakonia 164
Lamia 181
Latin 13, 26, 142, 145, 188, 189, 190
Latium 13, 19
Latvian 40
Laud Chronicle 161
Laurion 92
Lebadeia 37
Lebedos 159
Lecheion 173
Lefkandi 156
Lesbos 68, 95, 98, 164
Leuktra 69
Lex Hafniensis 162
Libya 31, 33, 55, 78, 82, 91, 151, 168
Libyrnian 154
Limnaia 158
Linear B tablets 156
Lithuanian 40, 155
Livius 144
Logone Birni 11
Lokris 47, 49, 159
Lokris, eastern, east 68, 164
Lokris, Epizypherian 181

Lokris, Opountian 159
Lokris, western, west 68, 164
London 61
Louis II 19, 27
Luxembourg 60
Lydia, Lydian 62, 142, 154
Lykia, Lykians 13, 47, 82, 142, 151, 157, 159, 175

Macedonia, Macedon, Macedonians 33, 39, 48, 49, 78, 81, 82, 84, 134, 138, 151, 152, 153, 168, 176, 187
Machiavelli 144
Magna Carta 161
Magna Graecia 153
Magnesia 108
Makari 11
Makassarese 20
Malay, Malayan 20, 25, 34, 141, 143, 144, 145, 188, 189
Malla dynasty 20
Malla, Yaksa 20
Mankessim 21, 143
Mantinea 53, 88, 89, 159, 170, 174, 175, 178, 179, 186
Mausolos, King 53
Maya, Mayan 13, 22, 27, 143, 188, 189
Mayapan 22
Mecca 19, 25, 141
Medina 19, 25, 141
Mediterranean 18, 27, 31, 33, 34, 46, 54, 70, 89, 134, 151, 169
Megalopolis 52, 54, 166, 167, 177
Megara 46, 62, 107, 159, 174, 179, 179, 184
Megara Hyblaia 44, 45, 53, 99, 157, 159, 173
Melaka 20, 141
Melos 53, 62, 159, 163, 165, 166
Menander Rhetor 158
Menelaos 155
Mesoamerica, Mesoamerican 13, 138, 144, 145, 148, 188
Mesopotamia 2, 7, 8, 9, 16, 17, 18, 25, 26, 27, 138, 188
Messene 166, 167
Messenia 47, 55, 91, 106
Metapontion 164, 165, 166, 176
Methana 164, 165
Mexico 10, 13, 22, 139, 140
Middle East 141
Mideia 129

Milan 19
Miletos 12, 34, 46, 62, 87, 94, 99, 102,
    108, 153, 157, 172, 173, 175, 177,
    179
Minoan 41
Mixtec, Mixteca 13, 138, 140, 143,
    189
Molossians 181
Molykreion 159
Monaco 60
Mongols, Mongolian 20, 143
Monte Alban 22, 27
Montesquieu 15
Morris, Ian 98
Mossynoikeans 153
Mounichia 176
Mozabites 13, 21, 25
Mozambique 21
Murray, Oswyn 181
Mycenean, Myceneans 39, 40, 41, 42,
    43, 137, 156
Mygdonia 164
Mykale 48
Mykalessos 174, 176, 186
Mykenai 41, 42, 129
Mykonos 182
Mylasa 186
Mytilene 95, 172, 185
Mzâb 138, 141, 144, 188

Nakona 185
Naukratis 176, 178, 181
Naulochon 174
Naupaktos 159
Nausithoos 42
Naxos (Sicily) 99, 173
Naxos (island) 46, 179
Neapolis 153
Near East, Near Eastern 7, 10, 13, 17,
    18, 20, 26, 31, 37, 43, 54, 98, 133,
    138, 144, 145, 188
Nemea 37, 159
Nemea, Battle of 177
Neo-Babylonian 18, 138, 142, 188
Neo-Hittite 10, 13, 27, 138, 142, 188
Neoptolemos 181
Nepal, Nepalese 14, 20, 21, 146, 188,
    190
Nestor 155, 156
Netherlands 26
New Spain 141
New York 16
Niger 13, 21, 22, 25, 141

Nigeria 8, 13
Nikias, Peace of 158
Nile 134
Nimrud 43
Ninive 155
Nisyros 165, 174
Nordic 156
North Africa 18, 33, 138
North America 13
North American Indian 8
North Syria 27
Norway, Norwegian 9, 13, 19, 25, 45
Notion 186

Oaxaca 22
Odense 9
Odysseus 155
Odyssey 42, 43
Oinopes 179
Oinophyta 69
Oiteia 53, 167, 177
Olbia 31, 175
Old Assyrian 142
Old Indian 40
Old Oyo 188
Oldenburg 9
Ollie the Second v
Olympia 37, 175
Olympic Games 35, 152
Olympic gods 119, 133
Olympic stadion 153
Olympic victor(s) 37, 60
Olynthos, Olynthians 53, 75, 159, 165,
    171, 174
Omani 143
Orchomenos 174
Orneai 129
Orontes 121, 134
Oropos 37
Oyo 21, 139, 143

Pacific 13
Palembang 13, 20
Palestine, Palestinian 10, 13, 17, 18,
    26, 27, 138, 142, 188
Pallantion 54, 158
Palmyra 141
Pamphylians 153
Pamphyloi 179
Panathenaia 43
pan-Hellenic festivals, games 35, 37,
    51, 103, 127
Pantikapaion 107, 139, 166, 173, 177

Paphos 45
Paros 44, 46, 98
Parrhasian 185
Pausanias (Spartan) 182
Pausanias (writer) 165
Pax Romana 128, 133
Peiraieus 63, 71, 91, 92, 102, 173, 176
Peisistratos, Peisistratid, Peisistratids
    43, 156, 179
Pellene 166
Peloponnese 45, 46, 70, 78, 128, 130
Peloponnesian League 49, 128, 129,
    130
Peloponnesian War 52, 54, 71, 91,
    108, 128
Peneios 33, 152
Pennsylvania 16
Pergamon 158
Perikles 92, 141
Persia, Persian, Persians 36, 49, 62,
    129, 130, 151, 153
Persian Empire 13, 18, 34, 37, 54,
    134, 154, 157
Persian Wars 49, 95, 108, 153
Peukestas 153
Phaiakians, Phaiacians 42, 172
Phaistos 176
Phasis 173
Phigelea 174
Philip II 48, 49, 53, 157
Philista 181
Philistine, Philistines 10, 13, 18, 26,
    138, 142, 188, 189
Phleious 165
Phoenicia, Phoenicians, Phoenician
    10, 13, 18, 25, 26, 34, 38, 45, 138,
    141, 142, 188, 189
Phokaia 184
Phokis, Phokians 49, 53, 68, 80, 88,
    156, 159, 164, 166
Phrygia 154
Pillars of Hercules 33
Piraeus [=Peiraieus] 63, 176
Pisa 27
Pithekoussai 153, 173
Plataiai, Plataians 48, 53, 69, 73, 74,
    75, 108, 130, 159, 170, 175, 180
Plataiai, Battle of 107, 177
Plato 34, 89, 90, 94, 95, 123, 169, 183
Plato's *Laws* 108, 122, 174
    Republic 108, 122
Plutarch 123
Po Valley 91

Poland 9
Polis Centre 1, 2, 9, 14, 16, 73, 76, 82,
    83, 87, 143, 148
Polis Centre's Inventory 77, 79, 83,
    87, 96, 100, 106, 151, 170
Polybios 123
Pontos, Pontic region 78, 82, 151
Portuguese 141, 143
Poseidippos 37
Poseidon 182
Poseidon Hippios 175
Poseidonia 153
post-Mayapan 188
post-Mycenean 155
Powell, Barry 43
Praeneste 19
pre-Homeric society 95
Priam 155
Priene 74, 75, 166, 174
Procopius 50
Propontis 151
proto-Corinthian 157
Pseudo-Skylax 33, 34, 38, 160
Pteria 154
Ptolemy 113
Purushattum 18
Pydna 166
Pylos 41, 42
Pyrenees 9, 31
Pythian Games 52

Ramesses III 18, 26
Rhegion 153, 177
Rhodes, Rhodos, Rhodian 84, 133,
    151, 168, 173, 177, 179
Ribe 9
Robert, Louis 161
Roman city-states 141
Roman *comitiae* 144
Roman control 133
Roman Empire 27, 31, 50, 132
Roman Imperial period 39, 49, 52
Roman period 54, 128, 130, 151
Roman times 71
Roman province 128
Rome, Romans 13, 15, 19, 38, 138,
    139, 144, 148, 154
Rousseau, Jean-Jacques 15, 144
Royal Danish Academy 148

Sahara 13, 21, 141
Salamis (in Cyprus) 45
Salamis (the island) 48, 108

Samos 95, 172, 175, 179
San Marino 11, 60
Sanskrit 20, 154, 189
Sardinia 18
Sargon of Akkad 10, 17, 27
Scandinavia 14, 26
Scheria 42, 156
Schwyz 140
Selby 61
Seleukids 134
Selinus 185
Senate 113
Sestos 166
Shang 143
Sicilia 18
Sicily, Sicilian 26, 44, 45, 55, 78, 81,
    82, 91, 99, 102, 137, 138, 184
Side 153
Sidgwick, Henry 149
Sidon 18
Siena 27
Sierra Zapoteca 22
Sikanians 81
Sikels 81
Sikyon 179
Silk Route 20
Singapore 11
Siphai 131, 186
Siphnos 175
Siris 54
Skandeia 173
Skaphai 54
Skillous 181
Skolos 54
Skylax of Karyanda 33
Skythia, Skythian, Skythians 33, 38,
    153, 160
Smyrna 46, 99, 157, 181
Social War 19
Somalia 21
Sombart, Werner 90, 91, 92, 93, 94,
    97
South America 13
South East Asia 13
Spain, Spaniards, Spanish 9, 12, 14,
    18, 22, 23, 33, 36, 82, 138, 167
Sparta, Spartan, Spartans 34, 41, 46,
    48, 49, 53, 55, 71, 87, 88, 91, 95,
    96, 99, 100, 104, 106, 107, 108,
    116, 122, 123, 124, 128, 129, 139,
    157, 170, 174, 176, 177, 179, 182,
    183, 184
Spartiates 71

Spercheios 53
Sriwijaya 20, 143, 188
Stanford University 70
Strabo 153, 165
Styra 54, 159, 177
Sumatra 13, 20
Sumer, Sumerian, Sumerians 2, 9, 10,
    13, 17, 25, 27, 31, 69, 138, 140,
    144, 188, 189, 190
Swahili 13, 21, 141, 143, 144, 189
Swiss city-states 12, 19, 145, 188, 190
Swiss confederacy 15, 140
Switzerland 13, 14, 19, 27, 111
Sybaris 53, 184
Syracuse 42, 44, 45, 53, 55, 62, 87,
    94, 99, 107, 108, 126, 139, 152,
    159, 173, 176, 177, 179, 181, 184
Syria, Syrian 10, 13, 17, 25, 27, 33,
    82, 138, 142, 151, 188

Tai 189
Tai city-states 188
Tai Müang 143
Taklamakan 13, 20, 143, 188
Tamynai 176
Tanagra 69, 167, 174, 186
Tanzania 13, 21
Taras 127, 153
Tarim Basin 20
Tarquinia 19
Tegea 183
Tegyra 69
Tehuantepec 22, 143
Telos 165
Tenochtitlan 23, 139, 188
Teos 95, 98, 159, 160, 166, 172
Texcoco 23
Thailand, Thai 13, 20
Thales 160
Thasos 41, 182, 185
Thebes, Theban, Thebans 41, 48, 49,
    51, 52, 53, 54, 59, 60, 71, 73, 74,
    87, 93, 129, 130, 139, 159, 167,
    172, 174, 175, 176, 179, 186
Theophilos 60
Thera 52, 155
Therme 152
Theseus 51
Thespiai 130, 131, 172, 174
Thessalonike 54, 160
Thessaly, Thessalians 33, 47, 49, 78,
    80, 84, 95, 151, 160, 168
Thisbai 131, 186

Third Sacred War 53
Thirty Tyrants 175
Thorikos 176
Thourioi 166, 184
Thrace, Thracian, Thracians 33, 78, 82, 151, 152, 160, 168
Thucydides 36, 38, 53, 71, 73, 74, 91, 95, 123, 157
Tibet 20
Tibur 19
Tigris 17
Timesitheos of Trapezunt 153
Tiryns 42, 129, 170, 172
Tlacopan 23
Toriaion 158
Trapezunt 153
Triphylia 68, 88, 164
Troas 84, 151, 168
Trojan War 95
Troy 42, 43, 156, 172
Turkey 7
Tuscany 27, 188
Tyche 121, 133
Tyre 18, 45
Tyrtaios 41, 98

Ukraine 31
United Nations 60
Unterwalden 140
Ur 17, 27
Uri 140
Uruk 9, 17
USA 2, 16
Utrecht, Treaty of 15
Utrecht, Union of 20

Vathy Limenari 44
Venice 9, 11, 19, 92, 139
Viking Age 8, 9, 26
Viking city-states 138, 142, 157, 188
Vikings 19, 45
Vulci 19

Weber, Max 85, 86, 89, 90, 92, 93, 94, 95, 96, 97, 168, 169, 171
Weberian 83, 89, 168
Welsh 61
West Africa, West African 2, 10, 13, 21, 26, 138, 139
Western Zhou 143
Westminster 161
Westphalia, Peace of 14
Winchester 161
Wulfila 156

Xenophon 36, 38, 88, 94, 123, 181

Yakö 8
Yoruba 13, 21, 143, 144, 145, 161, 189, 190
Yucatan 13, 22

Zähringen 19, 27
Zagora 44, 155
Zankle 184
Zapotec 13, 27, 138
Zeus 51, 104, 182
    Boulaios 121
Zhou 20, 27

General Index

abstract public power, *polis* as 57, 64, 106

Ackerbürger (city farmers) 70, 83, 86, 89–91, 93–6

administration of justice 64, 86, 113–15, 120, 131

agora (market) 50, 95–6, 103, 133

agoranomoi (inspectors of the market) 94

akropolis 40, 56–7, 73, 96, 101–4, 126, 133

andrapodismos (enslaving of a *polis*) 53, 128–9

apoikia (colony) 34

apoikismos (colonisation) 52

arbitration between *poleis* 134

archai (magistrates) 94, 103, 111, 115, 119–20, 126, 130, 132

archeia (offices of *archai*) 103

aristocracy 108, 111

army 35, 71, 107, 109, 114, 115, 116–17, 130

Assembly, see *ekklesia*

aste (female citizen) 111

astos (male citizen) 40, 66, 111–12

asty (town, city) 40, 56, 59, 66, 67, 87, 99

autonomia (independence) 48–50, 64–5, 125–6, 130

autonomia (self-government) 49–50, 86, 132, 134

barbarian *poleis* 38

barbarians 33–8

basileus (king) 111

Boiotian federation 130–1

boule (Council) 50, 103, 112, 115, 130, 132–4

bouleuterion (Council-house) 103, 133

chora, ge (territory, hinterland) 56–8, 60, 64, 67–72, 77–84, 103, 106–7, 131

citizens, see *aste, astos, politai*

citizenship 35, 61, 110–11, 116, 131,

134

city, *polis* as 38, 40, 56–7, 62–3, 66–105, 109, see also *asty, polisma*

city, size of 73–6

city-state empire 107

civic centre (not city), *polis* as 88–9

civic subdivisions 101, 102, 114–15

civil war, see *stasis*

coinage 37, 52, 113, 115, 131

colonies 31, 33–4, 35–6, 44–7, 52–54, 78, 81, 84, 106, 125–6, 134

commune, see *demos*

constitution, see *politeia*

consumer cities 85–6, 90–3, 97

council, see *boule*

Cretan Bronze Age city-states 41, 137

decree (*psephisma*) 110, 114–15, 127

demise of the *polis* 48–50

demokratia (democracy) 50, 111, 112, 116, 121, 123–4, 125, 132

Demokratia (goddess) 121

demos (commune) 54, 59, 63, 68, 102, 114–15, 133

demos (people) 57, 60, 64, 106, 111

dependent *poleis* 48–50, 63–5, 101, 107, 115, 124–6, 129–30, 132

desmoterion (prison) 115

destruction of *poleis* 53, 128–9

dialects 36–7

dikasteria (courts) 36, 103, 132–4

dioikismos (breaking up of a *polis*) 53–4

disappearance of *poleis* 31, 41, 53–5, 129–30

douloi (slaves) 35, 41, 53, 88, 107, 109–10, 120, 128–9

ekklesia (Assembly) 50, 57, 103, 111–12, 115, 116, 119, 121, 123, 132–4

ekklesiasterion (Assembly place) 103

eleutheria (freedom) 50, 123

emergence of *poleis* 51–3, 54, 98–100

emergence of the *polis* 31, 39–47

emporion (commercial harbour) 101, 104

envoys, see *presbeis*
ephebeia 105, 132–3
epineion (harbour) 101
ethnic identity 35, 63–4, 125
ethnikon (adj. derived from toponym and used as name) 59–61
etymology of the word *polis* 39–41, 99

face-to-face society 63, 86, 89–90
farmsteads 67–72
federation (*koinon, ethnos*) 49, 52, 55, 58, 60, 64–5, 116, 130, 134
financial administration 113–14
foreign policy 114–15, 127–31
foundation myth of a *polis* 51
freedom, see *eleutheria*
free foreigners, see *metoikoi*
fusion of state and society 122–4

gates 104
gene (lineages, clans) 114, 118
German *Städte* 62–3, 94
Greek language 36–7, 134
grid-planned *poleis* 74–5, 133
gymnasia 105, 133–4

harbour, see *emporion, epineion, limen*
harbour-towns 101
hegemonic *poleis* 49, 126, 129
hekastotyes (hundredths) 102, 115
Hellas, extent of 33
Hellenic *poleis* 33–4
Hellenised *poleis* 47, 52, 77, 82, 84, 133
Hellenistic *poleis* 35, 39, 49, 52, 71, 102, 103, 121, 126, 130, 132–4
heralds, see *kerykes*
hierarchical systems of *poleis* 65, 101, 130
hiereis (priests) 119
hinterland, see *chora, ge*
hippodromos 105
Homeric *poleis* 41–3, 98
homonoia (unity) 126, 133
honourary decrees 114
hoplites 107, 109, 116–17
horoi (boundary markers) 104
household (*oikia, oikos*) 54, 70, 74–5, 85, 108–10
hypekooi poleis (dependent *poleis*) 64, 129

independence, see *autonomia*

institutions of a *polis* 40, 44, 57, 64, 86, 112–15, 125, 134

kathartai (purifiers) 120
kerykes (heralds) 127
koina (semi-private associations) 133
koine (common language) 37
koinonia (community) 57, 110
kome (village) 54, 59, 63, 68–9, 72, 109, 114–15, 133
Kyrene's moderate oligarchy 113

landscape surveys 68–71, 75–6, 80, 82, 97, 101
leagues of *poleis* 49, 55, 116, 128–30
legislation 113–15
lex hafniensis 59, 87–8
limen (harbour) 34, 101, 104

magistrates, see *archai*
manteis (soothsayers) 120
market, see *agora*
meanings and uses of the word *polis* 39–41, 56–9, 67, 87–8, 98–9, 101, 106
mercenaries 35, 36, 117
metoikoi (free foreigners) 34, 41, 109–10, 117, 132
metropolis 34, 130
Mycenean city-states 39, 41, 137
myriandros polis (*polis* with 10,000 citizens) 84, 108–9

names of *poleis* 59–60
naturalisation 113–14
navy 108, 116
New Palace period 41, 46
nomoi (laws) 115
number of *poleis* 31, 73, 77, 79–80, 82

oligarchy 50, 111–12, 125, 132
oracles 35, 37, 114

palaces 42, 102, 133
palaistra (wrestling hall) 105
pan-Hellenic festivals 35, 37, 51, 103, 127
patriotism 64, 116, 125
pentkostyes (fiftieths) 115
perioikoi (free non-Spartans in Lakedaimon) 129
periplous (peregrination) 33
phalanx (formation of hoplites) 116

phratries 102, 114–15, 133
phyle (tribe) 59, 114–15, 133
polis kata komas oikoumene (conurbation) 99, 101
polisma (town) 67, 87
politai (citizens) 35, 40, 56–7, 66, 107, 110–12, 119, 122–3
politeia (constitution) 109–14
politeia (Aristotelian citizen-constitution) 111, 116
population of all *poleis*, total 31, 77–84
po-to-ri-jo (Mycenean form of *polis*) 39
presbeis, presbytai (envoys) 52, 114, 127
priests (*hiereis*) 118–21
prison, see *desmoterion*
property qualification 109, 113
protecting deity 121
proxenoi (consuls) 52, 127–8
prytaneion (town hall) 103, 115, 121
ptolis 39, 43

religion 36–7, 50, 118–21, 126, 133
religious festivals 37, 103, 105, 114–15, 119, 126
Roman *poleis* 31, 39, 49, 52, 71, 128, 132–4
rural population, size of 70–2, 80–3, 133

sanctuaries 103, 114, 115, 118–21
schools 105
self-government 40, 44, 49, 51, 59, 85, 96, 101, 125–6, 129–30, 132
settlement, *polis* as 34, 40, 43–4, 56, 58, 62–3, 67–72, 80, 85, 101–2, 110
shot-gun method 74, 84, 107
slaves, see *douloi*
Sparta as a *polis* in the urban sense 87, 99, 104
sporting contests 37
stadion 105
stasis (faction, civil war) 35, 125–6
state, *polis* as 38, 40, 41, 44, 58–61, 63–6, 88, 98–100, 108–15

stoa (portico) 105, 133
strategoi (generals) 113, 121
subsistence economy 85–6, 92, 94–7
suburbs 73, 75
synoikismos 52–4

temples 37, 42, 102–3, 105, 118–21
territory, see *chora, ge*
territory, size of 55, 70, 77–84, 90–1, 93
theatres 103, 105, 115, 133
theorodokoi (hosts of *theoroi*) 52
theoroi (envoys announcing a pan-Hellenic festival) 52, 127
thesmophoria (festival for Demeter celebrated by women) 119
trade 35, 90–7, 101, 104, 114
trading cities 93
tribe, see *phyle*
triremes 108
tyrants 102, 111–12, 132

unity, see *homonoia*
urban population, size of 63, 70–1, 79–83, 133
urbanisation 35, 44–5, 70–1, 77–84, 85–7, 89, 98–100

village 54, 59, 63, 67–72, 76, 81, 85, 87, 89, 101, 109, 114, 131, 133, see also *kome*

walls of *poleis* 44, 46, 56, 63, 70–1, 73–86, 95–6, 98–9, 101, 103–5, 128, 132–3
war 52, 69, 73, 104, 114, 116–17, 120, 127–9
water supply 102
Weberian 'Ideal type' 86, 96
women 110–11, 119–20, 132–4

xenia (guest-friendship) 127
xenoi (foreigners) 41

zoon politikon (political animal) 115